בס"ד

This Purim Guide belongs to ______________________

My Very Own Purim Guide 2.0
First Edition, 22 Sh'vat, 5775 / February, 2015
Second Edition Edition, 22 Adar 1, 5776 / March, 2016

Artwork by Chana Silver
www.ToolsforTorah.com / TAG613.com
Info@ToolsforTorah.com / 203-887-6044

Proceeds from the sales of this book will enable more
Tools for Torah to be created and published.

ISBN 978-1508444497

Dedication opportunities are available in honor or memory of a loved one.

Visit www.ToolsforTorah.com or email: Partner@ToolsforTorah.com

Table of Contents

Introduction & Credits

With gratitude to ה', My Very Own PURIM Guide finally joins the other Yom Tov Guides: Tishrei, Pesach and Chanukah.

I would like to acknowledge some of the sources used for this Purim Guide. "The Complete Story of Purim," by Nissan Mindel, published by Kehot Publications, "Purim" by Artscroll, and many other sources. The dates and timeline are from "The Chronological Index of Jewish History" by Rabbi Mattis Kantor.

The Megilah translation and commentary sources are credited in the book, on page 69.

150 Pages of Pure Purim for Ages 8 – 108.
Laws, Customs, Thoughts, Activities and Illumination.
Translated Kitzur Shulchan Aruch
Translation of the Whole Megilah (Original, Student – Friendly)
430 Compiled Commentaries on the Megilah!
Thoughtfully Illustrated, Textbook and Workbook
A Thorough, Fun Resource from which to Learn and Teach פּוּרִים.

Thank you to some people who helped me with this Purim book:

Mushkie Blau, for researching and writing much of the history, my daughters Shayna and Chana Mushka for contributing the Megilah commentary from Perek 5 on. Aidela Zirkind, Chanale Block & Rivky Springer for formatting help.

Chana Silver for the thoughtful illustrations* (email CSilver1205@gmail.com to hire her).
(*Drawings on pages 9, & some others are not Chana's Illustrations)

Rabbi Shmuel Rabin for reviewing the Halachos and expert proofreading.

Kitzur365.org for allowing us to include their Kitzur Quiz on Purim Halachos.

My wife, Sarah, for designing the beautiful cover and managing all our family & work responsibilities while I'm in Purim World.

Last, but not least, you, the students, teachers, principals, parents and educators who continue to encourage me to create more materials. ("We use your Tishrei, Pesach & Chanukah Guides... - When is your פּוּרִים book coming out...?") Thank you all!
May ה' brighten up our world with the ultimate, eternal light of the גְאוּלָה, now!

Rabbi Chayim B. Alevsky
כב שבט ה' תשע"ה - February 11, 2015
New York City

Please send your fixes, comments & suggestions to: Info@ToolsforTorah.com

Visit www.ToolsforTorah.com for more educational materials and Sponsorship Opportunities

PURIM פּוּרִים

WHY IS PURIM SO SPECIAL?!

So.... How will YOU dress up for Purim this year?! Will you be the beautiful Queen Esther? Saintly Mordechai? King Achashverosh? Perhaps a Jewish Superman, or maybe a Torah Scroll? The list is endless because there are so many ideas to choose from...

Help! I lost my costume! Please dress me up for Purim!

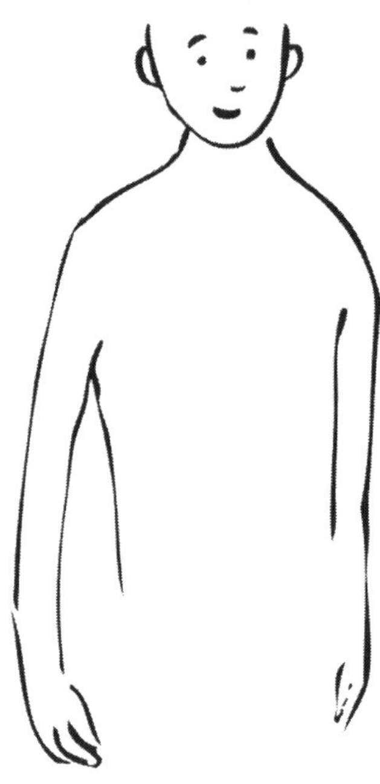

Why do we dress up on Purim? What is the meaning behind all the costumes and makeup? It's a lot of fun! However, fun is not the (main) reason why we dress up. All our laws and customs for the holiday have deeper meanings, ideas, and lessons that we can learn. So, why do we dress up?

Many answers are given to this question and we will see several of them later in the book. Now, we will discuss one, which is a central theme and "main idea" of Purim.

You may already know this song: "Hashem is here, Hashem is there Hashem is truly everywhere. Up, up, down, down, right, left and all around, here there and everywhere that's where Hashem is found!"

As the song says, Hashem is everywhere. If so, why do we not see Hashem? One of the reasons is that Hashem wanted to create a world, with people who will have free choice to follow Hashem's ways, study His Torah, and observe His Mitzvos.

Imagine if Hashem was revealed to us and we would actually see Hashem and how He creates and manages the universe!

We would love Hashem too much for us to do anything against His will! We wouldn't want to "disconnect" from Him by not following His Torah and Mitzvos.

We also wouldn't want to disappoint Hashem in any way. We would be in such awe of Him that we'd be scared to do anything besides His will.

PURIM  פּוּרִים

Seeing Hashem's glory, or even feeling Hashem's presence, would "force" us to do what Hashem wants and we wouldn't have freedom of choice. We would be just like the angels who see Hashem in his full glory - and therefore are like holy "robots" because they have no choice but to follow Hashem's will.

Hashem wanted us to serve Him differently. Hashem wanted us to make the right decisions on our own, without being forced to. Therefore, He hid Himself. We humans, have the freedom of choice, because we don't see Hashem, and we often don't "feel" His presence.

On Purim we celebrate a great miracle in which Hashem, although hidden, clearly saved us from plots of King Achashverosh and his wicked, evil adviser, Haman.

<u>TYPES OF MIRACLES</u>

What is a "miracle"? What is "nature"? Is nature "natural" or also a miracle?

Type of Miracle	Nature Frequent events	**נס גלוי** - Revealed Miracle *A clear and obvious miracle.*	**נס נסתר** - Hidden Miracle *Doesn't seem like a miracle at first, but we realize when looking back, that it really was!*
Examples	The sun rising daily	10 מכות in מצרים	Jews being saved on Purim
	Food giving us energy	Splitting of the sea	The countless stories we hear of extra-ordinary experiences
	Awaking rested after sleeping	Oil burning for 8 days on Chanukah	What unexpectedly wonderful thing happened to you?

In true reality, everything is a miracle! Nothing "needs" to be or happen. Hashem causes everything to happen: Natural and miraculous. It's all the same to Hashem. The difference is only for us, the way we see things: Events that occur frequently, we call "nature." Unfrequent events, we call "miracles."

Within the world of "unfrequent" miracles, some miracles are obviously miraculous, some not. Some are revealed, some hidden.

What kind of miracle was the **פורים** miracle?

The נס of פורים did not happen all at once. The story of מגילת אסתר occurred over a span of about nine long years, therefore they did not seem to be נסים at the time that they occurred, as the different parts of the story can all seem "regular":

PURIM  פּוּרִים

- Achashverosh throws a party at which he gets drunk and…
- gets rid of queen Vashti, allowing for…
- Esther to be appointed as the new Queen.
- Mordechai the Tzaddik hears Bigsan & Seresh's plot, and later on…
- Achashverosh cannot sleep…
- Haman is in the palace at just the right time…
- Esther finally reveals her identity… etc.

Only when we look back at all the events, can we see that Hashem was orchestrating and arranging all the events to occur in a precise order, leading to our miraculous ישועה – deliverance & annulling Haman's evil plot.

That explains why the Purim miracles are considered a "hidden" נס.

This is also the main reason why we dress up on Purim. Just as Hashem was "hiding" during the time and miracle of Purim, so too, we dress up and "hide" ourselves on Purim.

PURIM: THEN, OR NOW?

When we celebrate all of our Yomim Tovim (Jewish Holidays), we are not just celebrating something that happened many years ago. The "idea" or "message" of the holiday is happening in the here and now, and in all times and places. The holiday is just our reminder about that message.

Purim reminds us that Hashem is constantly involved in our world. What we call "nature" is really Hashem – working "behind the scenes." "Nature" is the program that Hashem created to hide His involvement in our world.

Even the word "הטבע," meaning "The Nature" has the same גמטריא as "א-להים" (Hashem) = 86, expressing that they are one and the same.

One of the main messages and lessons of Purim is, to realize that Hashem is running every detail of the world – although we do not see it.

One of the ways we call Hashem's interaction with the world is:

Hashgocha Protis.

PURIM  פּוּרִים

HP = HASHGOCHA PROTIS

Hashgocha Protis is often translated as Divine Providence.

One of the beautiful, encouraging teachings of the Baal Shem Tov is that every detail of Hashem's creation, is being continually recreated and directed by Hashem. Some people used to think, that after Hashem created the world, He left it to run by itself. Similar to a carpenter who "creates" a table out of wood, and after he builds it, does not need to be there anymore to keep the table in existence. Similar to you, when you build a beautiful castle out of Lego. You design and build it, and then, when Mommy says it's time to get to your home-work... you walk away, while your castle remains standing, tall and proud.

The major difference between Hashem's creation and a carpenter's - and your Lego creation is that you and the carpenter use existing material, wood and legos etc., and only change its form; from a tree to a table or from individual legos to a castle.

When Hashem creates, he makes <u>something</u> from <u>nothing</u>. There was nothing – no material - from which to create the world. Hashem created the material and formed the world, and all that resides in it.

So: The true, original "nature" of our world – is to <u>not</u> exist. For our world to "stay" and continue existing, Hashem continuously re-creates it at every moment.

The Baal Shem Tov explains that this is the meaning of our tefilla: המחדש בטובו בכל יום תמיד מעשה בראשית – Hashem "renews" and "recreates" every single creation, constatnly.

Now we understand one of Purim's beautiful messages. Even though we do not physically see it with our eyes, Hashem is with us always. He is creating us continuously and directing everything that exists; here, there and everywhere, up, down, right, left and all around.

Hashem is hiding in nature.

Hashem re-creates & directs everything in the world all the time.

You are invited…

To participate in this most JOYOUS month!

WHO: Every Jewish Person

WHEN: The ENTIRE month of Adar.*

WHY: Adar is a lucky month for Jewish people! **

HOW: Just Be Happy! ***

BRING: Your special strong Mazal! ****

*[When] some of the years are "leap years" is when we have two months of Adar. We are happy during both months and celebrate Purim Katan on the 14th day of the first month and the "real" Purim, in the second month. Also, if someone was born on a "regular" year with only one month of Adar, his/her birthday is celebrated in the second month of Adar.

** [Why] Purim celebrates the greatest joy that we as a nation are forever connected to Hashem. During the Purim story, we were in big trouble, nevertheless, our connection with Hashem stayed strong. The month of Adar, which Haman thought was our lowest (since Moshe Rabeinu passed away on Zayin Adar), actually brought about the joy that is the greatest- the joy that we as a nation, will forever be connected to Hashem.

*** [How] We try to schedule weddings in Adar. Also, since the mazal of the Jews is strong during Adar, if someone has a court case against a gentile, they should try to schedule it during Adar.

**** The mazal of Adar is fish. Haman thought he would swallow us like a fish. Instead, Hashem swallowed his plan and saved us.

PURIM  פּוּרִים

PURIM JOY!

The happy month of Adar is a fine preparation for the *awesomist* joy of Purim!

Purim is all about Joy. Not "oy," - joy! Not "just" joy. *Joy! Joy! Joy!*

The Shulchan Aruch quotes the Talmud, which instructs us to be so joyous on Purim: "עד דלא ידע בין ארור המן לברוך מרדכי" - that we don't know the difference between "cursed is Haman and blessed is Mordechai!" Wow. Aside from a good "lechayim," what does that even mean? Who doesn't know which are the good guys and the bad guys?

Also, back in the Purim story, the Jews were super happy because they were all saved. Now there's no Haman with his evil decree... so what's this joyous "not knowing" all about now?

Like *all* Jewish holidays, Purim isn't only about remembering an interesting story that happened long ago. It's about *living* Purim, our way, this year, now. How? Read on. Dive in.

Purim means "lots", or "raffles". When someone wins a lottery or raffle, did they pay for the "prize", earn or deserve it? No. It's what we call "luck." It doesn't "make sense" and there's no explanation. It just happens, "randomly."

Haman thought that somewhere, deep, deep, deep in Hashem, there's a "place" where Hashem doesn't *really* care about good and bad, and doesn't care about us Jews, and if he could just "reach" that place, Hashem would allow anything to happen to us "randomly."

Haman figured he could "reach" that "randomness" in Hashem by picking a "random" date using the lottery, called Purim. Then, on that date, he thought Hashem won't protect us.

Boy, was he wrong! Hashem chose each and every one of us to be His holy, special nation, knowing, wanting and loving each boy, girl, man and woman, no matter what we do or don't, even when there's no rhyme or reason, Hashem loves us to His core, as deep as can be!

When I think about, that the Creator of everything, physical and spiritual, who made and sustains everything, Who did, does and will do everything – that Hashem Himself chose *me* to be part of His special nation and wants *me* in this world to help Him make it a better place – wow! That's one MEGA reason for me to be happy! Really happy! Super happy!

Haman's evil plot taught us a valuable lesson: Every Jew is precious to Hashem beyond logic and our connection with Hashem is unlimited, even in the "randomist" places.

Now, just like Hashem loves us unconditionally, we, too, love Hashem unconditionally.

Nothing can get in the way. Even when it *doesn't* make sense! Even when it's *really* difficult and we need to sacrifice things or suffer, we still love, and listen to Hashem, "עד דלא ידע."

When we think about, that no matter what we've done or not done, Hashem loves and cares for us "עד דלא ידע," we can reach a happiness on that level.

This Purim, think about how it doesn't make sense that we have this amazing connection with Hashem. We don't always really deserve it. And, since it doesn't make sense, we can be infinitely happy! Without any boundaries! "שמחה פורץ גדר", *joy breaks all boundaries.*

PURIM  פוּרִים

The Purim History: Short Version

Very Short Version: We were in trouble. Hashem saved us. Let's eat!
Ok. That was too short. Now, here's the simple scoop.

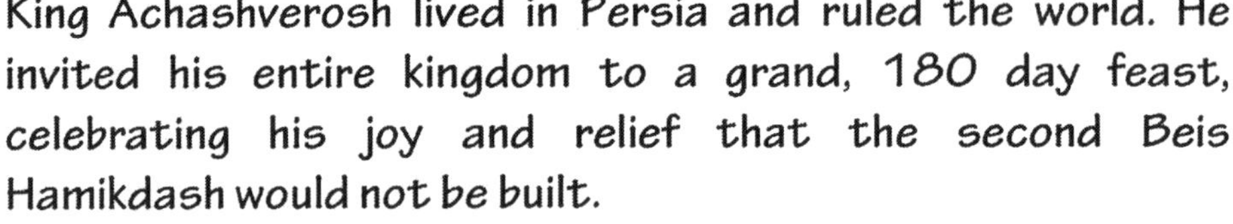

It started in the year 3395, after the destruction of the First Beis Hamikdash, King Achashverosh lived in Persia and ruled the world. He invited his entire kingdom to a grand, 180 day feast, celebrating his joy and relief that the second Beis Hamikdash would not be built.

While drunk, Achashverosh ordered his queen Vashti to come and show off her beauty. Vashti refused to do so and was killed.

Achashverosh arranged a beauty contest and chose Esther to replace Vashti. Queen Esther hid her Jewish identity and secretly kept in touch with her cousin Mordechai who was the head of the Sanhedrin.

Mordechai overheard Bigsan & Seresh plotting to kill the king, passing the message along the appropriate channels, and so he saved the king's life. This was recorded in the king's diary.

At this time, the wicked Haman rose to power and demanded that everyone bow to him. Mordechai's refusal to bow angered Haman, who wanted to take revenge by killing all the Jews. He cast a lot (raffle) to choose a date for his evil plan. It fell out on the 13th day of Adar. Haman then arranged permission from Achashverosh to carry out his evil plot.

Mordechai found out and publicly mourned the decree, informing Queen Esther about it, and instructing her to beg the king to spare their people. Esther hesitated for fear of being killed, but agreed on condition that all the Jews fast for 3 days.

Esther then invited the king to a wine-party with Haman and later invited them both to join her at a second party, the next day.

PURIM  פּוּרִים

Leaving the palace in high spirits, Haman noticed Mordechai – the man who refused to bow to him. Now furious, Haman decided to begin building the gallows on which to hang Mordechai that night. Only after he started did he decide to go to the palace to ask permission from the king to finish the project.

Meanwhile… back at the ranch, no, not ranch, royal palace, the king couldn't sleep. His servant, trying to help, read from his royal diary about when Mordechai saved the king from the plot of Bigsan and Seresh.

hen he found out that Mordechai was not yet rewarded, Achashverosh instructed Haman - who was at the palace to ask for permission to hang Mordechai… - to honor Mordechai by leading him through the city, wearing the king's royal robes, riding the king's horse.

The next day at the second feast, Queen Esther identified Haman as the one who wants to kill her and her people. The angry king had Haman hung on the same gallows he had prepared for Mordechai, and then appointed Mordechai to Haman's position of Prime Minister.

The Ancient Persian laws forbade cancelling a royal decree, so Mordechai and Esther wrote another decree, that the Jewish people should defend themselves from those who want to hurt them – and so they did.

On the 13th of Adar, the Jewish people killed many of their enemies, along with Haman's ten sons. They rested from the battle and celebrated on the 14th of Adar, while the people of Shushan the capital battled for one more day and rested on the 15th of Adar.

Mordechai and Esther established that we celebrate the holiday of Purim and commemorate the miracles for all future generations by:

1. Megilah: Reading the story from the Megilah
2. Mishloach Manos: Giving gifts of food to friends
3. Matonos la'evyonim: Giving Tzedaka to the poor
4. Mishteh: Eating a Purim feast

PURIM  פּוּרִים

THE פורים HISTORY IN NOT-SO-SHORT

Throughout the ages, עַם יִשְׂרָאֵל has been persecuted and mistreated by other nations of the world. Although we have our very own Holy Land, אֶרֶץ יִשְׂרָאֵל, for most of our history we were chased away from it and scattered throughout the four corners of the earth.

Even when we lived in our holy land, we weren't always our own boss. Nations of the world ruled us, tortured us and destroyed our holy בֵּית הַמִקְדָשׁ twice.

It was - and still is - very much גָלוּת.

There were four main nations who ruled over us, and we refer to the time periods they ruled us as the "Four גָלוּיוֹת/Exiles."
גָלוּת מִצְרַיִם is not counted in this group as one of the גָלוּיוֹת of our People, because we were exiled in מִצְרַיִם before we became an independent nation.

The four גָלוּיוֹת are:

- גָלוּת בָּבֶל – Babylon (חוּרְבַּן בַּיִת רִאשׁוֹן – נְבוּכַדְנֶצַר)
- גָלוּת מָדַי-פָּרַס – Media & Persia (פּוּרִים)
- גָלוּת יָוָן – Greece (חֲנוּכָּה)
- גָלוּת אֱדוֹם – Rome (in which we will remain until מָשִׁיחַ comes)

One of the most obvious miracles of ה׳, is that against all odds - we are still here. The nations that tried so hard to destroy us are now mere subjects in history books. With Hashem's help, the Jewish Nation is still alive and vibrant. The fact that you – a Jewish boy or girl – are in a Jewish school or home - and you are reading these lines is a true miracle.

Why, do you think, did ה׳ save us? Why, do you think, does Hashem want YOU here, and now?

Basic Timeline of Rulers

גָלוּת בָּבֶל Year 3319: Nevuchanetzar becomes the king of Bavel, an empire that ruled most of the world. After a few years he conquers אֶרֶץ יִשְׂרָאֵל.

3327: Nevuchanetzar exiles the Jewish king יכני'ה מלך יהודה and many great people such as Mordechai, Daniel, Chananya, Mishoel, and Azarya.

3338 (423 BCE): Nevuchanetzar destroys the first Beis Hamikdash and sends most of the Jewish people out of Israel, into Galus – Galus Bavel.

3389: Belshatzar, grandson and successor of Nevuchanetzar, is killed by the Persians. Achashverosh marries his daughter Vashti.

גָלוּת מָדִי-פָּרַס

3390: Koresh (Cyrus) becomes king of Persia and Media. Koresh permits construction of Beis Hamikdash. Permission was taken away because of lies against the Jews, fabricated by their enemies.

3392 (369 BCE): Achashverosh rules.

3395: Achashverosh calls a feast to celebrate that the Beis Hamikdash was not built within the time that was prophesied by Yirmiyahu Hanavi to be rebuilt. (He miscalculated.)

3399: Esther becomes queen.

3404: Haman rises to power and plans to destroy the Jewish People. He casts the lot on 13 Nissan. It fell on 13 Adar. Esther decrees a 3 day fast: 14-16 Nissan. On 15 Nissan, Esther approaches the king; Haman is hanged on 16 Nissan.

3405: 13 Adar, Jews defend themselves against their enemies.
10 sons of Haman are hanged. 14 Adar is the Purim Celebration.

3406: Achashverosh dies. Daryavesh (Darius), Esther's son is king at the age of six years old.

3408: (353 BCE) Daryavesh permits the Jews to rebuild the Beis Hamikdash.

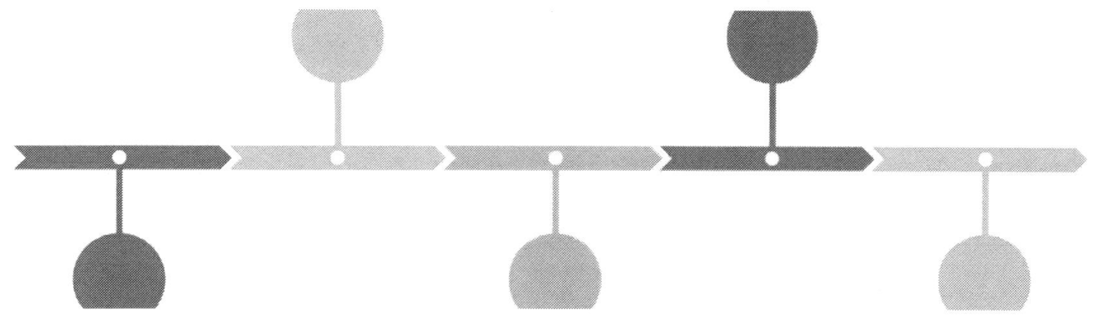

Achashverosh Rises to power

The miracle of Purim took place towards the end of גָלוּת בָּבֶל, after the destruction of the first Beis Hamikdash, in the years 3395-3405/ 366-356 BCE, about 200 years before Chanukah.

From reading Megilas Esther alone, it may seem like the Purim story happened all at once, in a very short time. The story in the Megilah actually occurred over the course of about nine years, beginning at Achashverosh's grand party all the way up until the final victory in Shushan.

The Megilah begins stating that Achashverosh was now the ruler of 127 countries, and tells the story of his hosting a grand feast.

WHY DID HE DECIDE TO THROW A PARTY NOW?

Reason #1 To show off his wealth.	Reason #2 To celebrate that the Beis Hamikdash hadn't been rebuilt.	Reason #3 To celebrate the completion of a new, magnificent throne.
Achashverosh did not come from royal ancestry. Raised as a stable boy, he gained power over the years, and rose higher in rank, amassing many riches and was then given Vashti, the granddaughter of Nevuchanetzar to marry, and became true royalty. Achashverosh knew that he himself was not of royal blood, so he was constantly worried about being undermined. Therefore, he tried to earn people's respect by impressing them with his power and riches Hoping this would distract from the fact that he was only royalty due to his marriage to Vashti.	ירמיהו הנביא prophesied that Bavel would rule Israel for 70 years, after which we would rebuild the Beis Hamikdash. Achashverosh miscalculated the time, and thought the 70 years had passed. Achashverosh reasoned that since ירמיהו's prophecy was "wrong," the Beis Hamikdash would never be rebuilt again. This made him very happy, because he knew that if the Beis Hamikdash was rebuilt, the Jewish people would be the greatest power in the world with Hashem's open miracles, as it was during the first Beis Hamikdash. Achashveirosh wouldn then lose his royal power, or the Jews as his subjects, if that happened.	Shlomo Hamelech's throne was famous as the most magical throne, brilliantly engineered with his superior wisdom. After Shlomo Hamelech's passing, many kings wanted his magical throne, including Achashverosh. It didn't go well for the few who managed to get it. Whoever tried to ascend the throne, was injured by the golden, mechanical animals sitting on the steps. Realizing he could not ascend the throne unharmed, Achashverosh ordered a team of engineers to construct a replica (copy) of Shlomo Hamelech's throne for himself. It was completed in the third year of his rule. To celebrate, Achashverosh made a party.

Shlomo Hamelech's Magnificant Throne

The throne was made of expensive ivory (a glossy white substance that comes from elephants' tusks and can be carved into intricate shapes) and covered in gold.

As Shlomo Hamelech ascended the throne, 2 mechanical creatures would automatically support him, helping him up to the next step.

Step One had a lion and an ox.

Step Two had a wolf and a lamb.

Step Three had a tiger and camel.

Step Four had an eagle and a peacock.

Step Five had a cat and a rooster.

Step Six had a hawk and dove.

When Shlomo Hamelech would sit on his royal throne, a golden eagle would soar towards him, holding King Shlomo's royal crown in its beak. The eagle would settle just behind King Shlomo's head and stay there, holding his royal crown just above his head, so it wouldn't feel heavy. A golden dove would fly over with the king's personal, little Sefer Torah and place it on his lap.

Kings and queens from all over the world would come to see and marvel at Shlomo Hamelech's wondrous throne.

PURIM  פּוּרִים

The Party

When Nevuchanetzar captured the Beis Hamikdash, he stole many treasures. Before he died though, he dumped them all in the sea. When Koresh allowed the Beis Hamikdash to be rebuilt, Hashem showed him the treasures. Achashverosh inherited them, becoming immensely wealthy.

After the first party, a monstrously large occasion that lasted 180 days, Achashverosh hosted another party for 7 days, just for the people in his capitol, Sushi. I mean Shushan. While there was of course, all the great reasons above to party and keep partying, Achashverosh's main purpose was to get the Jews to sin so Hashem would be upset with them. That way, they for sure wouldn't be able to build the Beis Hamikdash.

Some Jews joined the party even though their leader, Mordechai, forbade them to. The Jews who did go, were horrified at the desecration of the holy vessels which Achashverosh displayed and was showing off at the party, but they stayed, afraid of insulting the king.

VASHTI

The seventh and final day of the party was Shabbos. Achashverosh had held back from drinking until then, but on that last day he let loose, and became very drunk. High level representatives of the various countries in his kingdom, were debating about which country boasts the most beautiful women. Achashverosh drunkenly proclaimed his wife Vashti the most beautiful of all.

The jolly representatives challenged the king to show off Vashti, to prove his point.

Vashti was also hosting a party, at the same time, just for women. One of Vashti's evil customs was to force her Jewish servants to work for her on Shabbos, knowing that it was so painful for them to descrate their holy day. The Jewish girls were serving Vashti, when the king's servant's arrived.

PURIM  פּוּרִים

The king's servants interrupted the festivities, informing Vashti that the king requested for her to come, show herself off to everyone at his party, wearing her golden crown. Upon hearing this, Vashti flew into a rage.

She started mocking her husband, saying, "My father, King Belshatzar could drink 1,000 drinks and not get drunk but my husband has a few drinks and goes crazy!" The servants tried to calm her but she said, "I'm not a simple servant girl, tell my husband I refuse to come!"

Drunk as he was, Achashverosh still realized that Vashti disobeyed him, thereby humiliating him in public. According the law of the land, Vashti deserved to be put to death.

Unsure of how to respond, Achashveirosh asked the Jewish judges. Realizing that whatever advice they would give the king, he would later punish them for it, they said, "Your Majesty, ever since the Beis Hamikdash was destroyed, we've lost our power to judge serious cases of life and death."

Achashverosh then called in his regular, close advisors, hoping they might have some advice. However, before they had a chance to speak, Haman (then known as Memuchan), at the time one of the younger, lower ranking officers, spoke out: "Your majesty, Vashti did something that not only affects you, but something that will drastically affect the entire kingdom. If you allow her to get away with it, all the other women in your kingdom will learn from her and stop listening to their husbands. The country will soon be in chaos! Right now, we need to teach EVERYONE a lesson. Vashti must never return to the throne, and must be replaced by another, better than she.

In his drunkedness, Achashverosh ordered Vashti executed.

Vashti was killed on the last day of the feast, Shabbos, mida k'neged mida for having tortured Jewish girls, making them suffer on the holy day of Shabbos.

PURIM  פּוּרִים

The New Queen

The day after the party, Achashverosh didn't remember what happened. When he realized that Vashti had been killed, he became uncontrollably angry, killing many of his own servants in his rage. Without Vashti, the king became depressed. The king's advisors knew they needed to figure out a plan to lift his spirits. Haman, the advisor who had told Achashverosh to kill Vashti, came up with another plan to cheer the king up. The kingdom would hold a grand beauty contest to find a new queen. Haman was hoping his daughter would be chosen as queen and then he would rule, with Achashverosh as only a puppet-king. Unluckily for him it didn't go according to his plan - Achashverosh didn't choose her. After a few years of searching, there was still no queen.

Until they found Esther. Esther had been hiding, not wanting to marry someone like King Achashverosh. She was married to her cousin, Mordechai, the leader of the Jews. When the messengers came to take Esther, Mordechai instructed her not to reveal that she was Jewish. He thought that maybe if she didn't reveal where she was from, the king wouldn't want to marry her.

Esther arrived at the palace and was put into the special rooms that prepared all the contestants. Every girl was given special beauty treatment for a whole year, as well as anything and everything she asked for. Esther refused to take anything to enhance her beauty. Still, Esther was graced with a special beauty, one that shone from within. She enchanted everyone around her. Esther made sure that even though she was in the palace, she still kept Torah and Mitzvos. She ate a strict vegetarian diet to keep kosher, and asked for seven different servants, one for each day of the week, so that no one would realize she kept Shabbos.

Finally, it was Esther's turn to meet the king. Achashverosh chose her as his Queen the moment he saw her, and asked where she was from. No matter how hard he tried, Esther's lips were sealed about her family and ancestry. She only revealed to him that she was an orphan.

Esther asked Achashverosh why he didn't have a Jewish advisor, as did all the kings before him. These Jewish advisors always offered the best, most honest and trustworthy advice.

Achashverosh listened to Esther's advice and appointed Mordechai.

One day Mordechai, who sat by the gate of the palace, overheard a secret plot to poison the king. Bigsan and Seresh were upset because they were demoted when Mordechai became the chief advisor. They wanted to make it look like when they took care of the king everything was fine, but once a Jew was in charge, the king was in danger.

Bigsan and Seresh were speaking to each other in a language that people in Shushan wouldn't know: their native language, Tarshish. What they didn't know, was that Mordechai had been a member of the Sanhedrin, the Jewish high court, and understood all the spoken languages of the time, including Tarshish.

Mordechai sent an urgent message to Esther, informing her of the plot. Esther told the king, making sure to give all the credit to Mordechai. Thanks to the warning, the king was prepared, and sure enough, his drink was found to be poisoned! Bigsan & Seresh were killed, and the story of how Mordechai saved the king was written in the king's chronicles (diary).

PURIM  פּוּרִים

Haman's Plot

Shortly after this, Haman started to rise higher in power. He rose so high that he soon became the Prime Minister! Arrogantly, he ordered everyone to bow to him whenever he walked by, but Mordechai refused. Haman got angrier and angrier. He was a descendent of Amalek, so he already hated the Jewish people, and it didn't take long before that anger turned into a fiery rage. Fuming at the blow to his honor when Mordechai repeatedly refused to bow to him, Haman decided to kill not only Mordechai, but all the Jews. The first thing he would need was the perfect day to do it. He drew lots (made a lottery - a 'pur') to determine which month was the best. The lot fell out on Adar. Haman was thrilled, since he knew Moshe Rabeinu passed away in that month (he forgot that Moshe had also been born in Adar!). Now all he needed was to convince the king to agree with his plan.

Not wasting time, Haman approached King Achashverosh with his terrible plan. "There is a nation scattered amongst us who are a bunch of good-for-nothings," said Haman, "They have so many holidays, every other day they don't work. They alienate themselves, they don't marry into our families, and they even ridicule *your kingship.*" In truth though, Haman barely needed these small excuses. Achashverosh also wanted to get rid of the Jews, but he was afraid to start up with them. Haman calmed him by saying, "Oh, don't worry about their G-d, they abandoned Him, so He won't save them." Haman then offered Achashverosh 10,000 silver ducats to make for the taxes the Jews would have given him. Achashverosh refused the money and gave Haman his signet ring to do whatever he wished. Haman quickly sent out secret letters to the leaders of every province stating that on the 13th of Adar, all gentiles were able to kill the Jews and take all their possessions.

MORDECHAI INSTRUCTS ESTHER: HER MISSION!

That night, Mordechai learned through *Ruach Hakodesh* about the evil scheme. He ripped his clothes in mourning, walked up and down the streets, and cried out to the Jews to do Teshuva and return to Hashem. It didn't take long for Esther to notice his behavior from her palace window. She sent her servant, Hasach, with a new change of clothes for Mordechai and to find out what was going on. After refusing to change into the clothes she offered him, Mordechai sent her a copy of the decree, and a message that she needed to go to the king and plead for her people.

Esther told Mordechai that she hadn't been called to the king for over 30 days, and without an invitation, the king might put her to death! Mordechai responded that Hashem will find a way to save the Jews, with or without Esther's help. However, this could be the reason she had ended up in the palace, and if she chooses not to go, she would not be looked upon favorably for all future generations.

Esther finally agreed to go to the king, on the condition that the Jewish people fast for three days. She and her maidservants, would fast as well.

Mordechai knew he needed to change things Above – in Shamayim – for the Jews to be saved. What could he do to convince Hashem? Who has the greatest power to change Heavenly decrees? Yes! That's right! It's the Jewish children!

Mordechai gathered 22,000 children! He learned Torah with them and had them daven to Hashem, begging Hashem to save the Jewish Nation from destruction.

The Three Boys

One day Haman and his friends saw Mordechai approaching 3 school children. They came near to hear the conversation, and this is what they learned:

Mordechai said to the children: " פסוק לי פסוקיך" – recite for me a Possuk you learned in school today! This is what the kids replied:

Child #1: " אל תירא מפחד פתאום ומשואת רשעים כי תבוא (משלי ג: כה)" – Have no fear of sudden terror... the destruction of the wicked is on its way!

Child #2: " עוצו עצה ותפר דברו דבר ולא יקום (ישעי'ה ח: י) " They can make plans – they will not succeed! Plan a plot – and it will not happen – because m is with US!

Child #3: "ועד זקנה אני הוא ועד שיבה אני אסבל אני עשיתי ואני אשא ואני אסבל ואמלט" (ישעי'ה מו:ד) When you are old – I will be with you. When you turn white – I will sustain you, I made you, I will "carry" you, and I will sustain you and rescue you!

Mordechai rejoiced when he heard these encouraging words!

He knew that Hashem sends messages in many ways, and this was a clear sign that all will be well for the Jews!

Haman, however was very upset, and promised to deal (in his evil decree) with the children first!

PURIM  פּוּרִים

Esther's Request

At the end of the three day fast, Esther, though weak from fasting, put on her most beautiful clothes. Leaning on two maidservants for support, she entered the throne room. Although she was famished from the fast – and naturally should not have looked as beautiful as she usually did, when Achashverosh saw Esther, she suddenly found favor in his eyes. Achashverosh stretched out his scepter, an invitation to her and a way to tell the guards not to kill her, and miraculously it extended, until it was long enough to touch Esther's hand from where she stood.

"Esther, what is it that you want?" he asked her. "You can ask for up to half my kingdom." Esther asked for Achashverosh to come to a party that she would be making for him, and to also invite Haman. (Esther wanted to make Achashverosh suspicious that she and Haman were up to something – maybe plotting something against him.)

Confused about why Haman was invited, Achashverosh nevertheless ordered Haman to come. That night at the party, Achashverosh offered again, for Esther to have up to half his kingdom, asking Esther what she *really* wanted. But Esther knew the time wasn't right. Instead, she invited Haman and Achashverosh to come back again the next night for another party.

Haman left the palace that day feeling *very* good about himself. That is, until he met Mordechai. In the face of the honor of moments before, Mordechai's refusal to bow made Haman absolutely furious! He decided that waiting until Adar was too long; he needed to get rid of him at once! Haman gathered his family and all his advisors to come up with a plan to get rid of Mordechai. After many suggestions, none of which were accepted, because Jewish people had survived such perils in the past (such as fiery furnace and lion's den), Zeresh, his wife, perhaps the only person who could equal him in evil intent, came up with a plan. "Why don't you hang Mordechai on a gallow?" she suggested. Haman liked the idea, and impatient to get rid of Mordechai as soon as possible, began to build right away, with the help of his sons. As soon as it was ready, Haman headed straight to the palace to get permission for the hanging.

The King Can't Sleep!

That same night, the king could not sleep. He ordered his attendant, who was actually one of Haman's sons, to read his chronicles. Haman's son opened the book, and lo and behold, it was the story of how Mordechai had saved the king! Not wanting to talk about any good deed of Mordechai's, he tried to turn the page, but a *mal'ach* kept flipping the page back until he was forced to read it.

"Was Mordechai ever rewarded?" the king questioned.

"No." was the reply. At that moment, Haman showed up at the palace.

His timing was not overlooked by King Achashverosh, who thought it incredibly suspicious for Haman to suddenly show up in the middle of the night. He'd already become curious after Esther had invited Haman to two private parties. Was he plotting to kill him?

The king called Haman over and asked him, "What shall be done to a man I wish to honor?"

"Surely the king is referring to me," Haman thought. "Well, dearest King, I believe you should let him wear your royal robe, your royal crown, and you should have him ride on your royal white horse through the streets of Sushi. I mean Shushan. Another officer should walk in front of him, and should call out: 'Thus shall be done to the man who the king wishes to honor'"

Haman's response raised Achashverosh's suspicion even more! Haman was saying he wanted to wear his crown?! It was almost like he was saying that he wanted to be the king...!

"Perfect," Achashverosh replied, "Go make sure that all you have just said is done to Mordechai the Jew, and *you* will parade him through the streets."

Haman, horrified, immediately protested but could not change the king's mind. Instead of the king agreeing to kill Mordechai that day, Haman was forced to treat Mordechai like a king!

PURIM  פּוּרִים

After a full day of parading through the streets, Haman came home dirty and tired. All day long, people had laughed at him, and some had even thrown garbage! He didn't even have time to change when the guards of the king came to drag him to the party, where the King and Esther were waiting.

The Redemption!

"Esther, what can I do for you?" the King asked again. "I will give you up to half of my kingdom."

This time, Esther knew it was time to speak.

"My king, there is a man who wants to kill me and my entire nation!" she cried out. "Please, save me!"

"WHAT?" Achashverosh was furious. "Who would dare try to kill my precious queen?!"

Esther immediately pointed at Haman. "It's Haman!"

Upon hearing this, Achashverosh was so furious he stormed out of the banquet hall for fresh air.

As he was walking through his gardens, Hashem sent *mal'achim* dressed as workers to chop down the king's orchard. "STOP!" bellowed the king, "What are you doing?" "Haman commanded us to chop all the trees down."

Further angered, Achashverosh stormed back into the room where he'd left Haman and Esther, only to see Haman hanging over Esther's couch, where he had been begging for his life before a mal'ach had pushed him over, just in time for the king to walk back in. "You dare attack my queen in my very own palace, right in front of me?!" Achashverosh yelled.

Just then, an officer named Charvona pointed to the gallows Haman had made.

"See those gallows? Haman plans to use them for hanging Mordechai, the Jewish advisor who saved your life."

PURIM  פּוּרִים

The king had had enough! "Hang Haman on those very gallows!" He ordered.

Haman was hanged. However, sadly, the decree was still in effect. In those days, once a decree had been stamped with the king's seal, it couldn't be revoked, no matter what. Instead, Achashverosh gave Mordechai the seal so he could draft another decree, one that would tell the Jews that they could defend themselves and kill any one of their enemies.

On Yud Gimmel Adar, the day that Haman had chosen as the day of destruction for the Jewish people, the Jews fought their enemies and hanged Haman's 10 wicked sons. On Yud Daled Adar, they celebrated the victory. However, the people in the capitol of Sushi, I mean Shushan, were faced with many more enemies than the ones in the rest of Achashverosh's kingdom, and were given permission to fight an extra day. They celebrated on Tes Vov Adar.

ד* נוסח חב"ד

The Fast of Esther - תענית אסתר

What's the problem Yossi? Tomorrow is Purim, why don't you look happy?

Today is Ta'anis Esther, the day before Purim. It's the day the Jews fasted when they went out to fight their enemies. Boys and girls over Bar/Bas Mitzvah fast today!

Does everyone need to fast? Is it like Yom Kippur?
What happens if the day before Purim falls out on Sunday, do we fast on Shabbos?

Adults over Bar/Bas Mitzvah fast.
Expecting and nursing mothers or anyone not feeling well, need not fast.
A Chosson and Kallah during their week of Sheva Brachos don't fast.
If Purim falls out on a Sunday, we fast the previous Thursday.

Do we **do** anything special on Ta'anis Esther?

Glad you asked! We "do" מחצית השקל."
Fathers give three (silver) ½ dollar coins to Tzedaka. This reminds us of the ½ shekel בני ישראל gave in the month of Adar for the Korban Tzibur- a korban that was given every day on behalf of all the Jews.
See more in the *Kitzur* section below!

Interesting! Thank you so much!

Purim  פּוּרִים

The 4 Mitzvos of Purim

	What	How	When
	Megilah: We read (or hear) the Megilah.	The Megilah is read in Shul or large gatherings. Men, women, and children need to hear every word.	Twice: Once at night and once during the day.
	Mishloach Manos: We send gifts of food to friends.	We send gifts of ready-to-eat foods to a friend. At least 2 kinds of food - to 1 person. Boys give boys, girls give girls. We send the gifts through a messenger.	During the day.
	Matonos La'evyonim: We give tzedaka to the poor.	We give at least one coin or bill to <u>two</u> poor people (or Jewish organization that supports Torah study etc.). If we cannot find poor people on Purim day, we must set the $ aside on Purim, to distribute another time.	During the day.
	Mishteh: We have a Purim Se'udah (Feast).	We celebrate with a feast on Purim, during which we drink until we are so drunk, we don't know the difference between ארור המן and ברוך מרדכי!	After Mincha. If Purim falls on a Friday, we have it after Shacharis

PURIM  פּוּרִים

PURIM CUSTOMS

	What	When	Why
	Dress up in costume!	Night & / or day	1. Hashem was hiding in the Purim story (- See intro notes). 2. Esther hid her Jewish identity. 3. Poor people shouldn't be embarrassed to ask for money and since they are dressed up, we cannot see who is asking.
	Shake the gragger (or make any noise).	During the Megilah reading, when we hear Haman's name.*	There's a Mitzvah to wipe out the memory of Amalek. Haman was from Amalek's family. We use a noisy instrument to "boo" evil Haman's name.
	Eat Kreplach, a pastry filled with chopped meat.	During the meal.	Kreplach have meat hidden inside the dough, symbolizing how Hashem was hidden throughout the whole Purim story.
	Eat Hamantashen	Anytime!	1. Haman's triangular hat or ears. 2. "Mon Tash" in German/Yiddish means (poppy) seed Pocket. 3. Hamantash means Haman being weakened (tash= weakened in Hebrew). 4. They are yummy!

*Chabad's custom is to make noise only when there is an adjective after Haman's name, describing him, such as "Haman Hara, Ha'agagi etc."

PuriMitzvos

מתנות Matanos La'evyoni לאביונים

Men, women, young and old must give Matonos La'evyonim.Even poor people who live from Tzedaka funds.
It's called "Gifts" for the poor, not tzedaka, since a gift shows closeness. People only give gifts to someone whom they appreciate. We are supposed to give to the poor in an extra kind way, like we are giving them a special gift.

משלוח mishloach מנות manos

We give mishloach manos to express the unity of our nation. No person, no matter how rich, is completely self-sufficient. We need each other and send gifts to express our appreciation for our friendships.

משתה mishteh

During the Purim Mishteh, we drink wine, until we are drunk.
Aside from the simple meaning of drunk, it means that we are "drunk" with happiness that Hashem loves us and takes care of us in a "drunken" way – beyond logic, more than we deserve.

מגילה megilah

Hashem's name is not mentioned in the Megillah, since the miracle of Purim was a hidden miracle.

It looked like Hashem wasn't part of the story at all. But if we look under the surface, we clearly see the amazing "natural" miraculous events!

HaמּantashHaמantash

We eat Hamantashen that have Haman's name since we want to destroy Haman, and when you eat something, you destroy it.

The 3 corners of the Hamantash represent the 3 Avos: Avraham, Yitzchak and Yaakov, who always daven for us and helped save us in the Purim story.

Mordechai hid the news of the decree in pastries and delivered it to all the Jews to convince them how serious the situation was and how important it was that they do Teshuva
- Alshich

In the story of Purim we see the idea of ונהפוך הוא – turning upside-down, aka Topsy Turvy. Hashem caused the יהודים to do serious תשובה (sweet) through wicked Haman (bitter). We eat the Hamantash - a sweet cookie, named after the bitter Haman, to represent this Topsy Turvy.

Write your own idea here

Riddle:
Who killed his wife at the urging of his friend, then killed his friend at the urging of his wife?

גראגer

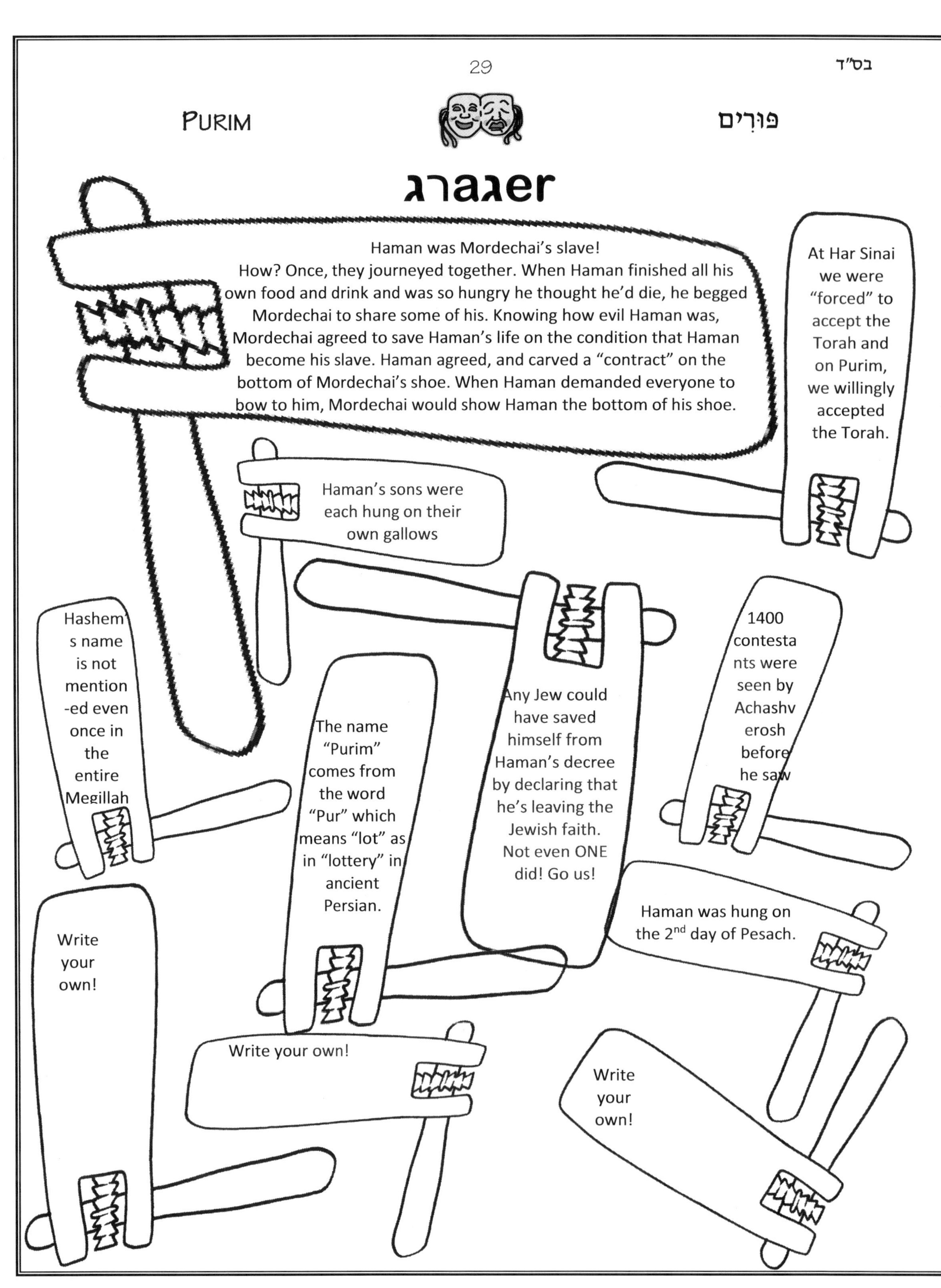
Haman was Mordechai's slave!
How? Once, they journeyed together. When Haman finished all his own food and drink and was so hungry he thought he'd die, he begged Mordechai to share some of his. Knowing how evil Haman was, Mordechai agreed to save Haman's life on the condition that Haman become his slave. Haman agreed, and carved a "contract" on the bottom of Mordechai's shoe. When Haman demanded everyone to bow to him, Mordechai would show Haman the bottom of his shoe.
At Har Sinai we were "forced" to accept the Torah and on Purim, we willingly accepted the Torah.
Haman's sons were each hung on their own gallows
Hashem's name is not mention-ed even once in the entire Megillah
The name "Purim" comes from the word "Pur" which means "lot" as in "lottery" in ancient Persian.
Any Jew could have saved himself from Haman's decree by declaring that he's leaving the Jewish faith. Not even ONE did! Go us!
1400 contestants were seen by Achashverosh before he saw
Haman was hung on the 2nd day of Pesach.
Write your own!
Write your own!
Write your own!

PURIM  פּוּרִים

חֲנוּכָּה Vs. פּוּרִים

On חֲנוּכָּה and פּוּרִים we celebrate and thank ה' for the wonderful miracles He made for us. Both חֲנוּכָּה and פּוּרִים are happy times of celebration. However, the way we celebrate on these two יָמִים טוֹבִים (Holidays) are very different.

WHAT	חֲנוּכָּה	פּוּרִים
Manner of Celebration	On חֲנוּכָּה, the main celebration is הַלֵּל and הוֹדָאָה - praise and thanksgiving to ה'. We celebrate in a רוּחָנִיוּת-spiritual way.	יְמֵי מִשְׁתֶּה וְשִׂמְחָה פּוּרִים days are - days of feasting and joy. We rejoice with a festive meal.
	Reason: Because on חֲנוּכָּה the (decree) was against our נְשָׁמוֹת. The Greeks didn't really want to kill our bodies, they mainly wanted us to stop serving ה' the way we do with such great אֱמוּנָה. The celebration too, is a spiritual one, of thanks and praise in our תְּפִילוֹת.	Reason: Because on פּוּרִים they wanted to kill us physically. They wanted our bodies. That is why we celebrate our victory with our bodies - with joyous feasts.
What came first?	חֲנוּכָּה happened after פּוּרִים	פּוּרִים happened before חֲנוּכָּה
Where?	חֲנוּכָּה happened in אֶרֶץ יִשְׂרָאֵל	פּוּרִים happened in Persia
Type of Miracle:	Revealed, clearly above the laws of nature	Hidden, not so obviously above the laws of nature
King:	אַנְטִיָּכוּס	אֲחַשְׁוֵרוֹשׁ
Our Heroes	The Macabees – חַשְׁמוֹנָאִים	אֶסְתֵּר & מָרְדְּכַי
Game/Toy	Dreidel	Gragger
Food	Oily: Latkes, donuts and dairy	Hamantashen

PURIM  פּוּרִים

PURIM POWER ILLUMINATED

Megillas Esther

Everyone knows the name of the Megilah is Megillas Esther. But Why? Why couldn't it be called "Megillas Mordechai", or "Megillas Esther and Mordechai"? After all, they wrote the Megilah together and Mordechai was the one who told Esther to go to the king! It would seem that he was really the one who the Megilah should be named after.

You see, Esther was the one who ACTUALLY went and made the story happen. Mordechai didn't go to the king and risk his life, Esther did. Mordechai did not tell the king about the evil Haman, Esther did. Mordechai did not ask the king to allow the Jews to fight back and save themselves, Esther did. Since Esther was the one who did the ACTION, the Megilah is named after her.

What can we learn from this?

Where is אסתר hiding?

ואנכי הסתר אסתי פני ביום ההוא:

And I will hide my face on that day...

Can you see "אסתר" hiding in these words?

This phrase from the Torah tells us about how Hashem was dealing with the world during the time of Purim: In a hidden manner.

The Power of children

"Me?! I'm just a kid! I'm not grown up; I go to school every day and do regular kid stuff. How can I actually accomplish something big?"

Do children really have the power to change the world?

When there was a heavy decree on the Jewish People, Mordechai knew the secret. Instead of calling all the great older sages and successful Jewish adults, Mordechai gathered 22,000 Jewish children, learned Torah and davened with them.

Why? Because children DO have the power to change the world! It was the learning and davening of the children that helped save the entire Jewish people!

Celebrate by giving

Why is Purim all about giving? We give gifts to the poor, we give gifts of food to our friends, and we invite everyone to a festive meal.

Why?

PURIM  פּוּרִים

The Jewish way to celebrate is by giving. When we are grateful to Hashem, we show Him how much we appreciate what He's done by helping - and making others happy. When we are glad, we give. When we are thankful, we give. When we want to celebrate our victory, we give.

Giving makes others happy and when they are happy, they too give to others.

So we go on and on and make more people happy until we affect the entire Jewish People. And when we are happy, we make Hashem happy as well.

True Happiness

In the Megilah there are two times it mentions happiness:

The first time was with Haman. When he was invited to the meal that Esther prepared for him and the king, it says that "Haman went out on that day joyful and happy".

The second time it's in reference to the Jews celebrating the victory of Purim.

What's the difference between the two?

Haman's happiness was superficial. It wasn't true happiness. Haman's happiness, changed drastically the moment Mordechai didn't bow to him. Haman had everything at that point; money, power, fame. Yet the moment one person refused to bow down to him, he couldn't be happy. Haman even told his wife that everything he has means nothing as long as Mordechai was alive and not bowing to him.

True happiness is not from power and fame. When the Jews celebrated it says, "The Jews had light and joy". The light refers to the Torah which we were now able to follow freely. Following the Torah brings real, everlasting happiness.

Haman's Ancestry

Many years before the Purim story, Shmuel Hanavi relates Hashem's instructions to King Shaul: "Wipe out the entire nation of Amalek. Do not spare one of them."

Shaul Hamelech has mercy on Agag, the King of Amalek and holds him captive. While in prison, Agag manages to marry, and father a child. Generations later, Haman descends from this child.

Another (opposite) story happened soon after Shaul's "mercy."

Shimi ben Gerah challenged Dovid Hamelech, (who was king right after Shaul). Legally, David could (should?) have had Shimi put to death, however, David spares Shimi. Generations later... Mordechai descends from Shimi.

From here we see a clear message. Mercy and kindness is only when it follows Hashem's instructions. Shaul had "mercy" on someone – after Hashem had instructed him to kill him... That didn't work out too well for us... We've suffered from that "kindness" for many generations.

Dovid Hamelech, however, went out of his way to be kind, and not take revenge. Dovid's act of true kindness produced the "cure" – Mordechai – for Shaul's mistaken mercy!

Drunk?! עד דלא ידע?!

Are we really supposed to get so drunk that we don't know the difference between "Boruch Mordechai and Arur Haman?!"

Well, for that you can check the Shulchan Aruch, below.

Here's another understanding of עד דלא ידע on Purim.

The word ידע – means knowing, related to understanding, logic.

During the time of the Purim story, בני ישראל acted in a way that would "logically" cause Hashem to allow for not good things to happen to them.

In the end, Hashem acted towards us in a "לא ידע" manner. We were not punished as we "logically" deserved. Hashem demonstrated a love for us that is greater than our "logical" connection to Him. So too, we, on Purim, celebrate in thanking Hashem in a על דלא ידע manner.

PURIM  פּוּרִים

Gragger vs. Dreidel

One of the differences between חֲנוּכָּה and פּוּרִים is expressed in the way we handle the toys of the day.

We spin the חֲנוּכָּה Dreidel from the top, and the פּוּרִים Gragger is spun from the bottom.

One explanation for this difference is because the miracle of חֲנוּכָּה was clearly from Above (the top), in a manner that was higher than nature, while the Miracle of פּוּרִים was not so clearly from above. It was a miracle that was "clothed" in nature – "below".

The miracle of פּוּרִים did not all happen at once in a clearly miraculous manner, rather, it happened over a few years and included many steps. Looking back at all that happened, we realize that it was all a slowly unfolding miracle, but it takes thought to understand it.

Another explanation:

On פּוּרִים, the Jewish people fasted and Davened, asking for ה׳'s help. They "worked hard" to annul Haman's decree, and they "earned" the miracle. That's why the Gragger's handle is on the bottom.

Draw your noisy gragger here

D.E.A.R.(H.) ד.ע.א.ר

INSTRUCTIONS — READING MINUTE - דַקַת קְרִיאָה — PURIM

Dear Student. Here is your D.E.A.R ***Purim*** *Kriyah* program!

DROP **E**VERYTHING **A**ND **R**EAD (HEBREW!) - is a fun reading program that helps improve your reading ability every day. One of the best things about this program is that you see - and keep track of - your daily improvements.

Teacher will give you a reading page to practice. Keep working with that page until Teacher gives you another – or until you can read the page very fast without any mistakes – however Teacher decides.

YOUR GOAL IS TO READ THE WHOLE PAGE SMOOTHLY, WITHOUT MISTAKES.

During each D.E.A.R. session, "Reader" will read for 1 or 2 minutes, while "Listener" listens. Then you switch and "Listener" becomes "Reader". This is how it works.

1. D.E.A.R. time begins when Teacher starts the timer: ...3 ...2 ...1 ...go! The timer will go for 1 or 2 minutes – as Teacher decides.

2. "Listener" holds your D.E.A.R. sheet while you read from his. Read each word, care-ful-ly pro-noun-cing **eve-ry sy-lla-ble,** as **"Listener"** carefully listens.

3. As you read, **"Listener"** holds your page and circles (in pencil) the line, word, letter or **נְקוּדָה** he thinks - you may still need to practice. Teacher will tell you whether to circle the line, word, letter or just the **נְקוּדָה**.

4. When the timer beeps – or the time is up, **"Listener" notes** in your chart, **the number of li**nes you read, and how many lines, words, etc. he circled for you to practice.

If "Listener" thinks you need to practice a word to read it better, s/he notes it in the chart. Even if you believe that you read the word correctly, don't worry. Just let him/her note it in your chart without a fuss.
You won't lose any points,
and it's a very healthy
self-control exercise.

5. Now it's your turn to be **"Listener"**.
Take "Reader's" page and do the same.

For each "D.E.A.R." session,
you read 1-5 times and listen 1-5 times.
In this manner: You read, switch papers, you listen.
Read, Switch, Listen. Read, Switch, Listen. Etc.

D.E.A.R.(H.) — ד.ע.א.ר

Purim — Reading Minute - דַּקַּת קְרִיאָה — פּוּרִים

L = Lines (# of lines you read) P = Practice (# of words you need to practice)

Sample	Day:	Sunday											
Sample	Date:	יא אדר א											
Sample	Time:	1 Minute											
Sample	Read:	וְעַל הַנִּסִּים		וְעַל הַנִּסִּים		וְעַל הַנִּסִּים		וְעַל הַנִּסִּים		וְעַל הַנִּסִּים		וְעַל הַנִּסִּים	
	L/P	L	P	L	P	L	P	L	P	L	P	L	P
Reading Rounds	1st	10	5										
Reading Rounds	2nd	13	3										
Reading Rounds	3rd	15	2										
Reading Rounds	4th	18	1										
Reading Rounds	5th	20	0										

1. וְעַל הַנִּסִּים,
2. וְעַל הַפֻּרְקָן,
3. וְעַל הַגְּבוּרוֹת,
4. וְעַל הַתְּשׁוּעוֹת,
5. וְעַל הַמִּלְחָמוֹת

(5. וְעַל הַנִּפְלָאוֹת)

6. שֶׁעָשִׂיתָ לַאֲבוֹתֵינוּ
7. בַּיָּמִים הָהֵם
8. בִּזְּמַן הַזֶּה.
9. בִּימֵי מָרְדְּכַי וְאֶסְתֵּר
10. בְּשׁוּשַׁן הַבִּירָה,
11. כְּשֶׁעָמַד עֲלֵיהֶם
12. הָמָן הָרָשָׁע,
13. בִּקֵּשׁ לְהַשְׁמִיד
14. לַהֲרֹג וּלְאַבֵּד
15. אֶת כָּל הַיְּהוּדִים,
16. מִנַּעַר וְעַד זָקֵן,
17. טַף וְנָשִׁים,
18. בְּיוֹם אֶחָד,
19. בִּשְׁלוֹשָׁה עָשָׂר
20. לְחֹדֶשׁ שְׁנֵים עָשָׂר,
21. הוּא חֹדֶשׁ אֲדָר,
22. וּשְׁלָלָם לָבוֹז.
23. וְאַתָּה
24. בְּרַחֲמֶיךָ הָרַבִּים
25. הֵפַרְתָּ אֶת עֲצָתוֹ,
26. וְקִלְקַלְתָּ אֶת מַחֲשַׁבְתּוֹ,
27. וַהֲשֵׁבוֹתָ לּוֹ
28. גְּמוּלוֹ בְּרֹאשׁוֹ,
29. וְתָלוּ אוֹתוֹ
30. וְאֶת בָּנָיו עַל הָעֵץ.

My [hiccup] Purim [hiccup] Experience

Don't Try This At Home. Or Anywhere Else. Ever.

I had 12 bottles of whiskey in my cellar and I was instructed by my wife to empty each and every bottle down the drain, so I proceeded with the task.

I withdrew the cork from the first bottle and poured the contents down the sink, with the exception of one glass which I drank.

I extracted the cork from the second bottle and did likewise, with the exception of one glass which I drank.

I then poured the contents down the sink, with the exception of one glass which I drank.

I then pulled the cork from the fourth sink, poured the bottles down the glass, which I drank.

I pulled the bottle from the cork of the next, and drank one sink out of it and threw the rest down the glass.

I pulled the sink out of the glass and poured the cork from the bottle. Then I corked the sink with the glass, bottled the drink and drank the pour.

When I had everything emptied, I steadied the house with one hand, counted the bottles, corks, glasses and sinks with the other, which were 29 and put the house in the bottle, which I drank.

I'm not under the affluence of incahol, but thinkle peep I am.

I'm not half as thunk as you might drink.
I fool so feelish I don't know who is me,
and the drunker I stand here the longer I get!

Hope you are having a blessed [hiccup] Purim!

From the original: The Eighteen Bottles, by Henry Morgan

PURIM  פּוּרִים

Cut out these letters. Shuffle them and compete with a friend to see who can put the sentence back in order first! Yes! Cut 'em right off this page! Don't worry! They will grow back!

ס	נַ	כְ	נִ	שֶׁ	מִ
			ר	דָ	אַ
	ם	י	בִּ	רְ	מַ
!	ה	חָ	מְ	שִׂ	בְּ

PuriMatch

Match the words on the left to their match on the right

1.	אגג	____	אסתר's son
2.	אסתר	____	בין ארור המן לברוך מרדכי
3.	בן יאיר בן שמעי בן קיש איש ימיני	____	דוד המלך spared his life
4.	דריוש	____	הדסה
5.	המן	____	מרדכי
6.	והעיר שושן	____	סעודת פורים
7.	ושתי	____	עמלק
8.	ושתי	____	שאול should have killed him...
9.	כורש	____	שושן פורים
10.	ככה ייעשה לאיש	____	began rebuilding the בית המקדש
11.	ליהודים היתה	____	he ruled for 45 years
12.	מרדכי	____	he was from שבט בנימין
13.	משנכנס אדר	____	wanted her husband to stop the rebuilding of the בהמ"ק
14.	נבוכדנצר	____	light and rejoicing
15.	עד דלא ידע	____	shouted and was glad
16.	עמלק	____	the descendant of עמלק
17.	שמעי	____	the first and worst enemy of the בני ישראל
18.	Adar 14th	____	the first queen
19.	Adar 15th	____	we must increase our rejoicing
20.	erase his name	____	whom the king wants to honor

Who-What-Aמ-I

Write the number of the correct source:

____משלוח מנות	____סעודת פורים	____תרש
____נדדה שנת המלך	____ושתי	____בגתן
____מרדכי	____עד דלא ידע	____מתנות לאביונים
____ועל הנסים	____רעשן	____אוזני המן
to dress up ____	____מסכות	____ככה ייעשה לאיש
____עד חצי המלכות	____הפיל פור	____אסתר
____המן	____אחשוורוש	____קריאת המגילה

Sources

1. Expression from the **מגילה**
2. "Character" in the **מגילה**
3. **מנהגי פורים**
4. **מצוות פורים**

Pesukiם Challenge!

Practice the Pesukim we all read out loud during the Megilah reading.

ב: ה אִ֣ישׁ יְהוּדִ֔י הָיָ֖ה בְּשׁוּשַׁ֣ן הַבִּירָ֑ה

וּשְׁמ֣וֹ מָרְדֳּכַ֗י בֶּ֣ן יָאִ֧יר בֶּן־שִׁמְעִ֛י בֶּן־קִ֖ישׁ אִ֥ישׁ יְמִינִֽי׃

ח: טו וּמָרְדֳּכַ֞י יָצָ֣א ׀ מִלִּפְנֵ֣י הַמֶּ֗לֶךְ בִּלְב֤וּשׁ מַלְכוּת֙ תְּכֵ֣לֶת וָח֔וּר

וַעֲטֶ֤רֶת זָהָב֙ גְּדוֹלָ֔ה וְתַכְרִ֥יךְ בּ֖וּץ וְאַרְגָּמָ֑ן

וְהָעִ֣יר שׁוּשָׁ֔ן צָהֲלָ֖ה וְשָׂמֵֽחָה׃

ח: טז לַיְּהוּדִ֕ים הָֽיְתָ֥ה אוֹרָ֖ה וְשִׂמְחָ֑ה וְשָׂשֹׂ֖ן וִיקָֽר׃

י: ג כִּ֣י ׀ מָרְדֳּכַ֣י הַיְּהוּדִ֗י

מִשְׁנֶה֙ לַמֶּ֣לֶךְ אֲחַשְׁוֵר֔וֹשׁ

וְגָדוֹל֙ לַיְּהוּדִ֔ים וְרָצ֖וּי לְרֹ֣ב אֶחָ֑יו

דֹּרֵ֥שׁ טוֹב֙ לְעַמּ֔וֹ וְדֹבֵ֥ר שָׁל֖וֹם לְכָל־זַרְעֽוֹ׃

The Baal Koreh needs to read ALL the names of Haman's ten sons in one breath. Can you?!

ט: ו ...חֲמֵ֥שׁ מֵא֖וֹת אִֽישׁ׃

ז וְאֵ֣ת ׀ פַּרְשַׁנְדָּ֗תָא וְאֵ֣ת ׀ דַּלְפ֛וֹן וְאֵ֥ת ׀ אַסְפָּֽתָא׃

ח וְאֵ֣ת ׀ פּוֹרָ֗תָא וְאֵ֥ת ׀ אֲדַלְיָ֖א וְאֵ֥ת ׀ אֲרִידָֽתָא׃

ט וְאֵ֣ת ׀ פַּרְמַ֗שְׁתָּא וְאֵ֣ת ׀ אֲרִיסַ֔י וְאֵ֥ת ׀ אֲרִדַ֖י וְאֵ֥ת ׀ וַיְזָֽתָא׃

י עֲשֶׂ֨רֶת בְּנֵ֨י הָמָ֧ן בֶּן־הַמְּדָ֛תָא

קִיצוּר שֻׁלְחָן עָרוּךְ

KITZUR SHULCHAN ARUCH

THIS SECTION CONTAINS THE LAWS OF PURIM
IN HEBREW WITH AN ORIGINAL TRANSLATION

THIS IS A **NON-LITERAL** TRANSLATION, **FOCUSING ON THE CONTENT** OF EACH HALACHAH

סי' קמ: סֵדֶר אַרְבַּע פָּרָשִׁיּוֹת

CHAP. 140: THE ORDER OF THE 4 PARSHIYOS

סי' קמא: הִלְכוֹת מְגִלָּה

CHAPTER 141: LAWS OF MEGILAH

סי' קמב: הִלְכוֹת מִשְׁלוֹחַ מָנוֹת אִישׁ לְרֵעֵהוּ וּמַתָּנוֹת לָאֶבְיוֹנִים וּסְעוּדַּת פּוּרִים

CHAPTER 142: LAWS OF: MISHLOACH MANOS,
MATONOS LA'EVYONIM, SE'UDAHS PURIM

THE KITZUR REVIEW SECTION IS ON PAGE 116
FOLLOWED BY A
SPECIAL, FUN, (YET PRETTY TOUGH!) MULTIPLE CHOICE QUIZZES
FROM KITZUR365.ORG! – THANK YOU!

Note: This is a loose translation, focusing on the content rather than the words.

#:	CHAP. 140: THE ORDER OF THE 4 PARSHIYOS	סי' קמ: סֵדֶר אַרְבַּע פָּרָשִׁיּוֹת	סְעִיף #:
1.	(There are 4 special Torah readings during the weeks before Purim & Pesach, and these 4 *Shabbosim* have special names, related to the special reading.)		
2.	The Shabbos before *Rosh Chodesh Adar** is called "*Shabbos Parshas Shekalim*". * On a leap-year, it would be *Adar* 2, the month just before *Nisan*.	שַׁבָּת שֶׁלִּפְנֵי רֹאשׁ חֹדֶשׁ אֲדָר הַסָּמוּךְ לְנִיסָן הוּא שַׁבַּת פָּרָשַׁת שְׁקָלִים,	א
3.	If *Rosh Chodesh* falls on *Shabbos*, we read from 3 *Sifrei Torah*. This is what we read, from the 3 *Sifrei Torah*:	וְאִם חָל רֹאשׁ חֹדֶשׁ בְּשַׁבָּת אֲזַי הוּא שַׁבַּת שְׁקָלִים, וּמוֹצִיאִין שְׁלֹשָׁה סִפְרֵי תוֹרָה,	
4.	Torah #1: We read 6 *Aliyos* of the regular *Parshas Hashavuah* – weekly Torah portion.	בָּרִאשׁוֹן קוֹרִין שִׁשָּׁה בְּפָרָשַׁת הַשָּׁבוּעַ.	
5.	Torah #2: We read the *Rosh Chodesh* reading for the 7th *Aliyah***, then say half *Kaddish*. ** Begin the reading from "וּבְיוֹם הַשַּׁבָּת".	בַּשֵּׁנִי קוֹרִין הַשְּׁבִיעִי בְּשֶׁל רֹאשׁ חֹדֶשׁ וּמַתְחִילִין וּבְיוֹם הַשַּׁבָּת וְאוֹמְרִים חֲצִי קַדִּישׁ,	
6.	Torah #3: We read *Parshas Shekalim* for the *Maftir Aliyah*.	בַּשְּׁלִישִׁי קוֹרִין מַפְטִיר בְּפָרָשַׁת שְׁקָלִים,	
7.	The *Haftorah* is a special one for *Parshas Shekalim*.	וּמַפְטִירִין הַפְטָרַת שְׁקָלִים.	
8.	If they mistakenly began reading *Parshas Shekalim* from the first Torah, they complete the reading.	וְאִם טָעוּ וְהִתְחִילוּ לִקְרוֹת תְּחִלָּה בְּפָרָשַׁת שְׁקָלִים גּוֹמְרִים,	
9.	They then read the *Rosh Chodesh* reading for *Maftir* and the usual *Shabbos / Rosh Chodesh Haftorah*.	וְהַמַּפְטִיר קוֹרֵא בְּשֶׁל רֹאשׁ חֹדֶשׁ וּמַפְטִיר גַּם כֵּן הַפְטָרַת שַׁבָּת וְרֹאשׁ חֹדֶשׁ.	
10.	The *Shabbos* before Purim is called "*[Shabbos] Parshas Zachor*."	שַׁבָּת שֶׁלִּפְנֵי פוּרִים הוּא פָּרָשַׁת זָכוֹר	ב
	The Shabbos before *Rosh Chodesh Nisan* is called "*Shabbos Parshas Hachodesh*."	וְהַשַּׁבָּת שֶׁלִּפְנֵי רֹאשׁ חֹדֶשׁ נִיסָן הוּא פָּרָשַׁת הַחֹדֶשׁ,	

Note: This is a loose translation, focusing on the content rather than the words.

11.	If *Rosh Chodesh* (*Nisan*) falls on *Shabbos*, it is still *Parshas Hachodesh*.	וְאִם חָל רֹאשׁ חֹדֶשׁ בְּשַׁבָּת אָז הוּא פָּרָשַׁת הַחֹדֶשׁ, וְדִינוֹ כְּמוֹ רֹאשׁ חֹדֶשׁ אֲדָר שֶׁחָל בְּשַׁבָּת.	
12.	The *Shabbos* before *Parshas Hachodesh* is called "*Shabbos Parshas Parah.*"	וְהַשַּׁבָּת שֶׁלְּפְנֵי פָּרָשַׁת הַחֹדֶשׁ הוּא פָּרָשַׁת פָּרָה.	
13.	Some say that our obligation to read *Parshas Zachor* and *Parah* are "*D'oraisa* – (Biblical, from the Torah *Shebichsav*" itself),	יֵשׁ אוֹמְרִים כִּי פָּרָשַׁת זָכוֹר וּפָרָשַׁת פָּרָה חַיָּבִים לִקְרוֹתָם מִדְּאוֹרַיְתָא,	ג
14.	And therefore, a "koton" (boy under *Bar Mitzvah*) should not be called for the *Maftir Aliyah*.	וְאֵין קוֹרִין בָּהֶם קָטָן לְמַפְטִיר,	
15.	Those who live in little *shtetels* that don't have a *minyan*, should make sure to go - on these *shabbosim* - to a community that has a *minyan*, (so they can hear the Torah readings).	וּבְנֵי הַיִּשׁוּבִים שֶׁאֵין לָהֶם מִנְיָן צְרִיכִין שֶׁיָּבֹאוּ לְמָקוֹם שֶׁיֵּשׁ מִנְיָן,	
16.	If this is not possible, they should, at least, read these portions with their proper trop.	וְאִם אִי אֶפְשָׁר לָהֶם, לְכָל הַפָּחוֹת יִקְרְאוּ אוֹתָן בִּנְגִינוֹת כָּרָאוּי.	

Can you hear the lines calling you? They are asking you to write a Purim Rhyme! Yes, You!

קִיצוּר שֻׁלְחָן עָרוּךְ – סִימָן קמא – הִלְכוֹת מְגִלָּה
Kitzur Shulchan Aruch – Chapter 141 – The Laws of Megillah
Note: This is a loose translation, focusing on the content rather than the words.

Chapter 141: Laws of Megilah	סי׳ קמא: הִלְכוֹת מְגִלָּה
1. When the month of Adar begins, we increase in joy*. {When you read this in class, surprise your teacher! Get up and dance!}	א "מִשֶּׁנִּכְנַס אֲדָר מַרְבִּים בְּשִׂמְחָה",
2. Schedule to settle your legal matters with others*, during this month.	וְיִשְׂרָאֵל שֶׁיֵּשׁ לוֹ דִין וּדְבָרִים עִם אֵינוֹ יְהוּדִי יִשְׁפּוֹט עִמּוֹ בְּחֹדֶשׁ זֶה.
3. In the times of Mordechai and Esther, the Jewish people gathered on the 13th of Adar to defend themselves and take revenge from their enemies.	ב בִּימֵי מָרְדֳּכַי וְאֶסְתֵּר נִקְהֲלוּ הַיְּהוּדִים בִּשְׁלֹשָׁה עָשָׂר לְחֹדֶשׁ אֲדָר לַעֲמוֹד עַל נַפְשָׁם וּלְהִנָּקֵם מֵאוֹיְבֵיהֶם,
4. They needed H's mercy.	וְהָיוּ צְרִיכִין לְבַקֵּשׁ רַחֲמִים מֵאֵת ה' יִתְבָּרַךְ שְׁמוֹ שֶׁיַּעְזְרֵם,
5. When Jews need mercy from H, they fast.	וּמָצִינוּ שֶׁכַּאֲשֶׁר הָיוּ יִשְׂרָאֵל בְּמִלְחָמָה, הִתְעַנּוּ שֶׁיַּעְזְרֵם ה',
6. Just like Moshe, who fasted on the day he battled Amalek.	וְגַם מֹשֶׁה רַבֵּינוּ עָלָיו הַשָּׁלוֹם בְּיוֹם שֶׁנִּלְחַם עִם עֲמָלֵק הִתְעַנָּה,
7. If so, it is reasonable to assume that they fasted on the 13th of Adar.	וְאִם כֵּן מִסְתָּמָא גַּם אָז בִּימֵי מָרְדֳּכַי וְאֶסְתֵּר הִתְעַנּוּ בְּיוֹם י"ג אֲדָר,
8. Therefore, the Jewish people accepted upon themselves this day as a fast day, called The Fast of Esther.	וְלָכֵן קִבְּלוּ עֲלֵיהֶם כָּל יִשְׂרָאֵל יוֹם זֶה לְתַעֲנִית צִבּוּר וְנִקְרָא "תַּעֲנִית אֶסְתֵּר",

Note: This is a loose translation, focusing on the content rather than the words.

9.	When we fast, we remember that our fasting and sincere Teshuva cause Hashem to see and hear everyone in their time of need,	כְּדֵי לִזְכּוֹר שֶׁהַבּוֹרֵא יִתְבָּרֵךְ שְׁמוֹ רוֹאֶה וְשׁוֹמֵעַ תְּפִלַּת כָּל אִישׁ בְּעֵת צָרָתוֹ, כַּאֲשֶׁר יִתְעַנֶּה וְיָשׁוּב אֶל ה' בְּכָל לְבָבוֹ	
10.	just as Hashem responded to our ancestors, when they needed His help.	כְּמוֹ שֶׁעָשָׂה לַאֲבוֹתֵינוּ בַּיָּמִים הָהֵם.	
11.	This fast is not as strict as the 4 fasts explicitly mentioned in Torah,	וּמִכָּל מָקוֹם אֵין תַּעֲנִית זֶה חוֹבָה כָּל כָּךְ, כְּמוֹ אַרְבָּעָה תַּעֲנִיתִים שֶׁכְּתוּבִים בַּמִּקְרָא,	
12.	therefore, we are lenient with this fast as needed, and these are some who need not fast:	וְלָכֵן יֵשׁ לְהָקֵל בּוֹ בְּעֵת הַצֹּרֶךְ, כְּגוֹן:	
13.	A pregnant or nursing woman, or a mother who gave birth within the past month, Someone who has a painful headache,	מְעֻבָּרוֹת וּמֵינִיקוֹת אוֹ אֲפִלּוּ חוֹלֶה קְצָת בִּכְאֵב עֵינַיִם שֶׁאִם מִצְטַעֲרִים הַרְבֵּה לֹא יִתְעַנּוּ, וְכֵן יוֹלֶדֶת כָּל שְׁלֹשִׁים יוֹם,	
14.	A Chosson (or Kallah) during the week of Sheva Brachos.	וְכֵן חָתָן בְּתוֹךְ שִׁבְעַת יְמֵי הַמִּשְׁתֶּה שֶׁלּוֹ אֵינוֹ צָרִיךְ לְהִתְעַנּוֹת	
15.	Those who skip this fast, make it up another time.	וְיִפְרְעוּ אֶת הַתַּעֲנִית אַחַר כָּךְ,	
16.	Healthy people should not excuse themselves from the fast – not to separate from the community -	אֲבָל שְׁאָר הַבְּרִיאִים לֹא יִפְרְשׁוּ אֶת עַצְמָם מִן הַצִּבּוּר,	
17.	Even travelers for whom it's difficult, should still fast.	וַאֲפִילוּ מִי שֶׁהוֹלֵךְ בַּדֶּרֶךְ וְקָשֶׁה עָלָיו הַתַּעֲנִית מִכָּל מָקוֹם צָרִיךְ לְהִתְעַנּוֹת.	
18.	Purim is on the 14th day of Adar.	בְּיוֹם י"ד אֲדָר הוּא פּוּרִים,	ג
19.	When Purim falls on a Sunday, we fast the previous Thursday.	וְאִם חָל פּוּרִים בְּיוֹם רִאשׁוֹן מַקְדִּימִין לְהִתְעַנּוֹת בְּיוֹם חֲמִישִׁי,	

קִיצוּר שֻׁלְחָן עָרוּךְ – סִימָן קמא – הִלְכוֹת מְגִלָּה

KITZUR SHULCHAN ARUCH – CHAPTER 141 – THE LAWS OF MEGILLAH

Note: This is a loose translation, focusing on the content rather than the words.

20.	 If there is a Bris on Thursday, the meal for the Bris should be at night.	וְאִם יֵשׁ אָז בְּרִית מִילָה יַעֲשׂוּ אֶת הַסְעֻדָּה בַּלַּיְלָה,	
21.	The Sandek and father of the baby may eat during the day,	אֲבָל הַסַנְדָּק וַאֲבִי הַבֵּן מֻתָּרִין לֶאֱכוֹל בַּיּוֹם,	
22.	and need not make up this fast on Friday.	וְאֵין צְרִיכִין לְהִתְעַנּוֹת בְּיוֹם שִׁשִּׁי,	
23.	Anyone else, who mistakenly ate on Thursday, should fast on Friday.	אֲבָל אָדָם אַחֵר שֶׁשָּׁכַח וְאָכַל בְּיוֹם חֲמִישִׁי יִתְעַנֶּה בְּיוֹם שִׁשִּׁי.	
24.	(*The question is here, when should we fast, because תענית אסתר is on the 13th of Adar – and this would be Shabbos – and we are not meant to fast on Shabbos – so what should we do?)		
25.	We dress in Shabbos clothing in honor of the Megilah reading. The home should be prepared with candles lit, table set and beds made.	לִכְבוֹד הַמְּגִלָּה יֵשׁ לִלְבּוֹשׁ בִּגְדֵי שַׁבָּת מִבָּעֶרֶב, וּכְשֶׁבָּא מִבֵּית הַכְּנֶסֶת יִמְצָא בְּבֵיתוֹ נֵרוֹת דּוֹלְקִים וְשֻׁלְחָן עָרוּךְ וּמִטָּה מֻצַּעַת.	ד...

קִיצוּר שֻׁלְחָן עָרוּךְ – סִימָן קמא – הִלְכוֹת מְגִלָּה

KITZUR SHULCHAN ARUCH – CHAPTER 141 – THE LAWS OF MEGILLAH

Note: This is a loose translation, focusing on the content rather than the words.

26.	This is the order of the evening: Maariv Kaddish Shalaim with Tiskabeil	עַרְבִית לְאַחַר שְׁמוֹנֶה עֶשְׂרֵה אוֹמְרִים קַדִּישׁ שָׁלֵם עִם "תִּתְקַבֵּל",	...ד
27.	Read the Megilah	וְקוֹרִין אֶת הַמְּגִלָּה,	
28.	V'Atah Kadosh	אַחַר כָּךְ אוֹמְרִים "וְאַתָּה קָדוֹשׁ*"	
29.	Kaddish Shalaim w/o Tiskabeil	וְאַחַר כָּךְ קַדִּישׁ שָׁלֵם בְּלֹא "תִּתְקַבֵּל",	
30.	On Motzei Shabbos after Megilah: 1. Vi'hi Noam 2. V'Atah Kadosh 3. Kaddish Shalaim w/o Tiskabeil 4. V'Yiten Lecha 5. Havdalah 6. Aleinu	וּבְמוֹצָאֵי שַׁבָּת "וִיהִי נֹעַם", "וְאַתָּה קָדוֹשׁ", קַדִּישׁ שָׁלֵם בְּלֹא "תִּתְקַבֵּל", "וְיִתֶּן לְךָ", וּמַבְדִּילִין עַל הַכּוֹס, "עָלֵינוּ."	
31.	* (שֶׁהוּא בְּמִזְמוֹר (תהלים כב) "לַמְנַצֵּחַ עַל אַיֶּלֶת הַשַּׁחַר", שֶׁנֶּאֱמַר עַל אֶסְתֵּר וְשָׁם נֶאֱמַר (ג) "אֱלֹהַי אֶקְרָא וְגוֹ'" דְּנֶאֱמַר עַל מִקְרָא מְגִלָּה, דְּאָמַר ר' יְהוֹשֻׁעַ בֶּן לֵוִי: חַיָּב אָדָם לִקְרוֹת אֶת הַמְּגִלָּה בַּלַּיְלָה וְלִשְׁנוֹתָהּ בַּיּוֹם, שֶׁנֶּאֱמַר "אֱלֹהַי אֶקְרָא יוֹמָם וְלֹא תַעֲנֶה וְלַיְלָה וְלֹא דוּמִיָּה לִי", וּסְמִיךְ לֵיהּ (ד) "וְאַתָּה קָדוֹשׁ וְגוֹ'"),		
32.	[Erev Purim] We give "Machatzis Hashekel." We use the coin that equals half of the local currency ($) of that time and place.*	נוֹהֲגִין לִתֵּן קֹדֶם פּוּרִים מַחֲצִית מִן הַמַּטְבֵּעַ הַקָּבוּעַ בְּאוֹתוֹ מָקוֹם וּבְאוֹתוֹ זְמַן,	ה
33.	to commemorate the half shekel the Jews would give in the month of Adar to support the community Korbanos.	זֵכֶר לְמַחֲצִית הַשֶּׁקֶל שֶׁהָיוּ נוֹתְנִין בַּאֲדָר לְצֹרֶךְ קָרְבְּנוֹת הַצִּבּוּר,	
34.	We use 3 coins because it says 3x in פָּרָשַׁת כִּי תִשָּׂא תְּרוּמָה.	וּמִנְהָג לִתֵּן שָׁלֹשׁ מַחֲצִית מִשּׁוּם דִּבְפָרָשַׁת כִּי תִשָּׂא כְּתִיב שָׁלֹשׁ פְּעָמִים תְּרוּמָה.	
35.	This is done Erev Purim, before we read the Megilah, and the money is given to poor people.	וְנוֹתְנִין בְּעֶרֶב לִפְנֵי קְרִיאַת הַמְּגִלָּה, וּמְחַלְּקִין אוֹתָן לַעֲנִיִּים.	
36.	Children under Bar/Bas Mitzvah need not participate in this custom – unless their father once "gave" for them, then they need to continue giving every year.	קָטָן פָּטוּר, וְאִם אָבִיו נָתַן בִּשְׁבִילוֹ פַּעַם אַחַת חַיָּב לְעוֹלָם,	

קִיצוּר שֻׁלְחָן עָרוּךְ – סִימָן קמא – הִלְכוֹת מְגִלָּה

KITZUR SHULCHAN ARUCH – CHAPTER 141 – THE LAWS OF MEGILLAH

Note: This is a loose translation, focusing on the content rather than the words.

37.	There's a Machlokes about the age when one must begin giving Machatzis Hashekel. Some say 13, some say 20.	בֶּן שְׁלשׁ עֶשְׂרֵה שָׁנָה יֵשׁ אוֹמְרִים דְּחַיָּב וְיֵשׁ אוֹמְרִים דְּפָטוּר עַד שֶׁיְּהֵא בֶּן עֶשְׂרִים.	
38.	(*In the USA we use a 50 cent coin. Most people don't have 50 cent coins. Usually, the local Shul puts out some of these coins on a plate and people exchange their regular money for the coins: They put in some money and take the 3 coins. Then they lift them and place them down 3 times and leave the coins and their money in the plate. The next person does the same etc.)		
39.	We say עַל הַנִּסִּים on Purim, in all three *tefillos* of *Shacharis, Mincha* and *Arvis* (& *Birkas Hamazon*)	בְּפוּרִים (דְּהַיְנוּ בְּיוֹם י"ד) עַרְבִית, שַׁחֲרִית וּמִנְחָה אוֹמְרִים עַל הַנִּסִּים,	ו
40.	If one forgets, the same rules of forgetting on Chanukah apply. See them there. <u>סִימָן קלט סְעִיף כא</u>	וְאִם שָׁכַח, דִּינוֹ כְּמוֹ בַּחֲנֻכָּה (עַיֵּן לְעֵיל <u>סִימָן קלט סְעִיף כא</u>).	
41.	Every man, woman and child must hear the Megilah at night and day.	חַיָּב כָּל אָדָם בֵּין אִישׁ בֵּין אִשָּׁה לִשְׁמוֹעַ קְרִיאַת הַמְּגִלָּה בַּלַּיְלָה וּבַיּוֹם,	ז
42.	Unmarried girls should also go to Shul.	וְלָכֵן גַּם הַבְּתוּלוֹת יֵשׁ לָהֶן לָלֶכֶת לְבֵית הַכְּנֶסֶת,	
43.	If one didn't make it to Shul, the Megilah must be read for them at home.	וְאִם אֵינָן הוֹלְכוֹת צְרִיכִין לִקְרוֹת לִפְנֵיהֶן בְּבַיִת	
44.	Even babies need to be educated to hear the Megilah	וְגַם אֶת הַקְּטַנִּים חַיָּבִים לְחַנֵּךְ אוֹתָם שֶׁיִּשְׁמְעוּ קְרִיאַת הַמְּגִלָּה,	
45.	Still, very small babies who will make noise and prevent others from hearing the Megilah should not be brought into the Shul.	וּמִכָּל מָקוֹם לֹא יָבִיאוּ לְבֵית הַכְּנֶסֶת קְטַנִּים בְּיוֹתֵר שֶׁמְּבַלְבְּלִים דַּעַת הַשּׁוֹמְעִים.	
46.	The Megilah reading at night must begin after the stars come out.	מְגִלָּה שֶׁל לַיְלָה אָסוּר לִקְרוֹת קֹדֶם צֵאת הַכּוֹכָבִים, אַף עַל פִּי שֶׁמִּצְטַעֵר הַרְבֵּה מֵחֲמַת הַתַּעֲנִית,	ח

קִיצוּר שֻׁלְחָן עָרוּךְ – סִימָן קמא – הִלְכוֹת מְגִלָּה
KITZUR SHULCHAN ARUCH – CHAPTER 141 – THE LAWS OF MEGILLAH
Note: This is a loose translation, focusing on the content rather than the words.

47.	If someone is suffering (feeling weak) from the fast, he may drink something before the Megilah reading.	אַךְ יָכוֹל לִטְעוֹם קְצָת קֹדֶם הַמְּגִלָּה, כְּגוֹן קָפֶה וְכַדּוֹמֶה, כְּדֵי לְהַחֲזִיק מְעַט מֵחֻלְשַׁת הַתַּעֲנִית.
48.	These are the "levels" of the best ways to read/hear the Megilah: The #1 best way is to hear the Megilah In Shul, in the presence of many people, as it says: "בְּרָב עָם הַדְרַת מֶלֶךְ" (The "glory" of the king is with many people).	ט מִצְוָה מִן הַמֻּבְחָר לִשְׁמוֹעַ קְרִיאַת הַמְּגִלָּה בְּבֵית הַכְּנֶסֶת בְּמָקוֹם שֶׁיֵּשׁ רֹב אֲנָשִׁים, מִשּׁוּם דִּ"בְּרָב עָם הַדְרַת מֶלֶךְ" (משלי יד, כח),
49.	If that is not an option, the next best is: With a Minyan.	וּלְכָל הַפָּחוֹת יִרְאֶה לִשְׁמוֹעַ אוֹתָהּ בְּמִנְיָן עֲשָׂרָה,
50.	If that is not an option, then each one should read from a Kosher Megilah, reciting (only) the Brachos before the Megilah	וְאִם אִי אֶפְשָׁר לִקְרוֹתָהּ בְּמִנְיָן, יִקְרָא אוֹתָהּ כָּל יָחִיד מִתּוֹךְ מְגִלָּה כְּשֵׁרָה עִם הַבְּרָכוֹת שֶׁלְּפָנֶיהָ,
51.	If only one person knows how to read the Megilah (correctly with the tune etc.): He should read while the others are יוצא even without a minyan.	וְאִם אֶחָד יוֹדֵעַ לִקְרוֹתָהּ וְהַשְּׁאָר אֵינָם יוֹדְעִים, יִקְרָא זֶה שֶׁהוּא יוֹדֵעַ וְהֵם יִשְׁמְעוּ וְיוֹצְאִים אַף עַל פִּי שֶׁאֵינָם עֲשָׂרָה,
52.	The brachos after the Megilah are only said with a minyan.	אֲבָל בְּרָכָה שֶׁלְּאַחֲרֶיהָ אֵין אוֹמְרִים רַק בַּעֲשָׂרָה,
53.	Anyone can say the Brachos after the Megilah, without Hashem name – even without a Minyan.	וְאַךְ בְּלֹא שֵׁם וּמַלְכוּת יָכוֹל גַּם יָחִיד לְאָמְרָהּ.

קִיצּוּר שֻׁלְחָן עָרוּךְ – סִימָן קמא – הִלְכוֹת מְגִלָּה

KITZUR SHULCHAN ARUCH – CHAPTER 141 – THE LAWS OF MEGILLAH

Note: This is a loose translation, focusing on the content rather than the words.

54.	The official Megilah Reader folds the Megilah "page over page" like a "letter," as it is called in the Megilah "the Purim letter."	מִנְהָג בְּכָל יִשְׂרָאֵל שֶׁהַקּוֹרֵא אֵינוֹ קוֹרֵא מִתּוֹךְ מְגִלָּה כְּרוּכָה, אֶלָּא פּוֹשֵׁט אוֹתָהּ וְכוֹפְלָהּ דַּף עַל דַּף כְּמוֹ אִגֶּרֶת, מִפְּנֵי שֶׁנִּקְרֵאת "אִגֶּרֶת הַפּוּרִים".	י
55.	The listeners need not fold it so.	אֲבָל הַשּׁוֹמְעִים אֵינָם צְרִיכִים לְפָשְׁטָהּ.	
56.	The Megilah Reader recites 3 brachos before the Megilah reading, at night and day: 1. עַל מִקְרָא מְגִלָּה 2. שֶׁעָשָׂה נִסִּים 3. שֶׁהֶחֱיָנוּ	הַקּוֹרֵא אֶת הַמְּגִלָּה בֵּין בַּיּוֹם וּבֵין בַּלַּיְלָה, מְבָרֵךְ לְפָנֶיהָ שָׁלֹשׁ בְּרָכוֹת, "עַל מִקְרָא מְגִלָּה", "שֶׁעָשָׂה נִסִּים" וְ"שֶׁהֶחֱיָנוּ".	יא
57.	After the reading, he rolls it up and recites "הָרָב אֶת רִיבֵנוּ".	וּלְאַחַר קְרִיאָתָהּ כּוֹרְכָהּ כֻּלָּהּ וּמַנִּיחָהּ לְפָנָיו, וּמְבָרְכִין בִּרְכַּת "הָרָב אֶת רִיבֵנוּ" וְכוּ'.	
58.	If a mourner reads the Megilah, another should recite the Brachos because he cannot recite the ברכה of שהחיינו.	אִם אָבֵל קוֹרֵא אֶת הַמְּגִלָּה, יְבָרֵךְ אַחֵר אֶת הַבְּרָכוֹת, מִשּׁוּם בִּרְכַּת "שֶׁהֶחֱיָנוּ".	
59.	While reciting the שֶׁהֶחֱיָנוּ during the day, each person should have in mind also the (other 3) Mitzvos of the day; Mishloach Manos, Matonos La'evyonim, Purim Se'udah.	בְּבִרְכַּת שֶׁהֶחֱיָנוּ שֶׁל יוֹם, יְכַוְּנוּ גַּם עַל מִצְוַת מִשְׁלוֹחַ מָנוֹת וּמַתָּנוֹת לָאֶבְיוֹנִים וּסְעֻדַּת פּוּרִים,	יב
60.	The Chazzan should have in mind to fulfill the congregation's obligation with his Bracha.	וְכֵן הַשְּׁלִיחַ צִבּוּר צָרִיךְ שֶׁיְּכַוֵּן לְהוֹצִיא אֶת הַצִּבּוּר גַּם עַל מִצְוֹת אֵלּוּ.	
61.	The Megilah Reader (Baal Koreh) must intend to include (have Kavana to be מוציא) all the listeners in his Mitzvah of reading the Megilah.	הַקּוֹרֵא אֶת הַמְּגִלָּה צָרִיךְ לְכַוֵּן לְהוֹצִיא אֶת כָּל הַשּׁוֹמְעִים.	יג
62.	The listeners must have in mind to fulfill their obligation (have Kavana to be יוצא) from his reading.	וְגַם הַשּׁוֹמֵעַ צָרִיךְ לְכַוֵּן לָצֵאת	
63.	The listeners must focus to hear every single word,	וְלִשְׁמוֹעַ כָּל תֵּבָה וְתֵבָה.	
64.	for if they miss just one word, they are not יוצא.	שֶׁאֲפִילוּ אִם רַק תֵּבָה אַחַת לֹא שָׁמַע אֵינוֹ יוֹצֵא,	

Note: This is a loose translation, focusing on the content rather than the words.

65.	The Reader must be extra careful to wait until ALL the gragger noise of "Haman" is completely quieted, before he resumes reading.	וְלָכֵן צָרִיךְ הַקּוֹרֵא לְהַשְׁגִּיחַ מְאֹד שֶׁבְּשָׁעָה שֶׁמַּרְעִישִׁין וּמְבַלְבְּלִין בְּהַכָּאַת הָמָן, יִשְׁתֹּק עַד יַעֲבֹר הָרַעַשׁ לְגַמְרֵי.	
66.	It's best for everyone to quietly read along with the Baal Koreh, in a Kosher Megilah, lest he miss a word.	וּמִכָּל מָקוֹם רָאוּי וְנָכוֹן שֶׁיִּהְיֶה לְכָל אֶחָד מְגִלָּה כְּשֵׁרָה כְּדֵי שֶׁיֹּאמַר בְּעַצְמוֹ מִלָּה בְּמִלָּה בְּלַחַשׁ, פֶּן לֹא יִשְׁמַע תֵּבָה אַחַת מִן הַקּוֹרֵא,	
67.	Women should also read along from a Kosher Megilah if they are able.	וְכֵן כָּל אִשָּׁה חַכְמַת לֵב שֶׁעוֹמֶדֶת בְּעֶזְרַת נָשִׁים, אִם אֶפְשָׁר מַה טּוֹב לִהְיוֹת לָהּ מְגִלָּה כְּשֵׁרָה לִקְרוֹת מִתּוֹכָהּ, כִּי שָׁם קָשֶׁה לִשְׁמוֹעַ	
68.	Women have the same obligation to hear the Megilah as men.	וְהַנָּשִׁים חַיָּבוֹת כְּמוֹ הָאֲנָשִׁים.	
69.	(See end of Siman 97 about what to do if they had not yet fulfilled the Mitzvah of קדוש לבנה (sanctifying the new moon), and the moon suddenly appeared during the Megilah reading.)	(אִם לֹא קִדְּשׁוּ אֶת הַלְּבָנָה וְנִרְאֲתָה בִּשְׁעַת קְרִיאַת הַמְּגִלָּה, עַיֵּן לְעֵיל סוֹף סִימָן צז).	
70.	Some things the Megilah Reader does: The Reader reads all 10 sons of Haman in one breath, (from the word "עֲשֶׂרֶת") as they were all hung together as one.	הַקּוֹרֵא צָרִיךְ שֶׁיֹּאמַר אֶת עֲשֶׂרֶת בְּנֵי הָמָן וְגַם תֵּבַת עֲשֶׂרֶת הַכֹּל בִּנְשִׁימָה אַחַת, לְהוֹדִיעַ שֶׁכֻּלָּם נֶהֶרְגוּ וְנִתְלוּ כְּאֶחָד.	יד
71.	Best to start from "חֲמֵשׁ מֵאוֹת אִישׁ" through the 10 sons of Haman, in one breath.	וְנוֹהֲגִין לְכַתְּחִלָּה לוֹמַר מִן "חֲמֵשׁ מֵאוֹת אִישׁ" הַכֹּל בִּנְשִׁימָה אַחַת,	
72.	If he didn't succeed - it's still OK.	וּבְדִיעֲבַד אֲפִילוּ הִפְסִיק בֵּין עֲשֶׂרֶת בְּנֵי הָמָן יָצָא,	
73.		וּמַה שֶּׁנּוֹהֲגִין בִּקְצָת מְקוֹמוֹת שֶׁכָּל הַקָּהָל אוֹמְרִים עֲשֶׂרֶת בְּנֵי הָמָן אֵינוֹ מִנְהָג נָכוֹן, אֶלָּא הַקּוֹרֵא לְבַד יֹאמְרֵם וְהַקָּהָל יִשְׁמְעוּ כְּמוֹ כָּל הַמְּגִלָּה,	

קיצור שֻׁלְחָן עָרוּךְ – סִימָן קמא – הִלְכוֹת מְגִלָּה

Kitzur Shulchan Aruch – Chapter 141 – The Laws of Megillah

Note: This is a loose translation, focusing on the content rather than the words.

74.	He raises his voice at "בַּלַּיְלָה הַהוּא נָדְדָה וְגוֹ'" for the main part of the miracle begins there. 2.	כְּשֶׁאוֹמֵר הַקּוֹרֵא "בַּלַּיְלָה הַהוּא נָדְדָה וְגוֹ'" יַגְבִּיהַּ קוֹלוֹ, כִּי שָׁם מַתְחִיל עִקַּר הַנֵּס,	
75.	When he says "הָאִגֶּרֶת הַזֹּאת" he shakes the Megilah.	וּכְשֶׁאוֹמֵר "הָאִגֶּרֶת הַזֹּאת" יְנַעֲנֵעַ אֶת הַמְּגִלָּה.	
76.	[Since we must hear every single word from a Kosher Megilah -] If someone is following the reading from an un-kosher Megilah (or a Chumash), he should not say the words along with the *Baal Koreh*,	מִי שֶׁיֵּשׁ לְפָנָיו מְגִלָּה פְּסוּלָה אוֹ חֻמָּשׁ, לֹא יִקְרָא עִם הַשְּׁלִיחַ צִבּוּר,	טו
77.	For, while he is reading from his un-Kosher Megilah, he cannot properly focus and listen to the *Baal Koreh*	כִּי אִם הוּא קוֹרֵא אֵינוֹ יָכוֹל לְכַוֵּן לִשְׁמוֹעַ מִן הַשְּׁלִיחַ צִבּוּר,	
78.	Even if he could focus, he should still not read from his non-Megilah, lest another might hear *him* read, instead of the *Baal Koreh* (and then he would not fulfill the Mitzvah to hear every word from a Kosher Megilah).	וַאֲפִילוּ אִם הוּא יְכַוֵּן, שֶׁמָּא יִשְׁמַע אַחֵר מַה שֶּׁהוּא קוֹרֵא וְלֹא יְכַוֵּן לִקְרִיאַת הַשְּׁלִיחַ צִבּוּר,	
79.	[For the same reason -] No-one should chant along with the Reader by heart.	וְכֵן לֹא יְסַיֵּעַ שׁוּם אָדָם בְּעַל פֶּה לְהַשְּׁלִיחַ צִבּוּר,	
80.	[There are 4 Pesukim at different parts of the Megilah that the congregation reads out loud. For the same reason as above:] The *Baal Koreh* must re-read from his Kosher Megilah, the 4 Pesukim that the congregation reads out loud.	וְלָכֵן אוֹתָן אַרְבָּעָה פְּסוּקֵי גְּאֻלָּה שֶׁאוֹמְרִים הַקָּהָל בְּקוֹל רָם, צָרִיךְ הַשְּׁלִיחַ צִבּוּר לַחֲזוֹר וְלִקְרוֹתָם מִתּוֹךְ הַמְּגִלָּה הַכְּשֵׁרָה.	

Note: This is a loose translation, focusing on the content rather than the words.

81.	If one already heard the Megilah and is going to read it for another; the one listening should say the Brachos if he knows how.	מִי שֶׁכְּבָר יָצָא בִּקְרִיאַת מְגִלָּה וְקוֹרֵא לְהוֹצִיא אַחֵר, אִם זֶה שֶׁהוּא צָרִיךְ לָצֵאת יוֹדֵעַ בְּעַצְמוֹ לְבָרֵךְ אֶת הַבְּרָכוֹת יְבָרֵךְ בְּעַצְמוֹ,	טז
82.	If he's reading for a woman, the *Baal Koreh* should say the Bracha and change the end to "אֲשֶׁר קִדְּשָׁנוּ בְּמִצְוֹתָיו וְצִוָּנוּ לִשְׁמוֹעַ מְגִלָּה."	וְאִם הִיא אִשָּׁה, טוֹב יוֹתֵר שֶׁהַקּוֹרֵא יְבָרֵךְ, וְיֹאמַר "אֲשֶׁר קִדְּשָׁנוּ בְּמִצְוֹתָיו וְצִוָּנוּ לִשְׁמוֹעַ מְגִלָּה."	
83.	We are allowed to touch/hold/move/carry the Megilah on Shabbos.	בְּשַׁבָּת (שֶׁאֵינוֹ פּוּרִים) מֻתָּרִין לְטַלְטֵל אֶת הַמְּגִלָּה,	יז
84.	However, when Purim falls on Sunday, we cannot bring the Megilah to Shul on Shabbos – even in a place where there is an Eruv – because we are not allowed to prepare from Shabbos to a weekday.	וּמִכָּל מָקוֹם אִם חָל פּוּרִים בְּיוֹם א' אֵין לְהָבִיא בְּשַׁבָּת אֶת הַמְּגִלָּה לְבֵית הַכְּנֶסֶת, אֲפִלּוּ בְּעִיר שֶׁהוּא מְתֻקֶּנֶת בְּעֵרוּבִין, מִשּׁוּם דְּהָוֵי מֵכִין מִשַּׁבָּת לְחוֹל.	
85.	If there is no local Reader who knows the Trop (Megilah chanting tunes), one can still read from a Kosher Megilah, as long as he reads the words correctly and doesn't change their meaning.	צִבּוּר שֶׁאֵין לָהֶם שְׁלִיחַ צִבּוּר שֶׁיָּכוֹל לִקְרוֹת אֶת הַמְּגִלָּה עִם הַטְּעָמִים כָּרָאוּי, יָכוֹל לִקְרוֹת גַּם בְּלֹא טְעָמִים, רַק שֶׁיִּקְרָא אֶת הַתֵּבוֹת כָּרָאוּי שֶׁלֹּא יִשְׁתַּנֶּה הָעִנְיָן,	יח
86.	(A change in the Nekudos of a word can change its meaning.) If someone mistakenly reads "וּמָרְדְּכַי יָשַׁב" instead of "וּמָרְדְּכַי יֹשֵׁב" or "וְהָמָן נָפַל" instead of "וְהָמָן נֹפֵל," he [and all his listeners] do not fulfill the Mitzvah of Megilah and he needs to read it again.	שֶׁאִם קָרָא בִּמְקוֹם "וּמָרְדְּכַי יֹשֵׁב" - יָשַׁב אוֹ בִּמְקוֹם "וְהָמָן נֹפֵל" - נָפַל, וְכַדּוֹמֶה, אֲפִלּוּ בְּדִיעֲבַד אֵינוֹ יוֹצֵא,	
87.	In "urgent" cases (when there is no-one who can read [even just the words of] the Megilah properly) we may write the Nekudos and Trop inside the actual Megilah.	וִיכוֹלִין לַעֲשׂוֹת בַּמְּגִלָּה נְקֻדּוֹת וּטְעָמִים שֶׁיִּקְרָא כְּהֹגֶן, כֵּיוָן שֶׁהוּא שְׁעַת הַדְּחַק,	
88.	It is better to write the *nekudos* into the Megilah than for someone to help the *Baal Koreh* by reading quietly from a Chumash into the *Baal Koreh's* ear, hile the *Baal Koreh* reads aloud to the congregation. Since the "helper" is not reading from a Kosher Megilah, and cannot properly listen to the *Baal Koreh's* reading from the Kosher Megilah while he is helping him, he is not יוֹצֵא from that reading.	וְהָכִי עָדִיף טְפֵי מִמַּה שֶׁיִּקְרָא אַחֵר מִתּוֹךְ הַחֻמָּשׁ בְּלַחַשׁ, דְּכֵיוָן שֶׁזֶּה הַקּוֹרֵא מִתּוֹךְ הַחֻמָּשׁ, אֲפִילוּ הוּא קוֹרֵא בְּלַחַשׁ, אֵינוֹ יָכוֹל לְכַוֵּן דַּעְתּוֹ שֶׁיִּשְׁמַע מֵהַשְּׁלִיחַ צִבּוּר, וְנִמְצָא שֶׁקָּרָא רַק מִתּוֹךְ הַחֻמָּשׁ וְאֵינוֹ יוֹצֵא,	

קִיצוּר שֻׁלְחָן עָרוּךְ – סִימָן קמא – הִלְכוֹת מְגִלָּה
Kitzur Shulchan Aruch – Chapter 141 – The Laws of Megillah
Note: This is a loose translation, focusing on the content rather than the words.

89.	If it did happen, he would need to hear the Megilah again from a Kosher Megilah.	וְאִם אֵרַע כָּךְ, צָרִיךְ לַחֲזוֹר וּלְשָׁמְעָהּ מִתּוֹךְ מְגִלָּה כְּשֵׁרָה.	
90.	**ויהי בי׳ אוז ורוש** If a Megilah is missing just a few words in the middle – not a complete concept – we may still read from it, with the Brachos.	צִבּוּר שֶׁאֵין לָהֶם מְגִלָּה כְּשֵׁרָה כְּדִינָהּ, מִכָּל מָקוֹם אִם הִיא כְּתוּבָה כְּהִלְכָתָהּ רַק שֶׁחָסְרִים אֵיזֶה תֵּבוֹת בְּאֶמְצָעָהּ, כֵּיוָן שֶׁלֹּא חָסֵר בָּהּ עִנְיָן אֶחָד שָׁלֵם, יְכוֹלִין לִקְרוֹת מִתּוֹכָהּ עִם הַבְּרָכוֹת,	יט
91.	The *Baal Koreh* should chant the missing words by heart or have someone say them quietly to him from a Chumash.	וְהַטָּעוּת יִקְרָא הַקּוֹרֵא בְּעַל פֶּה, אוֹ יֹאמַר לְפָנָיו בְּלַחַשׁ מִתּוֹךְ הַחֻמָּשׁ,	
92.	If a complete concept is missing from anywhere in the Megilah or – even anything missing from the very beginning or end of the Megilah – [we cannot read from it, and] everyone should just read the Megilah on their own, from a Chumash, without a Bracha.	אֲבָל אִם אֵין לָהֶם מְגִלָּה כְּלָל, אוֹ שֶׁחָסֵר בָּהּ עִנְיָן אֶחָד שָׁלֵם, אוֹ שֶׁחָסֵר בָּהּ בַּתְּחִלָּה אוֹ בַּסּוֹף, קוֹרִין מִתּוֹךְ הַחֻמָּשׁ כָּל אֶחָד בִּפְנֵי עַצְמוֹ וְאֵין מְבָרְכִין.	
93.	One, who is alone and has only an un-kosher Megilah, should read from it without the Brachos.	וְיָחִיד שֶׁאֵין לוֹ רַק מְגִלָּה פְּסוּלָה, קוֹרֵא בָּהּ בְּלֹא בְּרָכוֹת.	
94.	A mourner (Aveil) – within the seven days of "Shiva" observes the laws of Shiva	אָבֵל תּוֹךְ שִׁבְעָה נוֹהֵג בְּכָל דִּינֵי אֲבֵלוּת,	כ
95.	and is forbidden to see (celebrate?) joyous occasions – even on Purim.	וְאָסוּר לִרְאוֹת כָּל מִינֵי שִׂמְחָה,	
96.	He may however, wear leather shoes and sit on a regular height chair/bench,	אַךְ בִּנְעִילַת הַסַּנְדָּל וִישִׁיבָה עַל גַּבֵּי סַפְסָל מֻתָּר,	
97.	because these are noticeable in public (and on Purim we only observe the Shiva laws in private, in a manner that is not noticeable to the public)	מִפְּנֵי שֶׁהֵן דְּבָרִים הַנִּרְאִין לַכֹּל.	
98.	Purim evening, a mourner should have the Megilah reading at his home.	בַּלַּיְלָה אִם יָכוֹל לֶאֱסוֹף מִנְיָן לְבֵיתוֹ לִקְרוֹת הַמְּגִלָּה מוּטָב,	
99.	If he cannot arrange this, he should Daven Maariv at home and go to Shul to hear the Megilah reading.	וְאִם לָאו, יִתְפַּלֵּל בְּבֵיתוֹ וְיֵלֵךְ לְבֵית הַכְּנֶסֶת לִשְׁמוֹעַ הַמְּגִלָּה.	
100.	When Purim falls on Motzei Shabbos, a mourner should go to Shul during Shabbos, after Se'udah Shlishis (aka "Shaloshudis").	אִם חָל בְּמוֹצָאֵי שַׁבָּת, יֵלֵךְ לְבֵית הַכְּנֶסֶת לְאַחַר סְעֻדָּה שְׁלִישִׁית בְּעוֹד יוֹם.	
101.	On Purim morning, a mourner goes to Shul for Davening and Megilah.	וּבַיּוֹם הוֹלֵךְ לְבֵית הַכְּנֶסֶת לִתְפִלָּה וְלַמְּגִלָּה.	

Note: This is a loose translation, focusing on the content rather than the words.

102.	[An "Onein" is someone whose close relative passed away and has not yet been buried.] On the night of Purim, an Onein: Should hear the Megilah from another Reader.	מִי שֶׁמֵּת לוֹ מֵת בְּתַעֲנִית אֶסְתֵּר וּבַלַּיְלָה הוּא אוֹנֵן קֹדֶם הַקְּבוּרָה, יִשְׁמַע קְרִיאַת הַמְּגִלָּה מֵאַחֵר,	כא
103.	Should not eat meat or drink wine,	וְלֹא יֹאכַל בָּשָׂר וְלֹא יִשְׁתֶּה יַיִן,	
104.	for the Mitzvah of the feast doesn't apply at night	כִּי בַּלַּיְלָה אֵינוֹ חַיָּב בְּמִשְׁתֶּה,	
105.	During the day of Purim, after the burial, the Onein should Daven and read or hear the Megilah.	וּבַיּוֹם לְאַחַר יְצִיאָה מִבֵּית הַכְּנֶסֶת קוֹבְרִין אֶת הַמֵּת, וְאַחַר כָּךְ יִתְפַּלֵּל וְיִקְרָא אֶת הַמְּגִלָּה אוֹ יִשְׁמַע מֵאַחֵר,	
106.	If he heard the Megilah before the burial, he fulfilled the Mitzvah (- was יוצא),	וְאִם שָׁמַע קְרִיאַת הַמְּגִלָּה קֹדֶם הַקְּבוּרָה יָצָא,	
107.	Nevertheless, he should re-read the Megilah without the Brachos.	וּמִכָּל מָקוֹם נָכוֹן שֶׁיַּחֲזוֹר וְיִקְרָא בְּלֹא בְּרָכוֹת.	
108.	The Onein (is not obligated in some of the positive Matzos, and therefore) should not wrap Tefillin even after the burial, since it is the first day of his mourning.	וּתְפִלִּין לֹא יַנִּיחַ אֲפִילוּ אַחַר הַקְּבוּרָה, כֵּיוָן שֶׁהוּא יוֹם רִאשׁוֹן בְּאֶבְלוֹ.	
109.	On Purim, an Onein is allowed to eat meat and drink wine.	וְאוֹנֵן בְּפוּרִים בְּיוֹם מֻתָּר בְּבָשָׂר וּבְיַיִן.	
110.	[This is the order of Purim day:] 1. Go to Shul early 2. After Sh'moneh Esrei, say half Kaddish 3. Read the Torah about Amalek, in 3 Aliyos 4. Say half Kaddish 5. Return the Torah 6. Read the Megilah 7. After the Brachos, say "שׁוֹשַׁנַּת יַעֲקֹב" 8. Say Ashrei/Uva L'tziyon 9. Say complete Kaddish with Tiskabeil	שַׁחֲרִית מַשְׁכִּימִים לְבֵית הַכְּנֶסֶת, לְאַחַר שְׁמוֹנֶה עֶשְׂרֵה אוֹמְרִים חֲצִי קַדִּישׁ וְקוֹרִין בַּתּוֹרָה בְּפָרָשַׁת "וַיָּבֹא עֲמָלֵק" תְּלָתָא גַבְרֵי, וְאַחַר כָּךְ חֲצִי קַדִּישׁ, וּלְאַחַר שֶׁמַּכְנִיסִין אֶת הַסֵּפֶר תּוֹרָה קוֹרִין אֶת הַמְּגִלָּה, לְאַחַר בְּרָכָה אַחֲרוֹנָה אֵין אוֹמְרִים בְּשַׁחֲרִית "אֲשֶׁר הֵנִיא", וּלְאַחַר שֶׁסִּיֵּם "הָאֵל הַמּוֹשִׁיעַ" אוֹמְרִים "שׁוֹשַׁנַּת יַעֲקֹב" וְכוּ' וְאוֹמְרִים "אַשְׁרֵי", "וּבָא לְצִיּוֹן", קַדִּישׁ שָׁלֵם עִם "תִּתְקַבֵּל".	כב

Note: This is a loose translation, focusing on the content rather than the words.

111.	**Leave Tefillin on during Megilah reading because the word "וִיקָר" in the Megilah refers to Tefillin**	וְאֵין לַחֲלֹץ אֶת הַתְּפִלִּין עַד לְאַחַר קְרִיאַת הַמְּגִלָּה, מִשּׁוּם דִּכְתִיב בָּהּ (אסתר ח, טז) "וִיקָר", וְדָרְשִׁינַן "אֵלּוּ תְּפִלִּין".	
112.	**If there is a Bris, it should be before the Megilah reading, as the word "וְשָׂשׂוֹן" refers to a Bris**	אִם יֵשׁ מִילָה מָלִין קֹדֶם קְרִיאַת הַמְּגִלָּה מִשּׁוּם דִּכְתִיב "וְשָׂשׂוֹן" זוֹ מִילָה.	
113.	**The Megilah is read on the 15th day of Adar in a city surrounded by a wall since the times of Yehoshua.**	עִיר שֶׁהִיא מֻקֶּפֶת חוֹמָה מִימוֹת יְהוֹשֻׁעַ בִּן נוּן קוֹרִין בָּהּ בְּט"ו	כג
114.	**This is not common in our countries (Europe, where the author lived).**	(וְלָא שְׁכִיחִי בִּמְדִינוֹתֵינוּ).	

Note: This is a loose translation, focusing on the content rather than the words.

	CHAPTER 142: LAWS OF: MISHLOACH MANOS, MATONOS LA'EVYONIM, SE'UDAHS PURIM	סי' קמב: הִלְכוֹת מִשְׁלוֹחַ מָנוֹת אִישׁ לְרֵעֵהוּ וּמַתָּנוֹת לָאֶבְיוֹנִים וּסְעוּדַּת פּוּרִים	
1.	Every person must send 2 gifts (portions of food) to at least one other person.	חַיָּב כָּל אָדָם לִשְׁלוֹחַ לְכָל הַפָּחוֹת לְאָדָם אֶחָד שְׁתֵּי מַתָּנוֹת,	א
2.	As the Megilah says: "וּמִשְׁלוֹחַ **מָנוֹת** אִישׁ לְרֵעֵהוּ" – "מָנוֹת-portions" in plural form, meaning 2 portions to 1 friend.	דִּכְתִיב (אסתר ט, כב) "וּמִשְׁלוֹחַ מָנוֹת אִישׁ לְרֵעֵהוּ", מַשְׁמַע שְׁתֵּי מַתָּנוֹת לְאֶחָד.	
3.	The more Mishloach Manos you send the better.	וְכָל הַמַּרְבֶּה לִשְׁלוֹחַ מָנוֹת לְרֵעִים הֲרֵי זֶה מְשֻׁבָּח,	
4.	It's better to increase the Matonos La'evyonim than the Mishloach Manos and Purim Feast,	וּמִכָּל מָקוֹם מוּטָב לְהַרְבּוֹת בְּמַתָּנוֹת לָאֶבְיוֹנִים מִלְּהַרְבּוֹת בִּסְעֻדָּתוֹ וּבְמִשְׁלוֹחַ מָנוֹת לְרֵעִים,	
5.	for there is no greater joy to Hashem than uplifting the spirits of the poor, orphans and widows.	כִּי אֵין שִׂמְחָה גְדוֹלָה וּמְפֹאֶרֶת לִפְנֵי הַקָּדוֹשׁ בָּרוּךְ הוּא אֶלָּא לְשַׂמֵּחַ לֵב עֲנִיִּים וִיתוֹמִים וְאַלְמָנוֹת,	
6.	When we make them happy, we are compared to Hashem, as Hashem revives the spirits and hearts to the less fortunate. 	וְהַמְשַׂמֵּחַ לֵב הָאֻמְלָלִים הָאֵלּוּ דּוֹמֶה לַשְּׁכִינָה, שֶׁנֶּאֱמַר (ישעיה נז, טו) "לְהַחֲיוֹת רוּחַ שְׁפָלִים וּלְהַחֲיוֹת לֵב נִדְכָּאִים."	
7.	A "portion - מנה" is something edible (ready to eat) without any preparation.	לֹא נִקְרָא מָנוֹת אֶלָּא דָּבָר שֶׁרָאוּי לֶאֱכוֹל כְּמוֹת שֶׁהוּא בְּלִי תִּקּוּן,	ב
8.	i.e. cooked meat or fish - not raw. 	כְּגוֹן בָּשָׂר וְדָגִים מְבֻשָּׁלִים וְלֹא חַיִּין,	
9.	Sweets, fruits, wine or other drinks etc.	אוֹ מִינֵי מְתִיקָה אוֹ פֵּרוֹת אוֹ כּוֹס יַיִן וּמֵי דְבַשׁ וְכַיּוֹצֵא בּוֹ.	

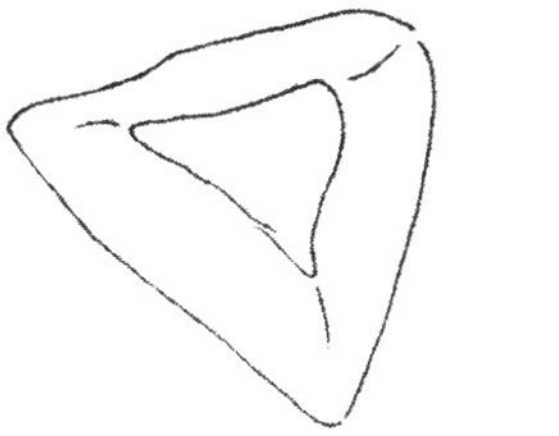

Note: This is a loose translation, focusing on the content rather than the words.

10.	Every person must give Matonos La'evyonim (Gifts of money to the poor). Even someone so poor who lives from Tzedaka himself – must still give at least 2 gifts to 2 poor people on Purim.	כָּל אָדָם אֲפִלּוּ עָנִי שֶׁבְּיִשְׂרָאֵל הַמְקַבֵּל צְדָקָה, חַיָּב לִתֵּן לְכָל הַפָּחוֹת שְׁתֵּי מַתָּנוֹת לִשְׁנֵי עֲנִיִּים,	ג
11.	Meaning: 1 gift to each one (of the 2 poor people).	דְּהַיְנוּ מַתָּנָה אַחַת לְכָל אֶחָד,	
12.	As it says: "וּמַתָּנוֹת לָאֶבְיוֹנִים" – plural, meaning (a total of) 2 gifts to 2 (separate) people.	דִּכְתִיב (<u>אסתר ט, כב</u>) "וּמַתָּנוֹת לָאֶבְיוֹנִים", מַשְׁמַע שְׁתֵּי מַתָּנוֹת לִשְׁנֵי אֶבְיוֹנִים,	
13.	On Purim, we give Tzedaka to whoever stretches out his hand (asking for Tzedaka).	וְאֵין מְדַקְדְּקִין בְּמָעוֹת פּוּרִים אֶלָּא כָּל הַפּוֹשֵׁט יָד לִטּוֹל נוֹתְנִים לוֹ.	
14.	If you are in a place where there aren't any poor people, set aside the money on Purim, and give or send it to a poor person when you can.	וּמִי שֶׁהוּא בְּמָקוֹם שֶׁאֵין שָׁם עֲנִיִּים, יְעַכֵּב אֶת הַמָּעוֹת אֶצְלוֹ עַד שֶׁיִּזְדַּמְּנוּ לוֹ עֲנִיִּים אוֹ יִשְׁלָחֵם לָהֶם.	
15.	Women are obligated (as men are) in the Mitzvah of Mishloach Manos and Matonos La'evyonim.	גַּם הַנָּשִׁים חַיָּבוֹת בְּמִשְׁלוֹחַ מָנוֹת וּמַתָּנוֹת לָאֶבְיוֹנִים,	ד
16.	For Mishloach Manos, women send to women, men send to men.	מִשְׁלוֹחַ מָנוֹת תִּשְׁלַח אִשָּׁה לְאִשָּׁה וְאִישׁ לְאִישׁ,	
17.	For Matonos La'evyonim, anyone can give to anyone.	אֲבָל מַתָּנוֹת לָאֶבְיוֹנִים יְכוֹלָה גַּם אִשָּׁה לִשְׁלוֹחַ לְאִישׁ וְכֵן בְּהִפּוּךְ.	
18.	Some women rely on their husbands to send Mishloach Manos for them – and this is not OK. Be strict / careful about this.	קְצָת נָשִׁים סוֹמְכוֹת עַל בַּעֲלֵיהֶן שֶׁהֵן שׁוֹלְחִים גַּם בִּשְׁבִילָן, וְאֵינוֹ נָכוֹן אֶלָּא יֵשׁ לְהַחֲמִיר.	
	It's a Mitzvah to eat, drink and rejoice on Purim.	חַיָּבִין לֶאֱכוֹל וְלִשְׁתּוֹת וְלִשְׂמוֹחַ בְּפוּרִים,	ה

Note: This is a loose translation, focusing on the content rather than the words.

19.	One should also do a little extra feasting on the eve of Purim.	גַּם בְּלֵיל י"ד יִשְׂמַח וְיַרְבֶּה קְצָת בִּסְעֻדָּה,
20.	When Purim falls on Motzei Shabbos, eat less during Se'udah Shlishis to make room for the meal on Purim eve.	וּכְשֶׁחָל בְּמוֹצָאֵי שַׁבָּת, אַף שֶׁצָּרִיךְ לַעֲשׂוֹת בְּשַׁבָּת סְעֻדָּה שְׁלִישִׁית, יְמַעֵט קְצָת בַּאֲכִילָתוֹ בַּיּוֹם לִתֵּן מָקוֹם לִסְעֻדַּת לֵיל פּוּרִים.
21.	The Mitzvah of Se'udahs Purim is only fulfilled during the day. As it says: "יְמֵי מִשְׁתֶּה – days of feast."	וּמִכָּל מָקוֹם בִּסְעֻדָּה שֶׁעוֹשִׂין בַּלַּיְלָה אֵין יוֹצְאִין יְדֵי חוֹבָתָן, דְּעִקַּר הַסְּעֻדָּה מִצְוָתָהּ שֶׁתְּהֵא בַּיּוֹם, דִּכְתִיב (שָׁם) "יְמֵי מִשְׁתֶּה",
22.	We light [celebratory] candles during the Purim day feast.	וְיֵשׁ לְהַדְלִיק נֵרוֹת דֶּרֶךְ שִׂמְחָה וְיוֹם טוֹב גַּם כְּשֶׁעוֹשִׂין הַסְּעֻדָּה בַּיּוֹם.
23.	On the eve of the 15th of Adar, we continue to rejoice (a bit).	וְגַם בְּלֵיל ט"ו צָרִיךְ לִשְׂמוֹחַ קְצָת.
24.	The Mitzvah of Matonos La'evyonim and Mishloach Manos can only be fulfilled during the day.	גַּם מַתָּנוֹת לָאֶבְיוֹנִים וּמָנוֹת לְרֵעֵהוּ צָרִיךְ לִהְיוֹת בַּיּוֹם,
25.	(Although the Se'udah must be during the day -) Since people are busy with Mishloach Manos during the day, we extend some of our Se'udah to the night.	וּמִשּׁוּם דִּטְרִידֵי בְּמִשְׁלוֹחַ מָנוֹת עוֹשִׂין מִקְצָת סְעֻדָּה בַּלַּיְלָה,
26.	We Daven Mincha early (during daylight), then make our Se'udah.	וּמִתְפַּלְּלִין מִנְחָה בְּעוֹד הַיּוֹם גָּדוֹל, וְעוֹשִׂין אֶת הַסְּעֻדָּה לְאַחַר מִנְחָה,
27.	The majority of the Purim Se'udah should take place during the day.	וּצְרִיכִין לַעֲשׂוֹת עַל כָּל פָּנִים רֹב סְעֻדָּה בַּיּוֹם.
28.	When Purim falls on Friday, we have the Se'udah in the morning, to honor Shabbos (so we have room for Se'udahs Shabbos in our tummy).	וּכְשֶׁחָל בְּעֶרֶב שַׁבָּת, עוֹשִׂין אוֹתָהּ בְּשַׁחֲרִית מִפְּנֵי כְּבוֹד שַׁבָּת.

קיצור שֻׁלְחָן עָרוּךְ – סִימָן קמב – הִלְכוֹת מְגִלָּה

KITZUR SHULCHAN ARUCH – CHAPTER 142 – THE LAWS OF PURIM

Note: This is a loose translation, focusing on the content rather than the words.

29.	**We should learn some Torah before the Se'udah,**	וְטוֹב לַעֲסוֹק קְצָת בַּתּוֹרָה קֹדֶם שֶׁמַּתְחִיל הַסְּעֻדָּה,	
30.	**Torah study is referred to in the Megilah, in the words "לַיְּהוּדִים הָיְתָה אוֹרָה" – as our Rabbis explain that "אוֹרָה - light" is תּוֹרָה.**	וְסֶמֶךְ לַדָּבָר "לַיְּהוּדִים הָיְתָה אוֹרָה" וְדָרְשִׁינַן (מגילה טז, ב) "אוֹרָה זוֹ תּוֹרָה".	
31.	**Some say we should eat various kinds of seeds on Purim to commemorate (remember) the seeds that Daniel and his friends ate in Bavel,**	יֵשׁ אוֹמְרִים שֶׁיֵּשׁ לֶאֱכוֹל מִינֵי זֵרְעוֹנִין בְּפוּרִים, זֵכֶר לַזֵּרְעוֹנִין שֶׁאָכְלוּ דָּנִיֵּאל וַחֲבֵרָיו בְּבָבֶל,	
32.	**and for the seeds that Esther ate, as the Gemara says about the Possuk "וַיְשַׁנֶּהָ וְאֶת נַעֲרוֹתֶיהָ לְטוֹב" that she was given seeds.**	וְזֵכֶר לַזֵּרְעוֹנִין שֶׁאָכְלָה אֶסְתֵּר, דְּאִיתָא בַּגְּמָרָא "וַיְשַׁנֶּהָ וְאֶת נַעֲרוֹתֶיהָ לְטוֹב", שֶׁהֶאֱכִילָהּ זֵרְעוֹנִים.	
33.	**(See the laws of Al Hanissim in the section on Birkas Hamazon Siman 44: Se'ifim 15 & 16.)**	(דִּינֵי עַל הַנִּסִּים בְּבִרְכַּת הַמָּזוֹן - עַיֵּן סִימָן מד סְעִיף טו, טז.)	
34.	**Since the miracle of Purim was (primarily) through wine, i.e.:**	כֵּיוָן שֶׁכָּל הַנֵּס הָיָה עַל יְדֵי הַיַּיִן,	ו
35.	**Vashti was removed at the wine feast and was replaced by Esther,**	וַשְׁתִּי נִטְרְדָה בְּמִשְׁתֵּה הַיַּיִן וּבָאָה אֶסְתֵּר בִּמְקוֹמָהּ,	
36.	**Haman's downfall was through wine -**	וְכֵן עִנְיַן הָמָן וּמַפַּלְתּוֹ הָיָה עַל יְדֵי יַיִן,	
37.	**- therefore our rabbis obligated us to drink wine**	לָכֵן חִיְּבוּ חֲכָמֵינוּ זִכְרוֹנָם לִבְרָכָה לְהִשְׁתַּכֵּר בְּיַיִן,	
38.	**until we are so drunk, we don't know the difference between "cursed is Haman" and "blessed is Mordechai."**	וְאָמְרוּ (שם ז, ב) "חַיָּב אֱינָשׁ לִבְסוּמֵי בְּפוּרְיָא עַד דְּלָא יָדַע בֵּין אָרוּר הָמָן לְבָרוּךְ מָרְדְּכַי".	

Note: This is a loose translation, focusing on the content rather than the words.

39.	(If getting drunk is not your thing...) At least drink more than "regular" to commemorate the miracle - and then take a nap,	וְלִפְחוֹת יִשְׁתֶּה יוֹתֵר מֵהֶרְגֵּלוֹ כְּדֵי לִזְכּוֹר אֶת הַנֵּס הַגָּדוֹל וְיִישַׁן,	
40.	for while you are sleeping, you won't "know" the difference between "cursed is Haman" and "blessed is Mordechai." (Nice trick eh?)	וּמִתּוֹךְ שֶׁיָּשֵׁן אֵינוֹ יוֹדֵעַ בֵּין אָרוּר הָמָן לְבָרוּךְ מָרְדְּכַי.	
41.	However: [These are the ones who should not get drunk at all:] Someone for whom it is unhealthy to drink wine.	וְאוּלָם מִי שֶׁהוּא חָלוּשׁ בְּטִבְעוֹ,	
42.	Someone who knows that drinking wine will cause him to compromise the observance of any Mitzvah, Bracha or Tefilla.	וְכֵן מִי שֶׁיּוֹדֵעַ בְּעַצְמוֹ שֶׁעַל יְדֵי כֵן יְזַלְזֵל חַס וְשָׁלוֹם בְּאֵיזֶה מִצְוָה, בִּבְרָכָה אוֹ בִּתְפִלָּה	
43.	Someone who may lose some control and conduct himself disrespectfully in any way.	אוֹ שֶׁיָּבֹא חַס וְשָׁלוֹם לְקַלּוּת רֹאשׁ,	
44.	These people should not drink too much,	מוּטָב שֶׁלֹּא לְהִשְׁתַּכֵּר,	
45.	And everyone should make sure all their actions are "L'Shaim Shamayim" for the sake of Heaven (Hashem).	וְכָל מַעֲשָׂיו יִהְיוּ לְשֵׁם שָׁמָיִם.	
46.	A mourner needs to give Matonos La'evyonim and send Mishloach Manos even during the 7 days of Shiva.	הָאָבֵל אֲפִלּוּ תּוֹךְ שִׁבְעָה חַיָּב בְּמַתָּנוֹת לָאֶבְיוֹנִים וְגַם לִשְׁלֹחַ מָנוֹת לְרֵעֵהוּ,	ז
47.	A mourner should not send "happy" gifts.	וּמִכָּל מָקוֹם לֹא יִשְׁלַח דָּבָר שֶׁל שִׂמְחָה,	
48.	A mourner does not receive [even "plain"] Mishloach Manos, all 12 months of his mourning period.	אֲבָל לְהָאָבֵל אֵין שׁוֹלְחִין מָנוֹת כָּל שְׁנֵים עָשָׂר חֹדֶשׁ אֲפִלּוּ דָּבָר שֶׁאֵינוֹ שֶׁל שִׂמְחָה.	
49.	If the mourner is poor, it is OK to send him money or "plain" food.	אִם הוּא עָנִי מֻתָּר לִשְׁלֹחַ לוֹ מָעוֹת אוֹ שְׁאָר דָּבָר שֶׁאֵינוֹ שֶׁל שִׂמְחָה,	
50.	If, on Purim, the only other local Jew is in mourning, you must send him Mishloach Manos, to fulfill the Mitzvah.	וְאִם אֵין בַּמָּקוֹם הַהוּא רַק הָאָבֵל עִם אֶחָד חַיָּב לִשְׁלֹחַ לוֹ כְּדֵי לְקַיֵּם הַמִּצְוָה מִשְׁלוֹחַ מָנוֹת.	

קִיצוּר שֻׁלְחָן עָרוּךְ – סִימָן קמב – הִלְכוֹת מְגִלָּה

Kitzur Shulchan Aruch – Chapter 142 – The Laws of Purim

Note: This is a loose translation, focusing on the content rather than the words.

51.	See the laws of the Onein in Siman 141:21	(דִּין הָאוֹנֵן עַיֵּן לְעֵיל סִימָן קמא סָעִיף כא)	
52.	On Purim we do not do "Melachos" (- creative work that is forbidden on Shabbos).	אֵין לַעֲשׂוֹת מְלָאכָה בְּפוּרִים,	
53.	"Melachos" that are done on Purim, will not bring any benefit.	וּמִי שֶׁעוֹשֶׂה בּוֹ מְלָאכָה אֵינוֹ רוֹאֶה מֵאוֹתָהּ מְלָאכָה סִימַן בְּרָכָה לְעוֹלָם,	
54.	A non-Jew may do any kind of Melacha / work for a Jew.	וְעַל יְדֵי אֵינוֹ יְהוּדִי מֻתָּר.	
55.	These are the kinds of work that may be done on Purim: Business activity is permitted on Purim.	וּמֻתָּר לַעֲסֹק בְּפְּרַקְמַטְיָא	
56.	It is OK to write: Letters to friends	וְכֵן מֻתָּר לִכְתּוֹב אֲפִילוּ אִגֶּרֶת שָׁלוֹם,	
57.	It is OK to write: Debt matters	וְכֵן חוֹבוֹתָיו	
58.	It is OK to write: Anything that doesn't take much concentration.	וְכָל דָּבָר שֶׁאֵינוֹ צָרִיךְ עִיּוּן גָּדוֹל,	
59.	It is OK to write: A Mitzvah matter - for sure!	וְכָל שֶׁכֵּן לִכְתּוֹב דְּבַר מִצְוָה אוֹ לַעֲשׂוֹת שְׁאָר דְּבַר מִצְוָה,	
60.	It is OK to do any Melacha, for the needs of Purim.	וְכֵן לְצֹרֶךְ פּוּרִים מֻתָּר לַעֲשׂוֹת אֲפִילוּ מְלָאכוֹת גְּמוּרוֹת.	
61.	The 15th of Adar is called "Shushan Purim." On Shushan Purim, we:	יוֹם ט"ו אֲדָר נִקְרָא אֶצְלֵנוּ שׁוּשַׁן פּוּרִים,	ט
62.	Do not say Tachanun Do not say Keil Erech Apayim Do not say Lam'natzei'ach	אֵין אוֹמְרִים בּוֹ תַּחֲנוּן וְלֹא אֵל אֶרֶךְ אַפַּיִם וְלֹא לַמְנַצֵּחַ,	
63.	Do not eulogize (make speeches about someone who passed at the funeral)Do not fast	וְאָסוּר גַּם בְּהֶסְפֵּד וְתַעֲנִית,	

Note: This is a loose translation, focusing on the content rather than the words.

64.	Do rejoice and feast a little	וְנוֹהֲגִין בּוֹ קְצָת מִשְׁתֶּה וְשִׂמְחָה
65.	Do not say Al Hanissim	אֲבָל אֵין אוֹמְרִים עַל הַנִּסִּים,
66.	Do make weddings,	וּמֻתָּרִין לַעֲשׂוֹת בּוֹ נִשּׂוּאִין
67.	since we don't read the Megilah then.	כֵּיוָן שֶׁאֵין אָנוּ קוֹרִין בּוֹ אֶת הַמְּגִלָּה,
68.	On the day of the Megilah reading, we do not make weddings,	אֲבָל בְּיוֹם שֶׁקּוֹרִין אֶת הַמְּגִלָּה שֶׁאָז עִקַּר הַשִּׂמְחָה, אֵין עוֹשִׂין נִשּׂוּאִין,
69.	because we do not mix 2 Simchos (to give each Simcha its proper attention).	מִשּׁוּם דְּאֵין מְעָרְבִין שִׂמְחָה בְּשִׂמְחָה.
70.	(On a leap year, when there are 2 months of Adar,) On the 14th and 15th of Adar 1, we also:	יוֹם י״ד וְט״ו שֶׁבַּאֲדָר הָרִאשׁוֹן, גַּם כֵּן אֵין אוֹמְרִים ׳
71.	Do not say Tachanun Do not say Keil Erech Apayim Do not say Lam'natzei'ach Do not eulogize Do not fast	לֹא תַּחֲנוּן וְלֹא אֵל אֶרֶךְ אַפַּיִם וְלֹא לַמְנַצֵּחַ, וַאֲסוּרִין בְּהֶסְפֵּד וְתַעֲנִית,
72.	We mark the 14th day of Adar 1 by adding (more or special foods) to our regular meal.	וּבְיוֹם י״ד מַרְבִּים קְצָת בִּסְעֻדָּה.

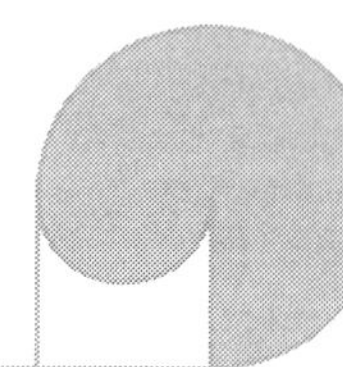

MY VERY OWN MEGILAH!

Student-Friendly,
Original - Literal - Translation

by Rabbi Chayim B. Alevsky, 5771-2011

Original translation for ages 8-118,
inspired by many previous translations, including:
Kehot Publications – Rabbi Yosef Marcus
Soncino / Judaica Press /
Kol Menachem-Slager Edition – Rabbi Chaim Miller
Mefarshei Hamikra; Rashi / Ibn Ezra / Malbim
Reviewed and improved by Rabbi JJ Hartmann

[These brackets] are used for:
a. words that are not in the Megilah text,
inserted to keep the English flow
b. words that are in the Megilah text,
but are not commonly used in English.
The words in (parentheses) are clarifications
that explain the literal translation.

This section contains the whole Megilah with its **translation**.
The next section contains the Megilah
with **Mefarshim – Commentaries**.

CHAPTER I: 1 And it was in the days of Achashverosh, he is [the same] Achashverosh who ruled from Hodu (India) to Cush (Ethiopia), one hundred twenty-seven provinces.

פרק א: א. וַיְהִי בִּימֵי אֲחַשְׁוֵרוֹשׁ הוּא אֲחַשְׁוֵרוֹשׁ הַמֹּלֵךְ מֵהֹדּוּ וְעַד־כּוּשׁ שֶׁבַע וְעֶשְׂרִים וּמֵאָה מְדִינָה:

2 In those days, when King Achashverosh sat on his royal throne, which was in Shushan the capital;

ב. בַּיָּמִים הָהֵם כְּשֶׁבֶת | הַמֶּלֶךְ אֲחַשְׁוֵרוֹשׁ עַל כִּסֵּא מַלְכוּתוֹ אֲשֶׁר בְּשׁוּשַׁן הַבִּירָה:

3 In the third year of his reign (rule), he made a feast for all his ministers and servants; the army of Persia and Media, the nobles and ministers of the provinces before him.

ג. בִּשְׁנַת שָׁלוֹשׁ לְמָלְכוֹ עָשָׂה מִשְׁתֶּה לְכָל־שָׂרָיו וַעֲבָדָיו חֵיל | פָּרַס וּמָדַי הַפַּרְתְּמִים וְשָׂרֵי הַמְּדִינוֹת לְפָנָיו:

4 When he showed the riches of his glorious kingdom and the splendorous beauty of his majesty for many days - one hundred and eighty days.

ד. בְּהַרְאֹתוֹ אֶת־עֹשֶׁר כְּבוֹד מַלְכוּתוֹ וְאֶת־יְקָר תִּפְאֶרֶת גְּדוּלָּתוֹ יָמִים רַבִּים שְׁמוֹנִים וּמְאַת יוֹם:

5 And when these days were completed, the king made - for all the people in Shushan the capital, from the great to the small (simple) - a feast for seven days, in the courtyard of the king's palace garden.

ה. וּבִמְלוֹאת | הַיָּמִים הָאֵלֶּה עָשָׂה הַמֶּלֶךְ לְכָל־הָעָם הַנִּמְצְאִים בְּשׁוּשַׁן הַבִּירָה לְמִגָּדוֹל וְעַד־קָטָן מִשְׁתֶּה שִׁבְעַת יָמִים בַּחֲצַר גִּנַּת בִּיתַן הַמֶּלֶךְ:

6 Hangings of white, green and blue, were held by cords of linen and purple wool on silver rods and marble pillars. There were beds (couches) of gold and silver on a floor of alabaster and marble [arranged in patterns of] rows and circles.

ו. חוּר | כַּרְפַּס וּתְכֵלֶת אָחוּז בְּחַבְלֵי־בוּץ וְאַרְגָּמָן עַל־גְּלִילֵי כֶסֶף וְעַמּוּדֵי שֵׁשׁ מִטּוֹת | זָהָב וָכֶסֶף עַל רִצְפַת בַּהַט־וָשֵׁשׁ וְדַר וְסֹחָרֶת:

7 And the drinks were served in golden vessels, and all kinds of vessels, and the royal wine was in plenty like the hand (ability) of the king.

ז. וְהַשְׁקוֹת בִּכְלֵי זָהָב וְכֵלִים מִכֵּלִים שׁוֹנִים וְיֵין מַלְכוּת רָב כְּיַד הַמֶּלֶךְ:

8 And the drinking was by the law, [there was] no forcing, for so had the king ordered all the managers of his household - to do like the will of each man.

ח. וְהַשְּׁתִיָּה כַדָּת אֵין אֹנֵס כִּי־כֵן | יִסַּד הַמֶּלֶךְ עַל כָּל־רַב בֵּיתוֹ לַעֲשׂוֹת כִּרְצוֹן אִישׁ־וָאִישׁ:

9 Also Vashti the Queen made a feast for the women, in the royal palace of King Achashverosh.

ט. גַּם וַשְׁתִּי הַמַּלְכָּה עָשְׂתָה מִשְׁתֵּה נָשִׁים בֵּית הַמַּלְכוּת אֲשֶׁר לַמֶּלֶךְ אֲחַשְׁוֵרוֹשׁ:

10 On the seventh day, when the king's heart was good (merry) with wine, he said to (ordered) Mehuman, Bizzesa, Charvona, Bigsa, Avagsa, Zeisar and Charkas, the seven chamberlains who served King Achashverosh;

י. בַּיּוֹם הַשְּׁבִיעִי כְּטוֹב לֵב־הַמֶּלֶךְ בַּיָּיִן אָמַר לִמְהוּמָן בִּזְּתָא חַרְבוֹנָא בִּגְתָא וַאֲבַגְתָא זֵתַר וְכַרְכַּס שִׁבְעַת הַסָּרִיסִים הַמְשָׁרְתִים אֶת־פְּנֵי הַמֶּלֶךְ אֲחַשְׁוֵרוֹשׁ:

11 To bring Vashti the Queen before the king with (wearing) the royal crown, to show the nations and ministers her beauty, for she was of beautiful appearance.

יא. לְהָבִיא אֶת־וַשְׁתִּי הַמַּלְכָּה לִפְנֵי הַמֶּלֶךְ בְּכֶתֶר מַלְכוּת לְהַרְאוֹת הָעַמִּים וְהַשָּׂרִים אֶת־יָפְיָהּ כִּי־טוֹבַת מַרְאֶה הִיא:

12 And the Queen Vashti refused to come – by the order of the king – the response which was brought by the chamberlains, and the king was very angry and his anger burned in him.

יב. וַתְּמָאֵן הַמַּלְכָּה וַשְׁתִּי לָבוֹא בִּדְבַר הַמֶּלֶךְ אֲשֶׁר בְּיַד הַסָּרִיסִים וַיִּקְצֹף הַמֶּלֶךְ מְאֹד וַחֲמָתוֹ בָּעֲרָה בוֹ:

13 And the king said to the wise men, those who knew the times - for this was the king's thing (way), [to bring such matters] before all who knew [the] law and judgment.

יג. וַיֹּאמֶר הַמֶּלֶךְ לַחֲכָמִים יֹדְעֵי הָעִתִּים כִּי־כֵן דְּבַר הַמֶּלֶךְ לִפְנֵי כָּל־יֹדְעֵי דָּת וָדִין:

14 And those closest to him were Carshina, Sheisar, Admasa, Sarshish, Meress, Marsina [and] Memuchan, the seven ministers of Persia and Media, who would (always) see the king's face, those who sat first in the kingdom.

יד. וְהַקָּרֹב אֵלָיו כַּרְשְׁנָא שֵׁתָר אַדְמָתָא תַרְשִׁישׁ מֶרֶס מַרְסְנָא מְמוּכָן שִׁבְעַת שָׂרֵי | פָּרַס וּמָדַי רֹאֵי פְּנֵי הַמֶּלֶךְ הַיֹּשְׁבִים רִאשֹׁנָה בַּמַּלְכוּת:

15 [He asked them:] According to the law, what to do with Queen Vashti, because she did not do (obey) the order of King Achashverosh, [brought to her] through the chamberlains.

טו. כְּדָת מַה־לַּעֲשׂוֹת בַּמַּלְכָּה וַשְׁתִּי עַל | אֲשֶׁר לֹא־עָשְׂתָה אֶת־מַאֲמַר הַמֶּלֶךְ אֲחַשְׁוֵרוֹשׁ בְּיַד הַסָּרִיסִים:

16 And Memuchan said before the king and the ministers: "[It is] not against the King alone that Vashti the Queen has sinned, but against all the ministers and against all the nations that are in all the provinces of King Achashverosh."

טז. וַיֹּאמֶר מומכן (מְמוּכָן) לִפְנֵי הַמֶּלֶךְ וְהַשָּׂרִים לֹא עַל־הַמֶּלֶךְ לְבַדּוֹ עָוְתָה וַשְׁתִּי הַמַּלְכָּה כִּי עַל־כָּל־הַשָּׂרִים וְעַל־כָּל־הָעַמִּים אֲשֶׁר בְּכָל־מְדִינוֹת הַמֶּלֶךְ אֲחַשְׁוֵרוֹשׁ:

17 "For word of the queen's deed will go out to all the women, to cause their husbands to be disgraced in their eyes. For they will say: 'The King Achashverosh said (commanded) to bring Queen Vashti before him, and [yet] she did not come!'

יז. כִּי־יֵצֵא דְבַר־הַמַּלְכָּה עַל־כָּל־הַנָּשִׁים לְהַבְזוֹת בַּעְלֵיהֶן בְּעֵינֵיהֶן בְּאָמְרָם הַמֶּלֶךְ אֲחַשְׁוֵרוֹשׁ אָמַר לְהָבִיא אֶת־וַשְׁתִּי הַמַּלְכָּה לְפָנָיו וְלֹא־בָאָה:

18 "And this day, the noblewomen of Persia and Media who have heard of the queen's deed will tell [about] it to all the King's nobles and there will be much disgrace and anger."

יח. וְהַיּוֹם הַזֶּה תֹּאמַרְנָה | שָׂרוֹת פָּרַס־וּמָדַי אֲשֶׁר שָׁמְעוּ אֶת־דְּבַר הַמַּלְכָּה לְכֹל שָׂרֵי הַמֶּלֶךְ וּכְדַי בִּזָּיוֹן וָקָצֶף:

19 "If it is good for (pleases) the king, a royal proclamation should go out from [before] him, and it should be written into the laws of Persia and Media and it will not be removed, that Vashti will never [again] come before King Achashverosh, and her reign - the King should give to her friend (another) who is better than she.

יט. אִם־עַל־הַמֶּלֶךְ טוֹב יֵצֵא דְבַר־מַלְכוּת מִלְּפָנָיו וְיִכָּתֵב בְּדָתֵי פָרַס־וּמָדַי וְלֹא יַעֲבוֹר אֲשֶׁר לֹא־תָבוֹא וַשְׁתִּי לִפְנֵי הַמֶּלֶךְ אֲחַשְׁוֵרוֹשׁ וּמַלְכוּתָהּ יִתֵּן הַמֶּלֶךְ לִרְעוּתָהּ הַטּוֹבָה מִמֶּנָּה:

20 "And it will be heard - the King's decree which he shall proclaim - in all of his kingdom, for it is great, and all the women will give respect to their husbands, from the great to the small (simple)."

כ. וְנִשְׁמַע פִּתְגָם הַמֶּלֶךְ אֲשֶׁר־יַעֲשֶׂה בְּכָל־מַלְכוּתוֹ כִּי רַבָּה הִיא וְכָל־הַנָּשִׁים יִתְּנוּ יְקָר לְבַעְלֵיהֶן לְמִגָּדוֹל וְעַד־קָטָן:

21 And the matter (idea) was good (pleasing) in the eyes of the king and the ministers, and the king did like the words (advice) of Memuchan.

כא. וַיִּיטַב הַדָּבָר בְּעֵינֵי הַמֶּלֶךְ וְהַשָּׂרִים וַיַּעַשׂ הַמֶּלֶךְ כִּדְבַר מְמוּכָן:

22 And he sent letters to all the king's provinces – to each province according to its script (writing) and to each nation according to its language, [ordering] that every man shall be master in his home and that he speak [like] the language of his nation.

כב. וַיִּשְׁלַח סְפָרִים אֶל־כָּל־מְדִינוֹת הַמֶּלֶךְ אֶל־מְדִינָה וּמְדִינָה כִּכְתָבָהּ וְאֶל־עַם וָעָם כִּלְשׁוֹנוֹ לִהְיוֹת כָּל־אִישׁ שֹׂרֵר בְּבֵיתוֹ וּמְדַבֵּר כִּלְשׁוֹן עַמּוֹ:

CHAPTER II 1 After these things (events), when the anger of King Achashverosh had calmed, he remembered Vashti and what she had done and [remembered] that which was decreed upon her.

פרק ב: א. אַחַר הַדְּבָרִים הָאֵלֶּה כְּשֹׁךְ חֲמַת הַמֶּלֶךְ אֲחַשְׁוֵרוֹשׁ זָכַר אֶת־וַשְׁתִּי וְאֵת אֲשֶׁר־עָשָׂתָה וְאֵת אֲשֶׁר־נִגְזַר עָלֶיהָ:

---

2 And the king's young attendants said: "Let them seek for the king, young, unmarried girls, beautiful in appearance.

ב. וַיֹּאמְרוּ נַעֲרֵי־הַמֶּלֶךְ מְשָׁרְתָיו יְבַקְשׁוּ לַמֶּלֶךְ נְעָרוֹת בְּתוּלוֹת טוֹבוֹת מַרְאֶה:

---

3 "And the King shall appoint officers in all the provinces of his kingdom, and they should gather every young, unmarried girl, beautiful in appearance to Shushan the capital, to the house of the women, [they should be given] into the charge of Heige, the king's chamberlain, the guard of the women, and their cosmetics should be given [to them].

ג. וְיַפְקֵד הַמֶּלֶךְ פְּקִידִים בְּכָל־מְדִינוֹת מַלְכוּתוֹ וְיִקְבְּצוּ אֶת־כָּל־נַעֲרָה־בְתוּלָה טוֹבַת מַרְאֶה אֶל־שׁוּשַׁן הַבִּירָה אֶל־בֵּית הַנָּשִׁים אֶל־יַד הֵגֶא סְרִיס הַמֶּלֶךְ שֹׁמֵר הַנָּשִׁים וְנָתוֹן תַּמְרֻקֵיהֶן:

---

4 "And the young girl who will be good (pleasing) in the eyes of the King, shall rule instead of Vashti." And the thing (advice) was good (pleasing) in the eyes of the king and he did so.

ד. וְהַנַּעֲרָה אֲשֶׁר תִּיטַב בְּעֵינֵי הַמֶּלֶךְ תִּמְלֹךְ תַּחַת וַשְׁתִּי וַיִּיטַב הַדָּבָר בְּעֵינֵי הַמֶּלֶךְ וַיַּעַשׂ כֵּן:

---

5 A Jewish man was in Shushan the capital, and his name was Mordechai, the son of Yair, the son of Shim'i, the son of Kish, a man from the tribe of Binyamin -

ה. אִישׁ יְהוּדִי הָיָה בְּשׁוּשַׁן הַבִּירָה וּשְׁמוֹ מָרְדֳּכַי בֶּן יָאִיר בֶּן־שִׁמְעִי בֶּן־קִישׁ אִישׁ יְמִינִי:

---

6 - Who was exiled from Yerushalayim with the exiled [group] that had been exiled with Yechoniah, the King of Yehudah, whom Nevuchanetzar the King of Bavel had exiled.

ו. אֲשֶׁר הָגְלָה מִירוּשָׁלַיִם עִם־הַגֹּלָה אֲשֶׁר הָגְלְתָה עִם יְכָנְיָה מֶלֶךְ־יְהוּדָה אֲשֶׁר הֶגְלָה נְבוּכַדְנֶאצַּר מֶלֶךְ בָּבֶל:

---

7 And he had raised Hadassah – [she is] Esther, the daughter of his uncle, for she did not have a father and mother. And the young girl was beautiful in [her] features and beautiful in appearance, and when her father and mother died, Mordechai took her for himself - as a daughter.

ז. וַיְהִי אֹמֵן אֶת־הֲדַסָּה הִיא אֶסְתֵּר בַּת־דֹּדוֹ כִּי אֵין לָהּ אָב וָאֵם וְהַנַּעֲרָה יְפַת־תֹּאַר וְטוֹבַת מַרְאֶה וּבְמוֹת אָבִיהָ וְאִמָּהּ לְקָחָהּ מָרְדֳּכַי לוֹ לְבַת:

---

8 And it was, when the king's order and his decree were heard, and when many young girls were gathered to Shushan the capital, under the charge of Heigai; and Esther was taken to the palace under the charge of Heigai, the guard of the women.

ח. וַיְהִי בְּהִשָּׁמַע דְּבַר־הַמֶּלֶךְ וְדָתוֹ וּבְהִקָּבֵץ נְעָרוֹת רַבּוֹת אֶל־שׁוּשַׁן הַבִּירָה אֶל־יַד הֵגָי וַתִּלָּקַח אֶסְתֵּר אֶל־בֵּית הַמֶּלֶךְ אֶל־יַד הֵגַי שֹׁמֵר הַנָּשִׁים:

9 And the girl was good (pleasing) in his eyes, and she gained his kindness, and he hurried her cosmetics and meals - to give her, and the seven maids that were befitting to give to her from the palace. And he changed (moved) her and her maids to the best [area] of the women's house.	ט. וַתִּיטַב הַנַּעֲרָה בְעֵינָיו וַתִּשָּׂא חֶסֶד לְפָנָיו וַיְבַהֵל אֶת־תַּמְרוּקֶיהָ וְאֶת־מָנוֹתֶהָ לָתֵת לָהּ וְאֵת שֶׁבַע הַנְּעָרוֹת הָרְאֻיוֹת לָתֶת־לָהּ מִבֵּית הַמֶּלֶךְ וַיְשַׁנֶּהָ וְאֶת־נַעֲרוֹתֶיהָ לְטוֹב בֵּית הַנָּשִׁים׃
10 Esther did not tell [about] her nation or birthplace (heritage), for Mordechai had instructed her that she should not tell.	י. לֹא־הִגִּידָה אֶסְתֵּר אֶת־עַמָּהּ וְאֶת־מוֹלַדְתָּהּ כִּי מָרְדֳּכַי צִוָּה עָלֶיהָ אֲשֶׁר לֹא־תַגִּיד׃
11 And every day Mordechai would walk about in front of the courtyard of the women's house, to know how Esther was faring and what would be done with her.	יא. וּבְכָל־יוֹם וָיוֹם מָרְדֳּכַי מִתְהַלֵּךְ לִפְנֵי חֲצַר בֵּית־הַנָּשִׁים לָדַעַת אֶת־שְׁלוֹם אֶסְתֵּר וּמַה־יֵּעָשֶׂה בָּהּ׃
12 And when it arrived - the turn of each young girl - to come to [the] King Achashverosh, at the end of her having – [like] the law of the women - twelve months, for this is how the days of their cosmetics (beauty-care) would be completed; six months with oil of myrrh and six months with perfumes and women's cosmetics.	יב. וּבְהַגִּיעַ תֹּר נַעֲרָה וְנַעֲרָה לָבוֹא | אֶל־הַמֶּלֶךְ אֲחַשְׁוֵרוֹשׁ מִקֵּץ הֱיוֹת לָהּ כְּדָת הַנָּשִׁים שְׁנֵים עָשָׂר חֹדֶשׁ כִּי כֵּן יִמְלְאוּ יְמֵי מְרוּקֵיהֶן שִׁשָּׁה חֳדָשִׁים בְּשֶׁמֶן הַמֹּר וְשִׁשָּׁה חֳדָשִׁים בַּבְּשָׂמִים וּבְתַמְרוּקֵי הַנָּשִׁים׃
13 And with this the young girl would come to the king; Whatever she would say (request) would be given to her, to come with her from the women's house to the king's palace.	יג. וּבָזֶה הַנַּעֲרָה בָּאָה אֶל־הַמֶּלֶךְ אֵת כָּל־אֲשֶׁר תֹּאמַר יִנָּתֵן לָהּ לָבוֹא עִמָּהּ מִבֵּית הַנָּשִׁים עַד־בֵּית הַמֶּלֶךְ׃
14 In the evening she would come [to the king], and in the morning she would return to the second house of the women, under the charge of Shaashgaz, the king's chamberlain, the guard of the concubines. She would not go anymore to the king, unless the king desired her, and she was called [to come] by [her] name.	יד. בָּעֶרֶב | הִיא בָאָה וּבַבֹּקֶר הִיא שָׁבָה אֶל־בֵּית הַנָּשִׁים שֵׁנִי אֶל־יַד שַׁעַשְׁגַז סְרִיס הַמֶּלֶךְ שֹׁמֵר הַפִּילַגְשִׁים לֹא־תָבוֹא עוֹד אֶל־הַמֶּלֶךְ כִּי אִם־חָפֵץ בָּהּ הַמֶּלֶךְ וְנִקְרְאָה בְשֵׁם׃
15 And when the turn came for Esther - daughter of Avichayil, the uncle of Mordechai, who took her as a daughter - to come to the king, she did not ask for a thing, aside from that which Heigai, the king's chamberlain, custodian of the women, had said (suggested her to bring). And Esther would find favor in the eyes of all who saw her.	טו. וּבְהַגִּיעַ תֹּר־אֶסְתֵּר בַּת־אֲבִיחַיִל דֹּד מָרְדֳּכַי אֲשֶׁר לָקַח־לוֹ לְבַת לָבוֹא אֶל־הַמֶּלֶךְ לֹא בִקְשָׁה דָּבָר כִּי אִם אֶת־אֲשֶׁר יֹאמַר הֵגַי סְרִיס־הַמֶּלֶךְ שֹׁמֵר הַנָּשִׁים וַתְּהִי אֶסְתֵּר נֹשֵׂאת חֵן בְּעֵינֵי כָּל־רֹאֶיהָ׃

16 And Esther was taken to King Achashverosh, to his palace, in the tenth month, which is the month of Tevet, in the seventh year of his kingdom (rule).	טז. וַתִּלָּקַח אֶסְתֵּר אֶל־הַמֶּלֶךְ אֲחַשְׁוֵרוֹשׁ אֶל־בֵּית מַלְכוּתוֹ בַּחֹדֶשׁ הָעֲשִׂירִי הוּא־חֹדֶשׁ טֵבֵת בִּשְׁנַת־שֶׁבַע לְמַלְכוּתוֹ׃
17 And the king loved Esther more than all the women and she "found" grace and kindness before him, more than all the [other] unmarried girls; And he placed the royal crown on her head and made her queen instead of Vashti.	יז. וַיֶּאֱהַב הַמֶּלֶךְ אֶת־אֶסְתֵּר מִכָּל־הַנָּשִׁים וַתִּשָּׂא־חֵן וָחֶסֶד לְפָנָיו מִכָּל־הַבְּתוּלוֹת וַיָּשֶׂם כֶּתֶר־מַלְכוּת בְּרֹאשָׁהּ וַיַּמְלִיכֶהָ תַּחַת וַשְׁתִּי׃
18 And the king made a grand feast for all his ministers and servants, "The Feast of Esther." And he arranged a discount for [the taxes of] the provinces, and he gave presents as fitting for the king.	יח. וַיַּעַשׂ הַמֶּלֶךְ מִשְׁתֶּה גָדוֹל לְכָל־שָׂרָיו וַעֲבָדָיו אֵת מִשְׁתֵּה אֶסְתֵּר וַהֲנָחָה לַמְּדִינוֹת עָשָׂה וַיִּתֵּן מַשְׂאֵת כְּיַד הַמֶּלֶךְ׃
19 And when the unmarried girls were gathered a second time [and] Mordechai was sitting at the king's gate.	יט. וּבְהִקָּבֵץ בְּתוּלוֹת שֵׁנִית וּמָרְדֳּכַי יֹשֵׁב בְּשַׁעַר־הַמֶּלֶךְ׃
20 Esther was not telling [anyone about] her birthplace and nation, just as Mordechai had instructed her. And Esther followed Mordechai's instructions just like [she did] when she was raised by him.	כ. אֵין אֶסְתֵּר מַגֶּדֶת מוֹלַדְתָּהּ וְאֶת־עַמָּהּ כַּאֲשֶׁר צִוָּה עָלֶיהָ מָרְדֳּכָי וְאֶת־מַאֲמַר מָרְדֳּכַי אֶסְתֵּר עֹשָׂה כַּאֲשֶׁר הָיְתָה בְאָמְנָה אִתּוֹ׃
21 In those days, [while] Mordechai sat at the king's gate, Bigsan and Seresh - two of the king's chamberlains from the guards of the threshold (entrance) - became angry, and sought (planned) to send a hand against (assassinate) King Achashverosh.	כא. בַּיָּמִים הָהֵם וּמָרְדֳּכַי יֹשֵׁב בְּשַׁעַר־הַמֶּלֶךְ קָצַף בִּגְתָן וָתֶרֶשׁ שְׁנֵי־סָרִיסֵי הַמֶּלֶךְ מִשֹּׁמְרֵי הַסַּף וַיְבַקְשׁוּ לִשְׁלֹחַ יָד בַּמֶּלֶךְ אֲחַשְׁוֵרֹשׁ׃
22 And the matter became known to Mordechai and he told [it] to Esther the Queen. And Esther told [it] to the king in the name of Mordechai.	כב. וַיִּוָּדַע הַדָּבָר לְמָרְדֳּכַי וַיַּגֵּד לְאֶסְתֵּר הַמַּלְכָּה וַתֹּאמֶר אֶסְתֵּר לַמֶּלֶךְ בְּשֵׁם מָרְדֳּכָי׃
23 And the matter was investigated and found (to be true), and they were hanged - both of them - on a gallows. And it was written in the Book of Chronicles before the king.	כג. וַיְבֻקַּשׁ הַדָּבָר וַיִּמָּצֵא וַיִּתָּלוּ שְׁנֵיהֶם עַל־עֵץ וַיִּכָּתֵב בְּסֵפֶר דִּבְרֵי הַיָּמִים לִפְנֵי הַמֶּלֶךְ׃

CHAPTER III 1 After these events, King Achashverosh promoted Haman, the son of Hamdasa, the Agagi and raised him (his position); He placed his seat (position) above all the ministers who were with him.

פרק ג: א. אַחַ֣ר ׀ הַדְּבָרִ֣ים הָאֵ֗לֶּה גִּדַּל֩ הַמֶּ֨לֶךְ אֲחַשְׁוֵר֜וֹשׁ אֶת־הָמָ֧ן בֶּֽן־הַמְּדָ֛תָא הָאֲגָגִ֖י וַֽיְנַשְּׂאֵ֑הוּ וַיָּ֙שֶׂם֙ אֶת־כִּסְא֔וֹ מֵעַ֕ל כָּל־הַשָּׂרִ֖ים אֲשֶׁ֥ר אִתּֽוֹ׃

2 And all the king's servants who were at the king's gate would kneel and bow to Haman, for so had the king commanded about him. And Mordechai would not kneel nor bow.

ב. וְכָל־עַבְדֵ֨י הַמֶּ֜לֶךְ אֲשֶׁר־בְּשַׁ֣עַר הַמֶּ֗לֶךְ כֹּרְעִ֤ים וּמִֽשְׁתַּחֲוִים֙ לְהָמָ֔ן כִּי־כֵ֖ן צִוָּה־ל֣וֹ הַמֶּ֑לֶךְ וּמָ֨רְדֳּכַ֔י לֹ֥א יִכְרַ֖ע וְלֹ֥א יִֽשְׁתַּחֲוֶֽה׃

3 And the king's servants who were at the king's gate said to Mordechai, "Why do you transgress the command of the King?"

ג. וַ֠יֹּאמְרוּ עַבְדֵ֥י הַמֶּ֛לֶךְ אֲשֶׁר־בְּשַׁ֥עַר הַמֶּ֖לֶךְ לְמָרְדֳּכָ֑י מַדּ֙וּעַ֙ אַתָּ֣ה עוֹבֵ֔ר אֵ֖ת מִצְוַ֥ת הַמֶּֽלֶךְ׃

4 And it was, when they said this to him every day and he did not listen to them; [and] they told [this] to Haman to see if Mordechai's words would stand, for he had told them that he is a Jew.

ד. וַיְהִ֗י באמרם (כְּאָמְרָ֤ם) אֵלָיו֙ י֣וֹם וָי֔וֹם וְלֹ֥א שָׁמַ֖ע אֲלֵיהֶ֑ם וַיַּגִּ֣ידוּ לְהָמָ֗ן לִרְאוֹת֙ הֲיַֽעַמְדוּ֙ דִּבְרֵ֣י מָרְדֳּכַ֔י כִּֽי־הִגִּ֥יד לָהֶ֖ם אֲשֶׁר־ה֥וּא יְהוּדִֽי׃

5 And Haman saw that Mordechai is not kneeling or bowing to him, and Haman became filled with anger.

ה. וַיַּ֣רְא הָמָ֔ן כִּי־אֵ֣ין מָרְדֳּכַ֔י כֹּרֵ֥עַ וּמִֽשְׁתַּחֲוֶ֖ה ל֑וֹ וַיִּמָּלֵ֥א הָמָ֖ן חֵמָֽה׃

6 And it was disgraceful in his eyes to send his hand (kill) Mordechai alone, for they had told him of Mordechai's nation. And Haman sought (wanted) to destroy all the Jews who were in Achashverosh's entire kingdom; [he wanted to destroy] Mordechai's nation.

ו. וַיִּ֣בֶז בְּעֵינָ֗יו לִשְׁלֹ֤ח יָד֙ בְּמָרְדֳּכַ֣י לְבַדּ֔וֹ כִּֽי־הִגִּ֥ידוּ ל֖וֹ אֶת־עַ֣ם מָרְדֳּכָ֑י וַיְבַקֵּ֣שׁ הָמָ֗ן לְהַשְׁמִ֧יד אֶת־כָּל־הַיְּהוּדִ֛ים אֲשֶׁ֛ר בְּכָל־מַלְכ֥וּת אֲחַשְׁוֵר֖וֹשׁ עַ֥ם מָרְדֳּכָֽי׃

7 In the first month, which is the month of Nissan, in the twelfth year of the King Achashverosh['s rule], he cast a "Pur," this is a lot, before Haman, for every day and every month, until [it fell on] the 12th month, which is the month of Adar.

ז. בַּחֹ֤דֶשׁ הָֽרִאשׁוֹן֙ הוּא־חֹ֣דֶשׁ נִיסָ֔ן בִּשְׁנַת֙ שְׁתֵּ֣ים עֶשְׂרֵ֔ה לַמֶּ֖לֶךְ אֲחַשְׁוֵר֑וֹשׁ הִפִּ֣יל פּוּר֩ ה֨וּא הַגּוֹרָ֜ל לִפְנֵ֣י הָמָ֗ן מִיּ֧וֹם ׀ לְי֛וֹם וּמֵחֹ֛דֶשׁ לְחֹ֥דֶשׁ שְׁנֵים־עָשָׂ֖ר הוּא־חֹ֥דֶשׁ אֲדָֽר׃

8 And Haman said to King Achashverosh, "There is one nation, scattered and dispersed among the nations, in all the provinces of your kingdom, and their laws are different from any other nation and the laws of the king – they do not do (obey), and for the king there is no value to let them be.

ח. וַיֹּ֤אמֶר הָמָן֙ לַמֶּ֣לֶךְ אֲחַשְׁוֵר֔וֹשׁ יֶשְׁנ֣וֹ עַם־אֶחָ֗ד מְפֻזָּ֤ר וּמְפֹרָד֙ בֵּ֣ין הָֽעַמִּ֔ים בְּכֹ֖ל מְדִינ֣וֹת מַלְכוּתֶ֑ךָ וְדָתֵיהֶ֞ם שֹׁנ֣וֹת מִכָּל־עָ֗ם וְאֶת־דָּתֵ֤י הַמֶּ֙לֶךְ֙ אֵינָ֣ם עֹשִׂ֔ים וְלַמֶּ֥לֶךְ אֵין־שֹׁוֶ֖ה לְהַנִּיחָֽם׃

9 "If it is good for (pleases) the king, let it be written (decreed) to destroy them, and ten thousand silver talents I will weigh - through the people who will do the job - to bring to the King's treasuries."	ט. אִם־עַל־הַמֶּלֶךְ טוֹב יִכָּתֵב לְאַבְּדָם וַעֲשֶׂרֶת אֲלָפִים כִּכַּר־כֶּסֶף אֶשְׁקוֹל עַל־יְדֵי עֹשֵׂי הַמְּלָאכָה לְהָבִיא אֶל־גִּנְזֵי הַמֶּלֶךְ:
10 And the king removed his [signet] ring from his hand and he gave it to Haman, the son of Hamdasa, the Agagi, oppressor of the Jews.	י. וַיָּסַר הַמֶּלֶךְ אֶת־טַבַּעְתּוֹ מֵעַל יָדוֹ וַיִּתְּנָהּ לְהָמָן בֶּן־הַמְּדָתָא הָאֲגָגִי צֹרֵר הַיְּהוּדִים:
11 And the king said to Haman, "The money is given to you (yours to keep), and the nation [is yours] to do with it, as is good in your eyes (as you please.)"	יא. וַיֹּאמֶר הַמֶּלֶךְ לְהָמָן הַכֶּסֶף נָתוּן לָךְ וְהָעָם לַעֲשׂוֹת בּוֹ כַּטּוֹב בְּעֵינֶיךָ:
12 And the king's scribes were called on the first month, on its thirteenth day, and it was written, just as Haman commanded to the king's messengers and the governors of every province and to the officials of each nation; [It was written] to each province according to its script and each nation according to its language. It was written in the name of King Achashverosh and sealed with the king's [signet] ring.	יב. וַיִּקָּרְאוּ סֹפְרֵי הַמֶּלֶךְ בַּחֹדֶשׁ הָרִאשׁוֹן בִּשְׁלוֹשָׁה עָשָׂר יוֹם בּוֹ וַיִּכָּתֵב כְּכָל־אֲשֶׁר־צִוָּה הָמָן אֶל אֲחַשְׁדַּרְפְּנֵי־הַמֶּלֶךְ וְאֶל־הַפַּחוֹת אֲשֶׁר | עַל־מְדִינָה וּמְדִינָה וְאֶל־שָׂרֵי עַם וָעָם מְדִינָה וּמְדִינָה כִּכְתָבָהּ וְעַם וָעָם כִּלְשׁוֹנוֹ בְּשֵׁם הַמֶּלֶךְ אֲחַשְׁוֵרֹשׁ נִכְתָּב וְנֶחְתָּם בְּטַבַּעַת הַמֶּלֶךְ:
13 And letters were sent by runners (couriers) to all the provinces of the king: to annihilate, to kill and cause to perish - all the Jews, from young to old, children and women, on one day – on the thirteenth day of the twelfth month, which is the month of Adar, and their possessions [were] for plunder (free to all to take).	יג. וְנִשְׁלוֹחַ סְפָרִים בְּיַד הָרָצִים אֶל־כָּל־מְדִינוֹת הַמֶּלֶךְ לְהַשְׁמִיד לַהֲרֹג וּלְאַבֵּד אֶת־כָּל־הַיְּהוּדִים מִנַּעַר וְעַד־זָקֵן טַף וְנָשִׁים בְּיוֹם אֶחָד בִּשְׁלוֹשָׁה עָשָׂר לְחֹדֶשׁ שְׁנֵים־עָשָׂר הוּא־חֹדֶשׁ אֲדָר וּשְׁלָלָם לָבוֹז:
14 Copies of the writing (decree) were to be given as law in every province, revealed [clearly] to all the nations, to be ready for this day.	יד. פַּתְשֶׁגֶן הַכְּתָב לְהִנָּתֵן דָּת בְּכָל־מְדִינָה וּמְדִינָה גָּלוּי לְכָל־הָעַמִּים לִהְיוֹת עֲתִדִים לַיּוֹם הַזֶּה:
15 The runners (couriers) went out – rushed by order of the king and the law was given in Shushan the capital. And the king and Haman sat to drink, and the city of Shushan was bewildered.	טו. הָרָצִים יָצְאוּ דְחוּפִים בִּדְבַר הַמֶּלֶךְ וְהַדָּת נִתְּנָה בְּשׁוּשַׁן הַבִּירָה וְהַמֶּלֶךְ וְהָמָן יָשְׁבוּ לִשְׁתּוֹת וְהָעִיר שׁוּשָׁן נָבוֹכָה:

CHAPTER IV 1 And Mordechai knew [about] all that happened, and Mordechai tore his clothes and put on sackcloth and ash. And he went out into the midst of the city and he cried a great bitter cry.

פרק ד: א. וּמָרְדֳּכַי יָדַע אֶת־כׇּל־אֲשֶׁר נַעֲשָׂה וַיִּקְרַע מָרְדֳּכַי אֶת־בְּגָדָיו וַיִּלְבַּשׁ שַׂק וָאֵפֶר וַיֵּצֵא בְּתוֹךְ הָעִיר וַיִּזְעַק זְעָקָה גְדוֹלָה וּמָרָה׃

2 And he came until before the king's gate, because it is not [proper] to enter the king's gate clothed in sackcloth.

ב. וַיָּבוֹא עַד לִפְנֵי שַׁעַר־הַמֶּלֶךְ כִּי אֵין לָבוֹא אֶל־שַׁעַר הַמֶּלֶךְ בִּלְבוּשׁ שָׂק׃

3 And in every province, each place that the word of the king and his law reaches, [there was] great mourning for the Jews, and fasting and crying and lamenting; sackcloth and ash were offered to the public.

ג. וּבְכׇל־מְדִינָה וּמְדִינָה מְקוֹם אֲשֶׁר דְּבַר־הַמֶּלֶךְ וְדָתוֹ מַגִּיעַ אֵבֶל גָּדוֹל לַיְּהוּדִים וְצוֹם וּבְכִי וּמִסְפֵּד שַׂק וָאֵפֶר יֻצַּע לָרַבִּים׃

4 And Esther's girls (maidens) and chamberlains came and told her [about it] and the queen was very afraid (terrified). And she sent clothing - to dress Mordechai, and to remove his sackcloth from upon him, but he did not accept [them].

ד. ותבואינה (וַתָּבוֹאנָה) נַעֲרוֹת אֶסְתֵּר וְסָרִיסֶיהָ וַיַּגִּידוּ לָהּ וַתִּתְחַלְחַל הַמַּלְכָּה מְאֹד וַתִּשְׁלַח בְּגָדִים לְהַלְבִּישׁ אֶת־מָרְדֳּכַי וּלְהָסִיר שַׂקּוֹ מֵעָלָיו וְלֹא קִבֵּל׃

5 And Esther called Hasach, [one] of the king's chamberlains whom he had placed before her (to serve her), and she commanded him regarding Mordechai, to find out what is this and for what [reason] is [he doing] this.

ה. וַתִּקְרָא אֶסְתֵּר לַהֲתָךְ מִסָּרִיסֵי הַמֶּלֶךְ אֲשֶׁר הֶעֱמִיד לְפָנֶיהָ וַתְּצַוֵּהוּ עַל־מָרְדֳּכָי לָדַעַת מַה־זֶּה וְעַל־מַה־זֶּה׃

6 And Hasach went out to Mordechai, to the city square that was in front of the king's gate.

ו. וַיֵּצֵא הֲתָךְ אֶל־מָרְדֳּכָי אֶל־רְחוֹב הָעִיר אֲשֶׁר לִפְנֵי שַׁעַר־הַמֶּלֶךְ׃

7 And Mordechai told him all that had happened to him, and the explanation of the silver that Haman said (ordered) to weigh (and deposit) to the king's treasuries for the Jews - to destroy them.

ז. וַיַּגֶּד־לוֹ מָרְדֳּכַי אֵת כׇּל־אֲשֶׁר קָרָהוּ וְאֵת ׀ פָּרָשַׁת הַכֶּסֶף אֲשֶׁר אָמַר הָמָן לִשְׁקוֹל עַל־גִּנְזֵי הַמֶּלֶךְ ביהודיים (בַּיְּהוּדִים) לְאַבְּדָם׃

8 And the copy of the written law (decree) that was given in Shushan to destroy them, he gave him to show Esther and to tell her [about it], and to order her to go to the king to plea to him and to request before him for her nation.

ח. וְאֶת־פַּתְשֶׁגֶן כְּתָב־הַדָּת אֲשֶׁר־נִתַּן בְּשׁוּשָׁן לְהַשְׁמִידָם נָתַן לוֹ לְהַרְאוֹת אֶת־אֶסְתֵּר וּלְהַגִּיד לָהּ וּלְצַוּוֹת עָלֶיהָ לָבוֹא אֶל־הַמֶּלֶךְ לְהִתְחַנֶּן־לוֹ וּלְבַקֵּשׁ מִלְּפָנָיו עַל־עַמָּהּ׃

9 And Hasach came and told to Esther the words of Mordechai.

ט. וַיָּבוֹא הֲתָךְ וַיַּגֵּד לְאֶסְתֵּר אֵת דִּבְרֵי מָרְדֳּכָי׃

10 And Esther said [this] to Hasach; and she ordered him to [tell] Mordechai:

י. וַתֹּאמֶר אֶסְתֵּר לַהֲתָךְ וַתְּצַוֵּהוּ אֶל־מָרְדֳּכָי׃

11 "All the king's servants and the people of the king's provinces know, that any man and woman who will come to the king, into the inner courtyard – who was not called [to come], his law is one; to be killed; except for whom the king extends his golden scepter, [only] he shall live. And I have not been called to come to the king for these [past] thirty days."	יא. כָּל־עַבְדֵי הַמֶּלֶךְ וְעַם־מְדִינוֹת הַמֶּלֶךְ יֹדְעִים אֲשֶׁר כָּל־אִישׁ וְאִשָּׁה אֲשֶׁר יָבוֹא־אֶל־הַמֶּלֶךְ אֶל־הֶחָצֵר הַפְּנִימִית אֲשֶׁר לֹא־יִקָּרֵא אַחַת דָּתוֹ לְהָמִית לְבַד מֵאֲשֶׁר יוֹשִׁיט־לוֹ הַמֶּלֶךְ אֶת־שַׁרְבִיט הַזָּהָב וְחָיָה וַאֲנִי לֹא נִקְרֵאתִי לָבוֹא אֶל־הַמֶּלֶךְ זֶה שְׁלוֹשִׁים יוֹם:
12 And they told [to] Mordechai the words of Esther.	יב. וַיַּגִּידוּ לְמָרְדֳּכָי אֵת דִּבְרֵי אֶסְתֵּר:
13 And Mordechai said to reply to Esther, "Do not imagine (think to yourself) to escape in[side] the king's palace from [the fate of] all the Jews.	יג. וַיֹּאמֶר מָרְדֳּכַי לְהָשִׁיב אֶל־אֶסְתֵּר אַל־תְּדַמִּי בְנַפְשֵׁךְ לְהִמָּלֵט בֵּית־הַמֶּלֶךְ מִכָּל־הַיְּהוּדִים:
14 "For if you will be [completely] silent at this time, relief and rescue will arise for the Jews from another place, and you and your father's house will perish. And who knows if for [just such] a time like this, you reached this [position of] royalty."	יד. כִּי אִם־הַחֲרֵשׁ תַּחֲרִישִׁי בָּעֵת הַזֹּאת רֶוַח וְהַצָּלָה יַעֲמוֹד לַיְּהוּדִים מִמָּקוֹם אַחֵר וְאַתְּ וּבֵית־אָבִיךְ תֹּאבֵדוּ וּמִי יוֹדֵעַ אִם־לְעֵת כָּזֹאת הִגַּעַתְּ לַמַּלְכוּת:
15 And Esther said to reply to Mordechai:	טו. וַתֹּאמֶר אֶסְתֵּר לְהָשִׁיב אֶל־מָרְדֳּכָי:
16 "Go, gather all the Jews who are in Shushan, and fast for my sake, and do not eat nor drink for three days, night and day. Also I and my maidens shall fast so. And thus I shall come to the king – which is not according to the law, and if I perish, I perish."	טז. לֵךְ כְּנוֹס אֶת־כָּל־הַיְּהוּדִים הַנִּמְצְאִים בְּשׁוּשָׁן וְצוּמוּ עָלַי וְאַל־תֹּאכְלוּ וְאַל־תִּשְׁתּוּ שְׁלֹשֶׁת יָמִים לַיְלָה וָיוֹם גַּם־אֲנִי וְנַעֲרֹתַי אָצוּם כֵּן וּבְכֵן אָבוֹא אֶל־הַמֶּלֶךְ אֲשֶׁר לֹא־כַדָּת וְכַאֲשֶׁר אָבַדְתִּי אָבָדְתִּי:
17 So Mordecai passed and did according to all that Esther had commanded him.	יז. וַיַּעֲבֹר מָרְדֳּכָי וַיַּעַשׂ כְּכֹל אֲשֶׁר צִוְּתָה עָלָיו אֶסְתֵּר:

CHAPTER V 1 Now it came to pass on the third day that Esther clothed herself regally, and she stood in the inner court of the king's house, opposite the king's house, and the king was sitting on his royal throne in the royal palace, opposite the entrance of the house.

פרק ה: א. וַיְהִי | בַּיּוֹם הַשְּׁלִישִׁי וַתִּלְבַּשׁ אֶסְתֵּר מַלְכוּת וַתַּעֲמֹד בַּחֲצַר בֵּית הַמֶּלֶךְ הַפְּנִימִית נֹכַח בֵּית הַמֶּלֶךְ וְהַמֶּלֶךְ יוֹשֵׁב עַל כִּסֵּא מַלְכוּתוֹ בְּבֵית הַמַּלְכוּת נֹכַח פֶּתַח הַבָּיִת:

2 And it came to pass when the king saw Queen Esther standing in the court that she won favor in his eyes, and the king extended to Esther the golden scepter that was in his hand, and Esther approached and touched the end of the scepter.

ב. וַיְהִי כִרְאוֹת הַמֶּלֶךְ אֶת אֶסְתֵּר הַמַּלְכָּה עֹמֶדֶת בֶּחָצֵר נָשְׂאָה חֵן בְּעֵינָיו וַיּוֹשֶׁט הַמֶּלֶךְ לְאֶסְתֵּר אֶת שַׁרְבִיט הַזָּהָב אֲשֶׁר בְּיָדוֹ וַתִּקְרַב אֶסְתֵּר וַתִּגַּע בְּרֹאשׁ הַשַּׁרְבִיט:

3 And the king said to her, "What concerns you, Queen Esther, and what is your petition? Even to half the kingdom, it will be given to you."

ג. וַיֹּאמֶר לָהּ הַמֶּלֶךְ מַה לָּךְ אֶסְתֵּר הַמַּלְכָּה וּמַה בַּקָּשָׁתֵךְ עַד חֲצִי הַמַּלְכוּת וְיִנָּתֵן לָךְ:

4 And Esther said, "If it pleases the king, let the king and Haman come today to the banquet that I have prepared for him."

ד. וַתֹּאמֶר אֶסְתֵּר אִם עַל הַמֶּלֶךְ טוֹב יָבוֹא הַמֶּלֶךְ וְהָמָן הַיּוֹם אֶל הַמִּשְׁתֶּה אֲשֶׁר עָשִׂיתִי לוֹ:

5 And the king said, "Rush Haman to do Esther's bidding," and the king and Haman came to the banquet that Esther had prepared.

ה. וַיֹּאמֶר הַמֶּלֶךְ מַהֲרוּ אֶת הָמָן לַעֲשׂוֹת אֶת דְּבַר אֶסְתֵּר וַיָּבֹא הַמֶּלֶךְ וְהָמָן אֶל הַמִּשְׁתֶּה אֲשֶׁר עָשְׂתָה אֶסְתֵּר:

6 And the king said to Esther during the wine banquet, "What is your petition? It shall be granted you. And what is your request? Even up to half the kingdom, it shall be fulfilled."

ו. וַיֹּאמֶר הַמֶּלֶךְ לְאֶסְתֵּר בְּמִשְׁתֵּה הַיַּיִן מַה שְּׁאֵלָתֵךְ וְיִנָּתֵן לָךְ וּמַה בַּקָּשָׁתֵךְ עַד חֲצִי הַמַּלְכוּת וְתֵעָשׂ:

7 Esther replied and said, "My petition and my request [are as follows]:

ז. וַתַּעַן אֶסְתֵּר וַתֹּאמַר שְׁאֵלָתִי וּבַקָּשָׁתִי:

8 If I have found favor in the king's eyes, and if it pleases the king to grant my petition and to fulfill my request, let the king and Haman come to the banquet that I will make for them, and tomorrow I will do the king's bidding."

ח. אִם מָצָאתִי חֵן בְּעֵינֵי הַמֶּלֶךְ וְאִם עַל הַמֶּלֶךְ טוֹב לָתֵת אֶת שְׁאֵלָתִי וְלַעֲשׂוֹת אֶת בַּקָּשָׁתִי יָבוֹא הַמֶּלֶךְ וְהָמָן אֶל הַמִּשְׁתֶּה אֲשֶׁר אֶעֱשֶׂה לָהֶם וּמָחָר אֶעֱשֶׂה כִּדְבַר הַמֶּלֶךְ:

9 And Haman went out on that day, happy and with a cheerful heart, but when Haman saw Mordechai in the king's gate, and he neither rose nor stirred because of him, Haman was filled with wrath against Mordechai.

ט. וַיֵּצֵא הָמָן בַּיּוֹם הַהוּא שָׂמֵחַ וְטוֹב לֵב וְכִרְאוֹת הָמָן אֶת מָרְדֳּכַי בְּשַׁעַר הַמֶּלֶךְ וְלֹא קָם וְלֹא זָע מִמֶּנּוּ וַיִּמָּלֵא הָמָן עַל מָרְדֳּכַי חֵמָה:

10 But Haman restrained himself, and he came home, and he sent and brought his friends and Zeresh his wife.	י. וַיִּתְאַפַּק הָמָן וַיָּבוֹא אֶל בֵּיתוֹ וַיִּשְׁלַח וַיָּבֵא אֶת אֹהֲבָיו וְאֶת זֶרֶשׁ אִשְׁתּוֹ:
11 And Haman recounted to them the glory of his riches and the multitude of his sons, and all [the ways] that the king had promoted him and that he had exalted him over the princes and the king's servants.	יא. וַיְסַפֵּר לָהֶם הָמָן אֶת כְּבוֹד עָשְׁרוֹ וְרֹב בָּנָיו וְאֵת כָּל אֲשֶׁר גִּדְּלוֹ הַמֶּלֶךְ וְאֵת אֲשֶׁר נִשְּׂאוֹ עַל הָרִים וְעַבְדֵי הַמֶּלֶךְ:
12 And Haman said, "Esther did not even bring [anyone] to the party that she made, except me, and tomorrow, too, I am invited to her with the king.	יב. וַיֹּאמֶר הָמָן אַף לֹא הֵבִיאָה אֶסְתֵּר הַמַּלְכָּה עִם הַמֶּלֶךְ אֶל הַמִּשְׁתֶּה אֲשֶׁר עָשָׂתָה כִּי אִם אוֹתִי וְגַם לְמָחָר אֲנִי קָרוּא לָהּ עִם הַמֶּלֶךְ:
13 But all this is worth nothing to me, every time I see Mordechai the Jew sitting in the king's gate."	יג. וְכָל זֶה אֵינֶנּוּ שֹׁוֶה לִי בְּכָל עֵת אֲשֶׁר אֲנִי רֹאֶה אֶת מָרְדֳּכַי הַיְּהוּדִי יוֹשֵׁב בְּשַׁעַר הַמֶּלֶךְ:
14 And Zeresh his wife and all his friends said, "Let them make a gallows fifty cubits high, and in the morning say to the king that they should hang Mordechai on it, and go to the king to the banquet joyfully." The matter pleased Haman, and he made the gallows.	יד. וַתֹּאמֶר לוֹ זֶרֶשׁ אִשְׁתּוֹ וְכָל אֹהֲבָיו יַעֲשׂוּ עֵץ גָּבֹהַּ חֲמִשִּׁים אַמָּה וּבַבֹּקֶר | אֱמֹר לַמֶּלֶךְ וְיִתְלוּ אֶת מָרְדֳּכַי עָלָיו וּבֹא עִם הַמֶּלֶךְ אֶל הַמִּשְׁתֶּה שָׂמֵחַ וַיִּיטַב הַדָּבָר לִפְנֵי הָמָן וַיַּעַשׂ הָעֵץ:

CHAPTER VI 1 On that night, the king's sleep was disturbed. And he said (ordered) to bring the book of records, the chronicles, and they were (would be) read before the king.

פרק ו: א. בַּלַּיְלָה הַהוּא נָדְדָה שְׁנַת הַמֶּלֶךְ וַיֹּאמֶר
לְהָבִיא אֶת־סֵפֶר הַזִּכְרֹנוֹת דִּבְרֵי הַיָּמִים וַיִּהְיוּ נִקְרָאִים
לִפְנֵי הַמֶּלֶךְ׃

2 And it was found written that Mordechai had informed on Bigsan and Seresh, two chamberlains of the king, from the guards of the threshold (entrance), who had sought (planned) to send their hand against (assassinate) the King Achashverosh.

ב. וַיִּמָּצֵא כָתוּב אֲשֶׁר הִגִּיד מָרְדֳּכַי עַל־בִּגְתָנָא וָתֶרֶשׁ
שְׁנֵי סָרִיסֵי הַמֶּלֶךְ מִשֹּׁמְרֵי הַסַּף אֲשֶׁר בִּקְשׁוּ לִשְׁלֹחַ יָד
בַּמֶּלֶךְ אֲחַשְׁוֵרוֹשׁ׃

3 And the king said; "What honor and greatness has been done (rewarded) to Mordechai for this?" And the king's young servants said "Nothing was done with (for) him."

ג. וַיֹּאמֶר הַמֶּלֶךְ מַה־נַּעֲשָׂה יְקָר וּגְדוּלָּה לְמָרְדֳּכַי עַל־זֶה
וַיֹּאמְרוּ נַעֲרֵי הַמֶּלֶךְ מְשָׁרְתָיו לֹא־נַעֲשָׂה עִמּוֹ דָּבָר׃

4 And the king said; "Who is in the courtyard?" And Haman had come to the outer courtyard of the king's palace to tell the king to hang Mordechai on the gallows that he had prepared for him.

ד. וַיֹּאמֶר הַמֶּלֶךְ מִי בֶחָצֵר וְהָמָן בָּא לַחֲצַר בֵּית־הַמֶּלֶךְ
הַחִיצוֹנָה לֵאמֹר לַמֶּלֶךְ לִתְלוֹת אֶת־מָרְדֳּכַי עַל־הָעֵץ
אֲשֶׁר־הֵכִין לוֹ׃

5 And the king's servants said to him; "Behold Haman is standing in the courtyard." And the king said, "Let him come."

ה. וַיֹּאמְרוּ נַעֲרֵי הַמֶּלֶךְ אֵלָיו הִנֵּה הָמָן עֹמֵד בֶּחָצֵר וַיֹּאמֶר
הַמֶּלֶךְ יָבוֹא׃

6 And Haman came, and the king said to him, "What [do you recommend] to do, for a man whom the king desires his honor (- for him to have honor). And Haman said in his heart (to himself), "To whom would the king wish to [cause] honor more than me?"

ו. וַיָּבוֹא הָמָן וַיֹּאמֶר לוֹ הַמֶּלֶךְ מַה־לַּעֲשׂוֹת בָּאִישׁ אֲשֶׁר
הַמֶּלֶךְ חָפֵץ בִּיקָרוֹ וַיֹּאמֶר הָמָן בְּלִבּוֹ לְמִי יַחְפֹּץ הַמֶּלֶךְ
לַעֲשׂוֹת יְקָר יוֹתֵר מִמֶּנִּי׃

7 And Haman said to the king, "[For] a man whom the king wishes his honor;

ז. וַיֹּאמֶר הָמָן אֶל־הַמֶּלֶךְ אִישׁ אֲשֶׁר הַמֶּלֶךְ חָפֵץ בִּיקָרוֹ׃

8 "Let them bring a royal garment that the king has worn, and a horse that the king rode upon, and on whose head the royal crown has been placed.

ח. יָבִיאוּ לְבוּשׁ מַלְכוּת אֲשֶׁר לָבַשׁ־בּוֹ הַמֶּלֶךְ וְסוּס אֲשֶׁר
רָכַב עָלָיו הַמֶּלֶךְ וַאֲשֶׁר נִתַּן כֶּתֶר מַלְכוּת בְּרֹאשׁוֹ׃

9 "And the garment and the horse shall be given into the hands of one of the king's noble ministers, and they shall dress the man whom the king wishes to honor, and they shall lead him on the horse in the city square, and they shall call out (proclaim) before him, 'So shall be done for the man whom the king desires his honor."

ט. וְנָתוֹן הַלְּבוּשׁ וְהַסּוּס עַל־יַד־אִישׁ מִשָּׂרֵי הַמֶּלֶךְ
הַפַּרְתְּמִים וְהִלְבִּישׁוּ אֶת־הָאִישׁ אֲשֶׁר הַמֶּלֶךְ חָפֵץ בִּיקָרוֹ
וְהִרְכִּיבֻהוּ עַל־הַסּוּס בִּרְחוֹב הָעִיר וְקָרְאוּ לְפָנָיו כָּכָה
יֵעָשֶׂה לָאִישׁ אֲשֶׁר הַמֶּלֶךְ חָפֵץ בִּיקָרוֹ׃

10 And The king said to Haman, "Hurry! Take the garment and the horse just as you spoke, and do so for Mordechai the Jew who sits at the king's gate. Do not leave out a thing from all that you spoke."

י. וַיֹּאמֶר הַמֶּלֶךְ לְהָמָן מַהֵר קַח אֶת־הַלְּבוּשׁ וְאֶת־הַסּוּס
כַּאֲשֶׁר דִּבַּרְתָּ וַעֲשֵׂה־כֵן לְמָרְדֳּכַי הַיְּהוּדִי הַיּוֹשֵׁב בְּשַׁעַר
הַמֶּלֶךְ אַל־תַּפֵּל דָּבָר מִכֹּל אֲשֶׁר דִּבַּרְתָּ׃

11 And Haman took the garment and the horse and he dressed Mordechai, and he led him in the city square and he called out (proclaimed) before him: 'So shall be done for the man whom the king desires his honor.

יא. וַיִּקַּח הָמָן אֶת־הַלְּבוּשׁ וְאֶת־הַסּוּס וַיַּלְבֵּשׁ אֶת־מָרְדֳּכָי
וַיַּרְכִּיבֵהוּ בִּרְחוֹב הָעִיר וַיִּקְרָא לְפָנָיו כָּכָה יֵעָשֶׂה לָאִישׁ
אֲשֶׁר הַמֶּלֶךְ חָפֵץ בִּיקָרוֹ׃

12 And Mordechai returned to the king's gate and Haman was rushed to his house, mourning and with a covered head.

יב. וַיָּשָׁב מָרְדֳּכַי אֶל־שַׁעַר הַמֶּלֶךְ וְהָמָן נִדְחַף אֶל־בֵּיתוֹ
אָבֵל וַחֲפוּי רֹאשׁ׃

13 And Haman told to Zeresh his wife and to all his friends [about] all that happened to him. And his wise men and Zeresh his wife said to him, "If Mordechai - before whom you have begun to fall - is of Jewish seed (descent) - you will not overcome (succeed against) him, but you will certainly fall before him."

יג. וַיְסַפֵּר הָמָן לְזֶרֶשׁ אִשְׁתּוֹ וּלְכָל־אֹהֲבָיו אֵת כָּל־אֲשֶׁר
קָרָהוּ וַיֹּאמְרוּ לוֹ חֲכָמָיו וְזֶרֶשׁ אִשְׁתּוֹ אִם מִזֶּרַע הַיְּהוּדִים
מָרְדֳּכַי אֲשֶׁר הַחִלּוֹתָ לִנְפֹּל לְפָנָיו לֹא־תוּכַל לוֹ כִּי־נָפוֹל
תִּפּוֹל לְפָנָיו׃

14 [While] they were still speaking with him - the chamberlains of the king arrived, and they rushed to bring Haman to the feast that Esther had made.

יד. עוֹדָם מְדַבְּרִים עִמּוֹ וְסָרִיסֵי הַמֶּלֶךְ הִגִּיעוּ וַיַּבְהִלוּ
לְהָבִיא אֶת־הָמָן אֶל־הַמִּשְׁתֶּה אֲשֶׁר־עָשְׂתָה אֶסְתֵּר׃

CHAPTER VII 1 And the king and Haman came to drink with Esther the Queen.

פרק ז: א. וַיָּבֹא הַמֶּלֶךְ וְהָמָן לִשְׁתּוֹת עִם־אֶסְתֵּר הַמַּלְכָּה׃

2 And the king said to Esther also on the second day at the wine feast, "What is your plea, Queen Esther - it will be given to you. And what is your request? Until half the kingdom - it will be done."

ב. וַיֹּאמֶר הַמֶּלֶךְ לְאֶסְתֵּר גַּם בַּיּוֹם הַשֵּׁנִי בְּמִשְׁתֵּה הַיַּיִן מַה־שְּׁאֵלָתֵךְ אֶסְתֵּר הַמַּלְכָּה וְתִנָּתֵן לָךְ וּמַה־בַּקָּשָׁתֵךְ עַד־חֲצִי הַמַּלְכוּת וְתֵעָשׂ׃

3 And Queen Esther replied and said: "If I have found favor in your eyes, O King, and if it is good for (pleases) the King, let my soul (life) be given to me for my plea, and my people for my request.

ג. וַתַּעַן אֶסְתֵּר הַמַּלְכָּה וַתֹּאמַר אִם־מָצָאתִי חֵן בְּעֵינֶיךָ הַמֶּלֶךְ וְאִם־עַל־הַמֶּלֶךְ טוֹב תִּנָּתֶן־לִי נַפְשִׁי בִּשְׁאֵלָתִי וְעַמִּי בְּבַקָּשָׁתִי׃

4 "For we have been sold – I and my people - to be annihilated, to be killed and to perish! And if we had been sold as slaves and maidservants I would have kept silent. But the oppressor is not (calculating, valuing or) bothered by the King's loss."

ד. כִּי נִמְכַּרְנוּ אֲנִי וְעַמִּי לְהַשְׁמִיד לַהֲרוֹג וּלְאַבֵּד וְאִלּוּ לַעֲבָדִים וְלִשְׁפָחוֹת נִמְכַּרְנוּ הֶחֱרַשְׁתִּי כִּי אֵין הַצָּר שֹׁוֶה בְּנֵזֶק הַמֶּלֶךְ׃

5 And King Achashverosh said [- and he said] to Queen Esther, "Who is this, and which one is he, whose heart fills him (with the chutzpa) to do so?"

ה. וַיֹּאמֶר הַמֶּלֶךְ אֲחַשְׁוֵרוֹשׁ וַיֹּאמֶר לְאֶסְתֵּר הַמַּלְכָּה מִי הוּא זֶה וְאֵי־זֶה הוּא אֲשֶׁר־מְלָאוֹ לִבּוֹ לַעֲשׂוֹת כֵּן׃

6 "And Esther said, "A man [who is] an oppressor and an enemy: This evil Haman!" And Haman was terrified before the king and the queen.

ו. וַתֹּאמֶר אֶסְתֵּר אִישׁ צַר וְאוֹיֵב הָמָן הָרָע הַזֶּה וְהָמָן נִבְעַת מִלִּפְנֵי הַמֶּלֶךְ וְהַמַּלְכָּה׃

7 And the king arose in anger from the wine feast [and went] to the palace garden. And Haman stood up to request (beg) for his life from Esther the Queen, for he saw, that the [intent to cause him] evil was decided against him – by the king.

ז. וְהַמֶּלֶךְ קָם בַּחֲמָתוֹ מִמִּשְׁתֵּה הַיַּיִן אֶל־גִּנַּת הַבִּיתָן וְהָמָן עָמַד לְבַקֵּשׁ עַל־נַפְשׁוֹ מֵאֶסְתֵּר הַמַּלְכָּה כִּי רָאָה כִּי־כָלְתָה אֵלָיו הָרָעָה מֵאֵת הַמֶּלֶךְ׃

8 And the king returned from the palace garden to the wine-feast house, and Haman was falling on the couch upon which Esther was. And the king said, "[Are you] also [trying] to conquer the queen with me in the palace?!" [As soon as] the words left the king's mouth - the face of Haman was covered.

ח. וְהַמֶּלֶךְ שָׁב מִגִּנַּת הַבִּיתָן אֶל־בֵּית ׀ מִשְׁתֵּה הַיַּיִן וְהָמָן נֹפֵל עַל־הַמִּטָּה אֲשֶׁר אֶסְתֵּר עָלֶיהָ וַיֹּאמֶר הַמֶּלֶךְ הֲגַם לִכְבּוֹשׁ אֶת־הַמַּלְכָּה עִמִּי בַּבָּיִת הַדָּבָר יָצָא מִפִּי הַמֶּלֶךְ וּפְנֵי הָמָן חָפוּ׃

9 And Charvonah, one of the chamberlains before the king, said, "Also, behold [there is] the gallows that Haman made for Mordechai, who spoke well for the King, standing at Haman's house, fifty cubits high!" And the king said "Hang him on it!"

ט. וַיֹּאמֶר חַרְבוֹנָה אֶחָד מִן־הַסָּרִיסִים לִפְנֵי הַמֶּלֶךְ גַּם הִנֵּה־הָעֵץ אֲשֶׁר־עָשָׂה הָמָן לְמָרְדֳּכַי אֲשֶׁר דִּבֶּר־טוֹב עַל־הַמֶּלֶךְ עֹמֵד בְּבֵית הָמָן גָּבֹהַּ חֲמִשִּׁים אַמָּה וַיֹּאמֶר הַמֶּלֶךְ תְּלֻהוּ עָלָיו׃

10 And they hanged Haman on the gallows that he prepared for Mordechai, and the king's anger calmed.

י. וַיִּתְלוּ אֶת־הָמָן עַל־הָעֵץ אֲשֶׁר־הֵכִין לְמָרְדֳּכָי וַחֲמַת הַמֶּלֶךְ שָׁכָכָה׃

CHAPTER VIII 1 On that day, King Achashverosh gave [to] Esther the Queen the house of Haman, oppressor of the Jews. And Mordechai came before the king, for Esther had told [the king] what he was to her (how he was related).	פרק ח: א. בַּיּוֹם הַהוּא נָתַן הַמֶּלֶךְ אֲחַשְׁוֵרוֹשׁ לְאֶסְתֵּר הַמַּלְכָּה אֶת־בֵּית הָמָן צֹרֵר היהודיים (הַיְּהוּדִים) וּמָרְדֳּכַי בָּא לִפְנֵי הַמֶּלֶךְ כִּי־הִגִּידָה אֶסְתֵּר מַה הוּא־לָהּ:
2 And the king removed his ring, which he had transferred from Haman - and gave it to Mordechai. And Esther put Mordechai in charge of Haman's house.	ב. וַיָּסַר הַמֶּלֶךְ אֶת־טַבַּעְתּוֹ אֲשֶׁר הֶעֱבִיר מֵהָמָן וַיִּתְּנָהּ לְמָרְדֳּכָי וַתָּשֶׂם אֶסְתֵּר אֶת־מָרְדֳּכַי עַל־בֵּית הָמָן:
3 And Esther continued and she spoke [again] before the king, and she fell before his feet, and she cried and begged him to avert (remove) the evil decree of Haman the Agagi, and his thought (plot) that he had plotted against the Jews.	ג. וַתּוֹסֶף אֶסְתֵּר וַתְּדַבֵּר לִפְנֵי הַמֶּלֶךְ וַתִּפֹּל לִפְנֵי רַגְלָיו וַתֵּבְךְּ וַתִּתְחַנֶּן־לוֹ לְהַעֲבִיר אֶת־רָעַת הָמָן הָאֲגָגִי וְאֵת מַחֲשַׁבְתּוֹ אֲשֶׁר חָשַׁב עַל־הַיְּהוּדִים:
4 And the king extended to Esther the golden scepter. And Esther arose and she stood before the king.	ד. וַיּוֹשֶׁט הַמֶּלֶךְ לְאֶסְתֵּר אֵת שַׁרְבִט הַזָּהָב וַתָּקָם אֶסְתֵּר וַתַּעֲמֹד לִפְנֵי הַמֶּלֶךְ:
5 And she said, " If it is good for (pleases) the king, and if I have found favor before him, and the matter is fitting (proper) before the King, and I am good (pleasing) in his eyes, let it be written (ordered) to return the letters [- the books containing] the plot of Haman, son of Hamdasa, the Agagi, [in] which he wrote (ordered) to cause to perish - the Jews that are in all the King's provinces.	ה. וַתֹּאמֶר אִם־עַל־הַמֶּלֶךְ טוֹב וְאִם־מָצָאתִי חֵן לְפָנָיו וְכָשֵׁר הַדָּבָר לִפְנֵי הַמֶּלֶךְ וְטוֹבָה אֲנִי בְּעֵינָיו יִכָּתֵב לְהָשִׁיב אֶת־הַסְּפָרִים מַחֲשֶׁבֶת הָמָן בֶּן־הַמְּדָתָא הָאֲגָגִי אֲשֶׁר כָּתַב לְאַבֵּד אֶת־הַיְּהוּדִים אֲשֶׁר בְּכָל־מְדִינוֹת הַמֶּלֶךְ:
6 "For how will I able to [tolerate and] see the evil that will find (befall) my nation? And how will I able to [tolerate and] see the destruction of my heritage?"	ו. כִּי אֵיכָכָה אוּכַל וְרָאִיתִי בָּרָעָה אֲשֶׁר־יִמְצָא אֶת־עַמִּי וְאֵיכָכָה אוּכַל וְרָאִיתִי בְּאָבְדַן מוֹלַדְתִּי:
7 And the King Achashverosh said to Esther the Queen and to Mordechai the Jew, "Behold, Haman's house - I have given to Esther, and they hung him on the gallows because he sent his hand against the Jews.	ז. וַיֹּאמֶר הַמֶּלֶךְ אֲחַשְׁוֵרֹשׁ לְאֶסְתֵּר הַמַּלְכָּה וּלְמָרְדֳּכַי הַיְּהוּדִי הִנֵּה בֵית־הָמָן נָתַתִּי לְאֶסְתֵּר וְאֹתוֹ תָּלוּ עַל־הָעֵץ עַל אֲשֶׁר־שָׁלַח יָדוֹ ביהודיים (בַּיְּהוּדִים):
8 "And you - write concerning the Jews as is good in your eyes (as you please) in the name of the king, and seal it with the king's ring. For a writing (order) that was written in the name of the King and was sealed with the king's ring – it is not [able] to be returned."	ח. וְאַתֶּם כִּתְבוּ עַל־הַיְּהוּדִים כַּטּוֹב בְּעֵינֵיכֶם בְּשֵׁם הַמֶּלֶךְ וְחִתְמוּ בְּטַבַּעַת הַמֶּלֶךְ כִּי־כְתָב אֲשֶׁר־נִכְתָּב בְּשֵׁם־הַמֶּלֶךְ וְנַחְתּוֹם בְּטַבַּעַת הַמֶּלֶךְ אֵין לְהָשִׁיב:

9 And the king's scribes were called at that time, in the third month, which is the month of Sivan, on its twenty-third day. And it was written according to all that Mordechai instructed the Jews, and the satraps, and the governors, and the ministers of the provinces [who were] from Hodu to Cush, one hundred twenty-seven provinces. [It was written to] each province according to its script and each nation according to its language, and to the Jews according to their script and their language.

ט. וַיִּקָּרְאוּ סֹפְרֵי־הַמֶּלֶךְ בָּעֵת־הַהִיא בַּחֹדֶשׁ הַשְּׁלִישִׁי הוּא־חֹדֶשׁ סִיוָן בִּשְׁלוֹשָׁה וְעֶשְׂרִים בּוֹ וַיִּכָּתֵב כְּכָל־אֲשֶׁר־צִוָּה מָרְדֳּכַי אֶל־הַיְּהוּדִים וְאֶל הָאֲחַשְׁדַּרְפְּנִים־וְהַפַּחוֹת וְשָׂרֵי הַמְּדִינוֹת אֲשֶׁר ׀ מֵהֹדּוּ וְעַד־כּוּשׁ שֶׁבַע וְעֶשְׂרִים וּמֵאָה מְדִינָה מְדִינָה וּמְדִינָה כִּכְתָבָהּ וְעַם וָעָם כִּלְשֹׁנוֹ וְאֶל־הַיְּהוּדִים כִּכְתָבָם וְכִלְשׁוֹנָם׃

10 And he wrote in the name of King Achashverosh and he sealed it with the king's ring.

And he sent the letters by the runners (couriers) on horseback, riders of the swift, royal camels (?):

י. וַיִּכְתֹּב בְּשֵׁם הַמֶּלֶךְ אֲחַשְׁוֵרֹשׁ וַיַּחְתֹּם בְּטַבַּעַת הַמֶּלֶךְ וַיִּשְׁלַח סְפָרִים בְּיַד הָרָצִים בַּסּוּסִים רֹכְבֵי הָרֶכֶשׁ הָאֲחַשְׁתְּרָנִים בְּנֵי הָרַמָּכִים׃

11 That the king had given [permission to] the Jews of every city to gather and stand up for their lives; to annihilate, kill and cause to perish, every army (force) of a nation and province that is oppressing them, [including their] children and women, and their possessions [are for the Jews] to plunder.

יא. אֲשֶׁר נָתַן הַמֶּלֶךְ לַיְּהוּדִים ׀ אֲשֶׁר בְּכָל־עִיר־וָעִיר לְהִקָּהֵל וְלַעֲמֹד עַל־נַפְשָׁם לְהַשְׁמִיד וְלַהֲרֹג וּלְאַבֵּד אֶת־כָּל־חֵיל עַם וּמְדִינָה הַצָּרִים אֹתָם טַף וְנָשִׁים וּשְׁלָלָם לָבוֹז׃

12 On one day in all the provinces of King Achashverosh, on the thirteenth of the twelfth month- this is the month of Adar.

יב. בְּיוֹם אֶחָד בְּכָל־מְדִינוֹת הַמֶּלֶךְ אֲחַשְׁוֵרוֹשׁ בִּשְׁלוֹשָׁה עָשָׂר לְחֹדֶשׁ שְׁנֵים־עָשָׂר הוּא־חֹדֶשׁ אֲדָר׃

13 A copy of the writing (order) was to be given (proclaimed) as law in every province, clearly, to all the nations, and that the Jews be ready for that day, to exact revenge from their enemies.

יג. פַּתְשֶׁגֶן הַכְּתָב לְהִנָּתֵן דָּת בְּכָל־מְדִינָה וּמְדִינָה גָּלוּי לְכָל־הָעַמִּים וְלִהְיוֹת היהודיים (הַיְּהוּדִים) עתודים (עֲתִידִים) לַיּוֹם הַזֶּה לְהִנָּקֵם מֵאֹיְבֵיהֶם׃

14 The runners (couriers), riders of the royal swift camels (?), went out rushed and pressed by the king's order, and the law was given (proclaimed) in Shushan the capital.

יד. הָרָצִים רֹכְבֵי הָרֶכֶשׁ הָאֲחַשְׁתְּרָנִים יָצְאוּ מְבֹהָלִים וּדְחוּפִים בִּדְבַר הַמֶּלֶךְ וְהַדָּת נִתְּנָה בְּשׁוּשַׁן הַבִּירָה׃

15 And Mordechai went out from before the king['s presence, dressed] in a royal garment of blue and white, and a large golden crown, and a cloak of fine linen and purple wool. And the city of Shushan cheered in delight and rejoiced.

טו. וּמָרְדֳּכַי יָצָא ׀ מִלִּפְנֵי הַמֶּלֶךְ בִּלְבוּשׁ מַלְכוּת תְּכֵלֶת וָחוּר וַעֲטֶרֶת זָהָב גְּדוֹלָה וְתַכְרִיךְ בּוּץ וְאַרְגָּמָן וְהָעִיר שׁוּשָׁן צָהֲלָה וְשָׂמֵחָה׃

16 For the Jews there was light and happiness, joy and honor.

טז. לַיְּהוּדִים הָיְתָה אוֹרָה וְשִׂמְחָה וְשָׂשֹׂן וִיקָר׃

17 And in every province and in every city – every place to which the king's order and law reached, [there was] happiness and joy for the Jews, feasting and a holiday.

And many of the people of the land converted to Judaism, for fear of the Jews had fallen on them.

יז. וּבְכָל־מְדִינָה וּמְדִינָה וּבְכָל־עִיר וָעִיר מְקוֹם אֲשֶׁר דְּבַר־הַמֶּלֶךְ וְדָתוֹ מַגִּיעַ שִׂמְחָה וְשָׂשׂוֹן לַיְּהוּדִים מִשְׁתֶּה וְיוֹם טוֹב וְרַבִּים מֵעַמֵּי הָאָרֶץ מִתְיַהֲדִים כִּי־נָפַל פַּחַד־הַיְּהוּדִים עֲלֵיהֶם׃

CHAPTER IX 1 And in the twelfth month, which is the month of Adar, on its thirteenth day, when the time arrived for the king's order and law to be done (executed), on the day that the enemies of the Jews had hoped to rule over them, [instead –] it was overturned (reversed): that the Jews ruled; they over their enemies.

פרק ט: א. וּבִשְׁנֵים עָשָׂר חֹדֶשׁ הוּא־חֹדֶשׁ אֲדָר בִּשְׁלוֹשָׁה עָשָׂר יוֹם בּוֹ אֲשֶׁר הִגִּיעַ דְּבַר־הַמֶּלֶךְ וְדָתוֹ לְהֵעָשׂוֹת בַּיּוֹם אֲשֶׁר שִׂבְּרוּ אֹיְבֵי הַיְּהוּדִים לִשְׁלוֹט בָּהֶם וְנַהֲפוֹךְ הוּא אֲשֶׁר יִשְׁלְטוּ הַיְּהוּדִים הֵמָּה בְּשֹׂנְאֵיהֶם׃

2 The Jews gathered in their cities in all the provinces of King Achashverosh to send a hand against (attack) those who sought their evil. And no man stood before them (in their way), for the fear of them (of the Jews) had fallen on all the nations.

ב. נִקְהֲלוּ הַיְּהוּדִים בְּעָרֵיהֶם בְּכָל־מְדִינוֹת הַמֶּלֶךְ אֲחַשְׁוֵרוֹשׁ לִשְׁלֹחַ יָד בִּמְבַקְשֵׁי רָעָתָם וְאִישׁ לֹא־עָמַד לִפְנֵיהֶם כִּי־נָפַל פַּחְדָּם עַל־כָּל־הָעַמִּים׃

3 And all the ministers of the provinces, and the satraps, and the governors and the king's staff elevated (respected) the Jews, for the fear of Mordechai had fallen on them.

ג. וְכָל־שָׂרֵי הַמְּדִינוֹת וְהָאֲחַשְׁדַּרְפְּנִים וְהַפַּחוֹת וְעֹשֵׂי הַמְּלָאכָה אֲשֶׁר לַמֶּלֶךְ מְנַשְּׂאִים אֶת־הַיְּהוּדִים כִּי־נָפַל פַּחַד־מָרְדֳּכַי עֲלֵיהֶם׃

4 For Mordechai was great in the palace of the king and his fame was spreading in all the provinces, for the man Mordechai was growing (in power).

ד. כִּי־גָדוֹל מָרְדֳּכַי בְּבֵית הַמֶּלֶךְ וְשָׁמְעוֹ הוֹלֵךְ בְּכָל־הַמְּדִינוֹת כִּי־הָאִישׁ מָרְדֳּכַי הוֹלֵךְ וְגָדוֹל׃

5 And the Jews struck at all their enemies [with the] strike of the sword and killing and destruction, and they did with their enemies as was their wish.

ה. וַיַּכּוּ הַיְּהוּדִים בְּכָל־אֹיְבֵיהֶם מַכַּת־חֶרֶב וְהֶרֶג וְאַבְדָן וַיַּעֲשׂוּ בְשֹׂנְאֵיהֶם כִּרְצוֹנָם׃

6 And in Shushan the capital, the Jews killed and destroyed five hundred men.

ו. וּבְשׁוּשַׁן הַבִּירָה הָרְגוּ הַיְּהוּדִים וְאַבֵּד חֲמֵשׁ מֵאוֹת אִישׁ׃

7 And Parshandasa, and Dalfon, and Aspasa;

ז. וְאֵת | פַּרְשַׁנְדָּתָא וְאֵת | דַּלְפוֹן וְאֵת | אַסְפָּתָא׃

8 and Porasa and Adalya and Aridasa;

ח. וְאֵת | פּוֹרָתָא וְאֵת | אֲדַלְיָא וְאֵת | אֲרִידָתָא׃

9 and Parmashta and Arisai and Aridai and Vaizasa,

ט. וְאֵת | פַּרְמַשְׁתָּא וְאֵת | אֲרִיסַי וְאֵת | אֲרִדַי וְאֵת | וַיְזָתָא׃

10 -- the ten sons of Haman, son of Hamdasa, oppressor of the Jews, they killed; but in the spoils (enemy's possessions) - they did not send their hands (take anything).

י. עֲשֶׂרֶת בְּנֵי הָמָן בֶּן־הַמְּדָתָא צֹרֵר הַיְּהוּדִים הָרָגוּ וּבַבִּזָּה לֹא שָׁלְחוּ אֶת־יָדָם׃

11 On that day, the number of those killed in Shushan the capital came (was reported) before the king.

יא. בַּיּוֹם הַהוּא בָּא מִסְפַּר הַהֲרוּגִים בְּשׁוּשַׁן הַבִּירָה לִפְנֵי הַמֶּלֶךְ׃

12 And the king said to Esther the Queen, "In Shushan the capital, the Jews killed and destroyed five hundred men and the ten sons of Haman; in the rest of the provinces of the king - what have they done?

"What is your plea - it will be given to you; And what else is your request - it shall be done."

יב. וַיֹּאמֶר הַמֶּלֶךְ לְאֶסְתֵּר הַמַּלְכָּה בְּשׁוּשַׁן הַבִּירָה הָרְגוּ
הַיְּהוּדִים וְאַבֵּד חֲמֵשׁ מֵאוֹת אִישׁ וְאֵת עֲשֶׂרֶת בְּנֵי־הָמָן
בִּשְׁאָר מְדִינוֹת הַמֶּלֶךְ מֶה עָשׂוּ וּמַה־שְּׁאֵלָתֵךְ וְיִנָּתֵן לָךְ
וּמַה־בַּקָּשָׁתֵךְ עוֹד וְתֵעָשׂ׃

13 And Esther said, " If it is good for (pleases) the king, tomorrow should also be given to the Jews who are in Shushan, to do according to the law (decree) of today, and the ten sons of Haman – they should hang on the gallows."

יג. וַתֹּאמֶר אֶסְתֵּר אִם־עַל־הַמֶּלֶךְ טוֹב יִנָּתֵן גַּם־מָחָר
לַיְּהוּדִים אֲשֶׁר בְּשׁוּשָׁן לַעֲשׂוֹת כְּדָת הַיּוֹם וְאֵת עֲשֶׂרֶת
בְּנֵי־הָמָן יִתְלוּ עַל־הָעֵץ׃

14 And the king ordered that this be done, and the law was given (proclaimed) in Shushan, and the ten sons of Haman were hanged.

יד. וַיֹּאמֶר הַמֶּלֶךְ לְהֵעָשׂוֹת כֵּן וַתִּנָּתֵן דָּת בְּשׁוּשָׁן וְאֵת
עֲשֶׂרֶת בְּנֵי־הָמָן תָּלוּ׃

15 And the Jews of Shushan gathered [again] also on the fourteenth day of the month of Adar, and they killed three hundred men in Shushan, but in the spoils (enemy's possessions) - they did not send their hands (take anything).

טו. וַיִּקָּהֲלוּ היהודיים (הַיְּהוּדִים) אֲשֶׁר־בְּשׁוּשָׁן גַּם בְּיוֹם
אַרְבָּעָה עָשָׂר לְחֹדֶשׁ אֲדָר וַיַּהַרְגוּ בְשׁוּשָׁן שְׁלֹשׁ מֵאוֹת
אִישׁ וּבַבִּזָּה לֹא שָׁלְחוּ אֶת־יָדָם׃

16 And the rest of the Jews who were in the king's provinces; they gathered and stood up for their lives and rested from their enemies and killed of those who hated them; seventy-five thousand, but in the spoils (enemy's possessions) - they did not send their hands (take anything).

טז. וּשְׁאָר הַיְּהוּדִים אֲשֶׁר בִּמְדִינוֹת הַמֶּלֶךְ נִקְהֲלוּ ׀ וְעָמֹד
עַל־נַפְשָׁם וְנוֹחַ מֵאֹיְבֵיהֶם וְהָרוֹג בְּשֹׂנְאֵיהֶם חֲמִשָּׁה
וְשִׁבְעִים אָלֶף וּבַבִּזָּה לֹא שָׁלְחוּ אֶת־יָדָם׃

17 On the thirteenth day of the month of Adar, and they rested on its fourteenth day and made it a day of feasting and joy.

יז. בְּיוֹם־שְׁלוֹשָׁה עָשָׂר לְחֹדֶשׁ אֲדָר וְנוֹחַ בְּאַרְבָּעָה עָשָׂר
בּוֹ וְעָשֹׂה אֹתוֹ יוֹם מִשְׁתֶּה וְשִׂמְחָה׃

18 And the Jews who were in Shushan gathered on its thirteenth and fourteenth [day], and rested on its fifteenth [day] and made it a day of feasting and happiness.

יח. והיהודיים (וְהַיְּהוּדִים) אֲשֶׁר־בְּשׁוּשָׁן נִקְהֲלוּ בִּשְׁלוֹשָׁה
עָשָׂר בּוֹ וּבְאַרְבָּעָה עָשָׂר בּוֹ וְנוֹחַ בַּחֲמִשָּׁה עָשָׂר בּוֹ
וְעָשֹׂה אֹתוֹ יוֹם מִשְׁתֶּה וְשִׂמְחָה׃

19 Therefore, the Jews of the villages, who dwell in un-walled cities, make the fourteenth day of the month of Adar [a day of] joy and feasting and a holiday, and [a day of] sending portions [of food] each man to his friend.

יט. עַל־כֵּן הַיְּהוּדִים הפרוזים (הַפְּרָזִים) הַיֹּשְׁבִים בְּעָרֵי
הַפְּרָזוֹת עֹשִׂים אֵת יוֹם אַרְבָּעָה עָשָׂר לְחֹדֶשׁ אֲדָר
שִׂמְחָה וּמִשְׁתֶּה וְיוֹם טוֹב וּמִשְׁלֹחַ מָנוֹת אִישׁ לְרֵעֵהוּ׃

20 And Mordechai wrote these things (events) and sent letters [books] to all the Jews who were in all the provinces of King Achashverosh, the near and far ones.

כ. וַיִּכְתֹּב מָרְדֳּכַי אֶת־הַדְּבָרִים הָאֵלֶּה וַיִּשְׁלַח סְפָרִים
אֶל־כָּל־הַיְּהוּדִים אֲשֶׁר בְּכָל־מְדִינוֹת הַמֶּלֶךְ אֲחַשְׁוֵרוֹשׁ
הַקְּרוֹבִים וְהָרְחוֹקִים׃

21 To [have them] establish (accept) upon themselves) to make (celebrate) the fourteenth day of the month of Adar and its fifteenth day, every year.

כא. לְקַיֵּם עֲלֵיהֶם לִהְיוֹת עֹשִׂים אֵת יוֹם אַרְבָּעָה עָשָׂר לְחֹדֶשׁ אֲדָר וְאֵת יוֹם־חֲמִשָּׁה עָשָׂר בּוֹ בְּכָל־שָׁנָה וְשָׁנָה׃

22 Like the days upon which the Jews rested from their enemies, and the month which had been overturned (transformed) for them from sorrow to joy, and from mourning to holiday, to make them days of feasting and joy, and sending portions [of food] to one another and [giving] gifts to the poor.

כב. כַּיָּמִים אֲשֶׁר־נָחוּ בָהֶם הַיְּהוּדִים מֵאֹיְבֵיהֶם וְהַחֹדֶשׁ אֲשֶׁר נֶהְפַּךְ לָהֶם מִיָּגוֹן לְשִׂמְחָה וּמֵאֵבֶל לְיוֹם טוֹב לַעֲשׂוֹת אוֹתָם יְמֵי מִשְׁתֶּה וְשִׂמְחָה וּמִשְׁלֹחַ מָנוֹת אִישׁ לְרֵעֵהוּ וּמַתָּנוֹת לָאֶבְיֹנִים׃

23 And the Jews accepted [upon themselves to continue] that which they had begun to do, and that about which Mordechai wrote to them.

כג. וְקִבֵּל הַיְּהוּדִים אֵת אֲשֶׁר־הֵחֵלּוּ לַעֲשׂוֹת וְאֵת אֲשֶׁר־כָּתַב מָרְדֳּכַי אֲלֵיהֶם׃

24 For Haman, son of Hamdasa, the Agagi, oppressor of all the Jews, thought (plotted) against the Jews to cause them to perish, and he cast a Pur, which is a lot, to stun (cause chaos and terrify) them and to cause them to perish.

כד. כִּי הָמָן בֶּן־הַמְּדָתָא הָאֲגָגִי צֹרֵר כָּל־הַיְּהוּדִים חָשַׁב עַל־הַיְּהוּדִים לְאַבְּדָם וְהִפִּל פּוּר הוּא הַגּוֹרָל לְהֻמָּם וּלְאַבְּדָם׃

25 And when she came before the king, he commanded through the letter (decree) that [Haman's] evil thought which he plotted against the Jews - be returned upon his [own] head, and they hanged him and his sons upon the gallows.

כה. וּבְבֹאָהּ לִפְנֵי הַמֶּלֶךְ אָמַר עִם־הַסֵּפֶר יָשׁוּב מַחֲשַׁבְתּוֹ הָרָעָה אֲשֶׁר־חָשַׁב עַל־הַיְּהוּדִים עַל־רֹאשׁוֹ וְתָלוּ אֹתוֹ וְאֶת־בָּנָיו עַל־הָעֵץ׃

26 Therefore, they called these days "Purim," named after “the Pur”. Therefore, because of all of the events of this letter, and what they saw about this matter – and what happened to them – [because of this -]

כו. עַל־כֵּן קָרְאוּ לַיָּמִים הָאֵלֶּה פוּרִים עַל־שֵׁם הַפּוּר עַל־כֵּן עַל־כָּל־דִּבְרֵי הָאִגֶּרֶת הַזֹּאת וּמָה־רָאוּ עַל־כָּכָה וּמָה הִגִּיעַ אֲלֵיהֶם׃

27 - The Jews established and accepted upon themselves, and upon their descendants, and upon all who joined with them, - and it will not be removed (end) - to make (celebrate) these two days according to their script and according to their dates, every year.

כז. קִיְּמוּ וקבל (וְקִבְּלוּ) הַיְּהוּדִים | עֲלֵיהֶם | וְעַל־זַרְעָם וְעַל כָּל־הַנִּלְוִים עֲלֵיהֶם וְלֹא יַעֲבוֹר לִהְיוֹת עֹשִׂים אֵת שְׁנֵי הַיָּמִים הָאֵלֶּה כִּכְתָבָם וְכִזְמַנָּם בְּכָל־שָׁנָה וְשָׁנָה׃

28 And these days are remembered and observed in every generation, by every family, in every province and every city. And these days of Purim will never pass from among the Jews, and their memory will not end from their descendants.

כח. וְהַיָּמִים הָאֵלֶּה נִזְכָּרִים וְנַעֲשִׂים בְּכָל־דּוֹר וָדוֹר מִשְׁפָּחָה וּמִשְׁפָּחָה מְדִינָה וּמְדִינָה וְעִיר וָעִיר וִימֵי הַפּוּרִים הָאֵלֶּה לֹא יַעַבְרוּ מִתּוֹךְ הַיְּהוּדִים וְזִכְרָם לֹא־יָסוּף מִזַּרְעָם׃

29 And Esther the Queen, daughter of Avichayil, and Mordechai the Jew, wrote about all the acts of power (the miracles), to establish [the holiday with] this second Purim letter.

כט. וַתִּכְתֹּב אֶסְתֵּר הַמַּלְכָּה בַת־אֲבִיחַיִל וּמָרְדֳּכַי הַיְּהוּדִי אֶת־כָּל־תֹּקֶף לְקַיֵּם אֵת אִגֶּרֶת הַפּוּרִים הַזֹּאת הַשֵּׁנִית׃

30 And he sent letters (books) to all the Jews, to one hundred and twenty-seven provinces of the kingdom of Achashverosh, words of peace and truth.

ל. וַיִּשְׁלַח סְפָרִים אֶל־כָּל־הַיְּהוּדִים אֶל־שֶׁבַע וְעֶשְׂרִים וּמֵאָה מְדִינָה מַלְכוּת אֲחַשְׁוֵרוֹשׁ דִּבְרֵי שָׁלוֹם וֶאֱמֶת׃

31 To confirm [that people will observe] these days of Purim in their [proper] times, just as Mordechai the Jew and Esther the Queen established for them, and just as they had accepted upon themselves and upon their descendants, the matters (observance) of the fasts and their cries.

לא. לְקַיֵּם אֵת־יְמֵי הַפֻּרִים הָאֵלֶּה בִּזְמַנֵּיהֶם כַּאֲשֶׁר קִיַּם עֲלֵיהֶם מָרְדֳּכַי הַיְּהוּדִי וְאֶסְתֵּר הַמַּלְכָּה וְכַאֲשֶׁר קִיְּמוּ עַל־נַפְשָׁם וְעַל־זַרְעָם דִּבְרֵי הַצּוֹמוֹת וְזַעֲקָתָם׃

32 And the word of Esther confirmed these matters of Purim and it (- this story of Purim) was written (included) in the [holy] Book[s of the Torah].

לב. וּמַאֲמַר אֶסְתֵּר קִיַּם דִּבְרֵי הַפֻּרִים הָאֵלֶּה וְנִכְתָּב בַּסֵּפֶר׃

Chapter 10 - פרק י

CHAPTER X 1 And King Achashverosh placed a tax upon the land and the islands of the sea.

פרק י: א. וַיָּשֶׂם הַמֶּלֶךְ אחשרש (אֲחַשְׁוֵרֹשׁ ׀) מַס עַל־הָאָרֶץ וְאִיֵּי הַיָּם׃

2 And all his mighty and powerful acts, and the description of Mordechai's greatness - to which the king had promoted him; are they not recorded in the Book of Chronicles of the kings of Media and Persia?

ב. וְכָל־מַעֲשֵׂה תָקְפּוֹ וּגְבוּרָתוֹ וּפָרָשַׁת גְּדֻלַּת מָרְדֳּכַי אֲשֶׁר גִּדְּלוֹ הַמֶּלֶךְ הֲלוֹא־הֵם כְּתוּבִים עַל־סֵפֶר דִּבְרֵי הַיָּמִים לְמַלְכֵי מָדַי וּפָרָס׃

3 For Mordechai the Jew – [was] second to King Achashverosh, and great amongst the Jews, and accepted by most of his brethren; Seeking goodness for his nation and speaking (arranging) peace for all their descendants.

ג. כִּי ׀ מָרְדֳּכַי הַיְּהוּדִי מִשְׁנֶה לַמֶּלֶךְ אֲחַשְׁוֵרוֹשׁ וְגָדוֹל לַיְּהוּדִים וְרָצוּי לְרֹב אֶחָיו דֹּרֵשׁ טוֹב לְעַמּוֹ וְדֹבֵר שָׁלוֹם לְכָל־זַרְעוֹ׃

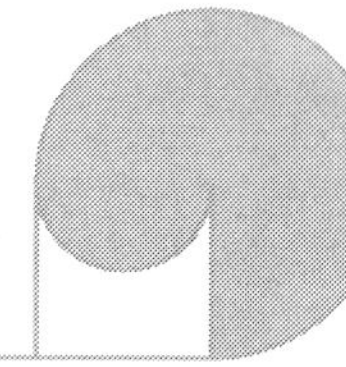

MY VERY OWN MEGILAH!

Student-Friendly, Original - Literal – Translation

with Commentary Compilation

by Rabbi Chayim B. Alevsky, 5771-2011

Original translation for ages 8-118,
inspired by many previous translations, including:
Kehot Publications – Rabbi Yosef Marcus
Soncino / Judaica Press /
Kol Menachem-Slager Edition – Rabbi Chaim Miller
Mefarshei Hamikra; Rashi / Ibn Ezra / Malbim
Reviewed and improved by Rabbi JJ Hartmann

[These brackets] are used for:
a. words that are not in the Megilah text,
inserted to keep the English flow
b. words that are in the Megilah text,
but are not commonly used in English.
The words in (parentheses) are clarifications
that explain the literal translation.

Commentary Compilation

The commentaries were culled from many sources as noted,
The Midrashim, primarily from the Torah Temima Megilah.
This edition contains many more Mefarshim than edition 2.0.
B'ezras Hashem, the next edition will include even more Mefarshim.

פרק א: א. וַיְהִי בִּימֵי אֲחַשְׁוֵרוֹשׁ הוּא אֲחַשְׁוֵרוֹשׁ הַמֹּלֵךְ מֵהֹדּוּ וְעַד־כּוּשׁ שֶׁבַע וְעֶשְׂרִים וּמֵאָה מְדִינָה:

CHAPTER I: 1 And it was in the days of Achashverosh, he is [the same] Achashverosh who ruled from Hodu (India) to Cush (Ethiopia), one hundred twenty-seven provinces.

1. וַיְהִי בִּימֵי: Every time the Torah uses the words "וַיְהִי בִּימֵי", it refers to a troublesome story. *–Megillah 10b*

2. וַיְהִי בִּימֵי אֲחַשְׁוֵרוֹשׁ: He killed his wife (Vashti) because of his friend, and his friend because of his wife. People would comment; וי וי – "woe to me woe to me" (that this fool is our king): *–Midrash Aba Guryon 1*

3. הוּא אֲחַשְׁוֵרוֹשׁ הַמֹּלֵךְ: Instead of "King Achashverosh", the verse just states "Achashverosh", showing he was not from a royal family. He was "king" because he married the royal Queen, Vashti. *–Rashi*

4. Some see the above as a positive note, some the opposite. The positive way to understand this is that Achashverosh was the only one worthy to be king at that time, even though he was not of royal descent. The other way to understand this is that he was so wealthy, he "bought" himself the position. *–Megillah 11a*

5. הוּא אֲחַשְׁוֵרוֹשׁ: He remained wicked – from beginning to end. *–Megillah 11a*

6. For example, even though in the end he cancelled the evil decree, he still did not allow B'nei Yisroel to rebuild the Beis Hamikdash *–Iyun Yaakov*

7. אֲחַשְׁוֵרוֹשׁ – שאחרית וראשית שלו: The name אֲחַשְׁוֵרוֹשׁ hints to the One who is the master over the beginning and end. He is everything and everywhere – hinting to Hashem. *–Me'orei Or*

8. When the word "מלך" appears in the Megillah on its own (without אֲחַשְׁוֵרוֹשׁ's name following) it often refers to Hashem. *–Midrash ER 3:10*

9. As we see in the above Midrashim, Hashem is hiding in the Megillah. This represents how Hashem interacts with the world – mostly in a hidden manner, and sometimes even through wicked kings like Achashverosh. So even when the Megillah mentions his name, it often refers to Hashem, showing that Achashverosh's importance is just the fact that he was Hashem's shaliach. *–The Rebbe.*

10. אֲחַשְׁוֵרוֹשׁ succeeded כורש as ruler of the Persian Empire toward the end of the Jews' seventy-year exile in בבל. *–Rashi*

11. אֲחַשְׁוֵרוֹשׁ: אח של ראש --he was like brother to the "head" of kings, נבוכדנצר, in his evil plots. *–Megillah 11a*

12. מֵהֹדּוּ וְעַד כּוּשׁ: The Gemara discusses whether these were two places across the world, or right next to each other. Either way, it means that Achashverosh ruled the world; if they were right next to each other, they were a world apart going the opposite way, since the world is round. *–Megillah 11a / Rama (Mechir Yayin)*

13. מֵהֹדּוּ וְעַד כּוּשׁ: הדו means thanks and glory (symbolizing humility), כּוּשׁ is darkness, referring to the two kinds of people in the kingdom: the refined and the opposite. Both kinds were under אֲחַשְׁוֵרוֹשׁ's influence, and wanted to please him. This makes the miracle even greater, as the whole world was ready to listen to Achashverosh and wipe out Bnei Yisroel Chas V'shalom-- and Hashem saved us. *–The Rebbe*

14. שֶׁבַע וְעֶשְׂרִים וּמֵאָה מְדִינָה: Similar to Sarah Imeinu's life of 127 years. *-Midrash Esther Rabba 1;8*

15. Rabbi Akiva was once teaching his students and they were falling asleep. He asked them: Why did Esther merit to rule over 127 provinces? Hashem said, "Let the daughter of Sarah (Imeinu) who lived for 127 years, rule over 127 provinces."

Why did this awaken his students?

We know that all of Sarah's 127 years were equally perfect. Rabbi Akiva was teaching that Sarah's careful time well spent was directly connected to the size of Esther's kingdom. Each careful year earned Esther a province, each month, a state, each week a city, each day a village, each hour a family, each minute a person etc.

It's the same with us. Every minute counts for us and our future generations. *–Chidushei HaRim*

16. שֶׁבַע וְעֶשְׂרִים וּמֵאָה מְדִינָה: Just as all 127 years of Sarah's life were equal in their being good, so too all Jews of all 127 provinces were equal in their commitment and mesiras nefesh—self sacrifice, to stay Jewish, even though converting would have saved them from Haman's decree! *–The Rebbe*

ב. בַּיָּמִים הָהֵם כְּשֶׁבֶת | הַמֶּלֶךְ אֲחַשְׁוֵרוֹשׁ עַל כִּסֵּא מַלְכוּתוֹ אֲשֶׁר בְּשׁוּשַׁן הַבִּירָה:

2 In those days, when King Achashverosh sat on his royal throne, which was in Shushan the capital;

17. כְּשֶׁבֶת: When he felt settled. He was relieved after he miscalculated the time that the rebuilding of the Beis Hamikdash would take place. –(see intro)

18. עַל כִּסֵּא מַלְכוּתוֹ: His personal throne was a replica of Shlomo Hamelech's. *–Midrash Abba Gurion, Esther Rabba 1:12* (see intro)

ג. בִּשְׁנַת שָׁלוֹשׁ לְמָלְכוֹ עָשָׂה מִשְׁתֶּה לְכָל־שָׂרָיו וַעֲבָדָיו חֵיל | פָּרַס וּמָדַי הַפַּרְתְּמִים וְשָׂרֵי הַמְּדִינוֹת לְפָנָיו:

3 In the third year of his reign (rule), he made a feast for all his ministers and servants; the army of Persia and Media, the nobles and ministers of the provinces before him.

19. בִּשְׁנַת שָׁלוֹשׁ לְמָלְכוֹ: In the year 3395.

20. עָשָׂה מִשְׁתֶּה בִּשְׁנַת שָׁלוֹשׁ לְמָלְכוֹ: He made a feast to celebrate:

a. That the בית המקדש had not been rebuilt.

b. His marriage to Vashti *–Ibn Ezra*

Three years with no successful rebellion (like a Chazakah) and he was happy. He was not from royal blood; Vashti was from the family of נבוכדנצר who was royalty. Being that אֲחַשְׁוֵרוֹשׁ was not of royal blood, he was all the more excited about it and celebrated his royal position. *–Midrash*

ד. בְּהַרְאֹתוֹ אֶת־עֹשֶׁר כְּבוֹד מַלְכוּתוֹ וְאֶת־יְקָר תִּפְאֶרֶת גְּדוּלָּתוֹ יָמִים רַבִּים שְׁמוֹנִים וּמְאַת יוֹם:

4 When he showed the riches of his glorious kingdom and the splendorous beauty of his majesty for many days - one hundred and eighty days.

21. עֹשֶׁר כְּבוֹד מַלְכוּתוֹ וְאֶת־יְקָר תִּפְאֶרֶת גְּדוּלָּתוֹ: נבוכדנצר buried 1,080 treasures in the Euphrates River. Later Koresh found it and אֲחַשְׁוֵרוֹשׁ inherited this fortune from him, and displayed six treasures a day to the guests at the party. This is hinted in the 6 expressions of wealth in the Possuk:

1) עֹשֶׁר 2) כְּבוֹד 3) מַלְכוּתוֹ 4) יְקָר 5) תִּפְאֶרֶת 6) גְּדוּלָּתוֹ

22. It took exactly 180 days to go through all his wealth; 180 x 6 = 1,080. *–Gra*

23. עֹשֶׁר כְּבוֹד מַלְכוּתוֹ: The vessels of the Beis Hamikdash were displayed and Achashverosh wore the clothing of the Kohen Gadol. *–Megillah 12a*

ה. וּבִמְלוֹאת | הַיָּמִים הָאֵלֶּה עָשָׂה הַמֶּלֶךְ לְכָל־הָעָם הַנִּמְצְאִים בְּשׁוּשַׁן הַבִּירָה לְמִגָּדוֹל וְעַד־קָטָן מִשְׁתֶּה שִׁבְעַת יָמִים בַּחֲצַר גִּנַּת בִּיתַן הַמֶּלֶךְ:

5 And when these days were completed, the king made - for all the people in Shushan the capital, from the great to the small (simple) - a feast for seven days, in the courtyard of the king's palace garden.

24. מִשְׁתֶּה: What did the Jews do to cause such an evil decree upon themselves? They enjoyed the feast of the wicked King Achashverosh. -*Megillah 12a*

25. Why is enjoying the feast such a serious matter? The Jews began enjoying their position in Galus. They stopped thinking about and relying on Hashem; why do they need to think about and trust in Hashem if even at the king's feast they are being respected and served kosher food?!

As a consequence of this attitude, that the Jews felt they could rely on the people/government etc. to take care of them, the Jews momentarily lost their merit to live above the laws of nature, as we usually do. -*The Rebbe*

26. Mordechai begged the Jews not to go but they didn't listen, with the excuse that they did not want to insult the king who even provided kosher food.

ו. חוּר | כַּרְפַּס וּתְכֵלֶת אָחוּז בְּחַבְלֵי־בוּץ וְאַרְגָּמָן עַל־גְּלִילֵי כֶסֶף וְעַמּוּדֵי שֵׁשׁ מִטּוֹת | זָהָב וָכֶסֶף עַל רִצְפַת בַּהַט־וָשֵׁשׁ וְדַר וְסֹחָרֶת:

6 Hangings of white, green and blue, were held by cords of linen and purple wool on silver rods and marble pillars. There were beds (couches) of gold and silver on a floor of alabaster and marble [arranged in patterns of] rows and circles.

27. חוּר כַּרְפַּס וּתְכֵלֶת: Colored sheets covered the couches. *–Rashi.*

28. חוּר: The Large ח in חור hints to the 8 clothes of the Kohen Gadol that אֲחַשְׁוֵרוֹשׁ wore at the party. -*Alkabetz*

29. מִטּוֹת זָהָב וָכֶסֶף: It was the ancient custom to recline at festive occasions *–Bereishis Rabba 46b* (as we know from our Pesach Seder).

30. חוּר כַּרְפַּס וּתְכֵלֶת: Hangings of white, green and blue. (1:6)

The event catered to all but one of the five senses: The feast was in an aromatic garden; there were beautiful hangings of white, green and blue; the food was suited to each person's taste, and the couches were delightful to the touch. But there is no mention of music, since what is music to one ear is noise to another. -*Akeidas Yitzchak*

31. By elaborating upon the great power and riches of Achashverosh, the Megillah emphasizes the power of any decree issued by him, and consequently, the greatness of the miracle. -*Akeidas Yitzchak*

ז. וְהַשְׁקוֹת בִּכְלֵי זָהָב וְכֵלִים מִכֵּלִים שׁוֹנִים וְיֵין מַלְכוּת רָב כְּיַד הַמֶּלֶךְ:

7 And the drinks were served in golden vessels, and all kinds of vessels, and the royal wine was in plenty like the hand (ability) of the king.

32. וְהַשְׁקוֹת בִּכְלֵי זָהָב: Although it makes Achashverosh sound very wealthy, people don't usually enjoy drinking from golden jugs. These were actually very refined colored (mirrored) glasses, that were as valuable as gold. -*Midrash*

33. The wine each person was served was older that s/he was. *-Rashi quoting Megillah 12a.*

ח. וְהַשְּׁתִיָּה כַדָּת אֵין אֹנֵס כִּי־כֵן | יִסַּד הַמֶּלֶךְ עַל כָּל־רַב בֵּיתוֹ לַעֲשׂוֹת כִּרְצוֹן אִישׁ־וָאִישׁ:

8 And the drinking was by the law, [there was] no forcing, for so had the king ordered all the managers of his household - to do like the will of each man.

34. כַּדָּת: They were not forced to drink a big cup, as was the custom, even in the previous party.

35. אֵין אֹנֵס: It was the custom for the host to "call the shots." Here, each person drank as they wished. *–Targum*

36. Achashverosh wanted the Jews to sin to anger Hashem so the בית המקדש wouldn't be rebuilt. Therefore he did not force anyone to

drink, he just tempted them, hoping they would drink and sin on their own and anger Hashem. *–Manos HaLevi*

37. לַעֲשׂוֹת כִּרְצוֹן אִישׁ־וָאִישׁ: Literally "with the will of each man and man"--the wishes of Mordechai and Haman who are referred to in the Book of Esther as "man" (in 2:5 and 7:6). (*Talmud, Megillah 12a;* To comply with their wishes, Achashverosh instructed that both kosher and non-kosher foods be provided.) *–Maharsha, ibid.*

38. This is an allusion to freedom of choice: The King of the World instructs that every person be given the choice to follow either the path of Mordechai or that of Haman. *-Midbar Kodesh*

39. Each golden goblet was only used once.

40. כִּי כֵן יִסַּד הַמֶּלֶךְ עַל כָּל רַב בֵּיתוֹ לַעֲשׂוֹת כִּרְצוֹן אִישׁ וָאִישׁ: Hashem, the King, arranges with the angels that we have free will; we can do what we want. *–The Rebbe*

41. כִּרְצוֹן אִישׁ וָאִישׁ: At Matan Torah, Hashem floated הר סיני above Bnei Yisroel forcing them to accept the Torah. During this story of Purim, קיימו מה שקבלו כבר, "they fulfilled what they accepted already". Hashem gave Bnei Yisroel the choice to do as they wished.

42. כִּרְצוֹן אִישׁ וָאִישׁ: Achashverosh ordered there to be kosher food to fulfill Mordechai's wish. (*Midrash*). The Megillah is teaching us that even in the capital city of a non-Jewish country, at the king's party where the chief minister is a Jew hater, we should not hide our Jewish identity. We should be tall and proud and demand kosher food be served. When we try to hide our identity, people don't respect us. When we are and act respectful of our privilege to be Hashem's chosen nation and openly proud of who we are, the world respects us. As the Megillah says: לַעֲשׂוֹת כִּרְצוֹן אִישׁ וָאִישׁ– that Hashem proclaims that the world, including the gentile kings, should grant us what we ask for. *–The Rebbe*

43. עַל כָּל רַב בֵּיתוֹ לַעֲשׂוֹת כִּרְצוֹן אִישׁ וָאִישׁ: Rashi says that this refers to the chief baker, butler and butcher. Why do we need to know this? Rashi is informing us that Achashverosh's instruction that every person be granted every wish at the feast applied to any and all areas-- not just the amount of wine they would drink. *–The Rebbe*

ט. גַּם וַשְׁתִּי הַמַּלְכָּה עָשְׂתָה מִשְׁתֵּה נָשִׁים בֵּית הַמַּלְכוּת אֲשֶׁר לַמֶּלֶךְ אֲחַשְׁוֵרוֹשׁ:

9 Also Vashti the Queen made a feast for the women, in the royal palace of King Achashverosh.

44. מִשְׁתֵּה נָשִׁים בֵּית הַמַּלְכוּת: Vashti arranged the women's feast in the same place where the men were feasting, as she and Achashverosh meant for immodest activity to happen. *-Megillah 12a*

י. בַּיּוֹם הַשְּׁבִיעִי כְּטוֹב לֵב־הַמֶּלֶךְ בַּיָּיִן אָמַר לִמְהוּמָן בִּזְּתָא חַרְבוֹנָא בִּגְתָא וַאֲבַגְתָא זֵתַר וְכַרְכַּס שִׁבְעַת הַסָּרִיסִים הַמְשָׁרְתִים אֶת־פְּנֵי הַמֶּלֶךְ אֲחַשְׁוֵרוֹשׁ:

10 On the seventh day, when the king's heart was good (merry) with wine, he said to (ordered) Mehuman, Bizzesa, Charvona, Bigsa, Avagsa, Zeisar and Charkas, the seven chamberlains who served King Achashverosh;

45. בַּיּוֹם הַשְּׁבִיעִי: It was Shabbos. *-Rashi from Megillah 12b*

46. בַּיּוֹם הַשְּׁבִיעִי: Vashti was punished מדה כנגד מדה. She would force her Jewish maidservants to work on Shabbos immodestly, so too, her punishment was on Shabbos– related to immodesty.

47. כְּטוֹב לֵב הַמֶּלֶךְ: As mentioned earlier, when it says מלך in the מגילה without mentioning Achashverosh, it refers to Hashem. Here, Hashem is happy about the Shabbos: Kiddush wine of Bnei Yisroel, along with their Divrei Torah. *-Megillah 12b*

48. When Bnei Yisroel drink wine on Shabbos, the "secrets" that are revealed from the effect of the wine are Divrei Torah. When others drink wine, the discussion is nonsense or worse. At the feast, there was a great debate amongst the drunken people as to which country produces the prettiest women. When Achashverosh claimed that his wife was the prettiest, he was challenged to prove it by showing her to the public. *–Megillah 12a*

49. The Gemara above teaches us that whenever a Jew sits to eat and drink, the meal should begin with Divrei Torah and praise to Hashem. *–The Rebbe*

50. Only on Shabbos was Achashverosh really happy. As mentioned earlier, he also wanted to please Mordechai, and now on Shabbos, Mordechai was happy that Bnei Yisroel were celebrating Shabbos with Kiddush and Divrei Torah. *–The Rebbe.*

יא. לְהָבִיא אֶת־וַשְׁתִּי הַמַּלְכָּה לִפְנֵי הַמֶּלֶךְ בְּכֶתֶר מַלְכוּת לְהַרְאוֹת הָעַמִּים וְהַשָּׂרִים אֶת־יָפְיָהּ כִּי־טוֹבַת מַרְאֶה הִיא:

11 To bring Vashti the Queen before the king with (wearing) the royal crown, to show the nations and ministers her beauty, for she was of beautiful appearance.

51. בְּכֶתֶר מַלְכוּת: Wearing only her crown. *–Midrash*

יב. וַתְּמָאֵן הַמַּלְכָּה וַשְׁתִּי לָבוֹא בִּדְבַר הַמֶּלֶךְ אֲשֶׁר בְּיַד הַסָּרִיסִים וַיִּקְצֹף הַמֶּלֶךְ מְאֹד וַחֲמָתוֹ בָּעֲרָה בוֹ:

12 And the Queen Vashti refused to come – by the order of the king - which was brought by the chamberlains, and the king was very angry and his anger burned in him.

52. וַתְּמָאֵן: She was struck with leprosy, so she should refuse to come and be killed. (See possuk י for the reason it happened on שבת). *-Rashi from Megillah 12b.*

53. The Angel גבריאל planted a tail on her. *-Megillah 12b*

54. Hashem caused Vashti to refuse and die because she convinced Achashverosh not to let the Jews rebuild the Bais Hamikdash, saying, "You want to build what my ancestors destroyed?" *–Midrash.*

55. וַתְּמָאֵן הַמַּלְכָּה וַשְׁתִּי: Notice the difference in the order of the words הַמַּלְכָּה and וַשְׁתִּי; in the previous Possuk, when Achashverosh called for her, the Possuk says וַשְׁתִּי הַמַּלְכָּה, first her name and then her

title, as Achashverosh was suggesting that she is just a regular person: "Vashti, who happens to be the queen." Here, when Vashti refused, it says הַמַּלְכָּה וַשְׁתִּי; Vashti was clarifying that she was the one with royal blood. *–Gra*

56. Just as the 127 provinces Esther ruled were connected to her ancestor Sarah's 127 years, so too Vashti's tail was connected to her grandfather Nevuchanetzar, who turned into a wild beast for several years. *–R' Pinchas Menachem of Piltz*

57. וַיִּקְצֹף: Vashti reminded Achashveirosh of his shameful past by embarrassing him. *–Rashi/Midrash*

יג. וַיֹּאמֶר הַמֶּלֶךְ לַחֲכָמִים יֹדְעֵי הָעִתִּים כִּי־כֵן דְּבַר הַמֶּלֶךְ לִפְנֵי כָּל־יֹדְעֵי דָּת וָדִין׃

13 And the king said to the wise men, those who knew the times - for this was the king's thing (way), [to bring such matters] before all who knew [the] law and judgment.

58. לַחֲכָמִים: These are the rabbis who are יֹדְעֵי הָעִתִּים, who know how to calculate the Jewish calendar. Achashverosh asked the rabbis what to do with Vashti. They knew that whatever they would answer would cause them trouble: if they would advise him to kill her he would be angry with them after he sobers, and if they would advise to let her be, they'd be disrespecting the royal king. Therefore, they replied that ever since the Bais Hamikdash was destroyed and Bnei Yisroel were exiled, their ability to advise in serious matters has diminished and he should ask others-- which he did in the next Possuk. *–Megillah 12b*

59. Rabbis who knew how the laws of the times were decided in the courts. *-Ibn Ezra*

60. כִּי כֵן דְּבַר הַמֶּלֶךְ: One good quality we see in Achashverosh is that he always asked others for advice in serious matters. *-Midrash*

יד. וְהַקָּרֹב אֵלָיו כַּרְשְׁנָא שֵׁתָר אַדְמָתָא תַרְשִׁישׁ מֶרֶס מַרְסְנָא מְמוּכָן שִׁבְעַת שָׂרֵי | פָּרַס וּמָדַי רֹאֵי פְּנֵי הַמֶּלֶךְ הַיֹּשְׁבִים רִאשֹׁנָה בַּמַּלְכוּת׃

14 And those closest to him were Carshina, Sheisar, Admasa, Sarshish, Meress, Marsina [and] Memuchan, the seven ministers of Persia and Media, who would (always) see the king's face, those who sat first in the kingdom.

61. כַּרְשְׁנָא שֵׁתָר אַדְמָתָא תַרְשִׁישׁ מֶרֶס מַרְסְנָא מְמוּכָן: Although the names in the Possuk are Persian, our Rabbis taught many connections to their Hebrew meanings. Here is one:

Each of the names refers to another avodah in the Beis Hamikdash. The angels mentioned these to Hashem to intercede on behalf of Bnei Yisroel. They said:
Does anyone else aside from B'nei Yisroel...
כַּרְשְׁנָא - כר (בן) שנה – sacrifice a 1 year old bull to you?
שֵׁתָר - שני תורים – offer you 2 doves?
אַדְמָתָא - מזבח אדמה – build an alter מזבח of earth for you?
תַּרְשִׁישׁ - serve you while wearing the תַּרְשִׁישׁ stone in the בגדי כהונה?
מֶרֶס [mixing] – mix the blood of the קרבן so it should not harden?
מַרְסְנָא [mixing] – mix the ingredients of the קרבן מנחה for you?
מְמוּכָן - prepare a שלחן or מזבח for you?
–Megillah 12b / Midrash

62. The Megillah hints that these names refer to קרבנות by writing וְהַקָּרֹב without a ו, hinting to קרבן. Another hint is the unusual list of names without a ו in between each person, as the Torah usually does when it mentions a list of names. *-Rokeach*

טו. כְּדָת מַה־לַּעֲשׂוֹת בַּמַּלְכָּה וַשְׁתִּי עַל ׀ אֲשֶׁר לֹא־עָשְׂתָה אֶת־מַאֲמַר הַמֶּלֶךְ אֲחַשְׁוֵרוֹשׁ בְּיַד הַסָּרִיסִים׃

15 [He asked them:] According to the law, what to do with Queen Vashti, because she did not do (obey) the order of King Achashverosh, [brought to her] through the chamberlains.

63. כְּדָת מַה לַּעֲשׂוֹת: Why did Achashverosh even ask anyone? Wasn't it obvious that Vashti deserved to die for not listening to the king? One reason is because the king had ordered that "אין אונס"– no one should be forced to do what they don't want to do. In this case, Vashti did not want to come. However, there was also a direct command for her to come, so Achashverosh was confused about how to deal with this. Therefore his adviser(s) came up with the idea (in the next Possuk) that it's not just about this event here and now; Vashti's refusal to come will negatively affect the whole country. *-The Rebbe*

64. Who is מְמוּכָן? There are 2 opinions. Some say he is המן; others say he is דניאל.

65. וַיֹּאמֶר מְמוּכָן: ממוכן is Haman. His name ממוכן hints that he was מוכן- prepared for trouble. מְמוּכָן spoke up first, although he was the last on the list of Achashverosh's close advisors. From here we learn that הדיוט קופץ בראש– an ignoramus is often the first to speak. *-Megillah 12b*

טז. וַיֹּאמֶר מומכן (מְמוּכָן) לִפְנֵי הַמֶּלֶךְ וְהַשָּׂרִים לֹא עַל־הַמֶּלֶךְ לְבַדּוֹ עָוְתָה וַשְׁתִּי הַמַּלְכָּה כִּי עַל־כָּל־הַשָּׂרִים וְעַל־כָּל־הָעַמִּים אֲשֶׁר בְּכָל־מְדִינוֹת הַמֶּלֶךְ אֲחַשְׁוֵרוֹשׁ׃

16 And Memuchan said before the king and the ministers: "[It is] not against the king alone that Vashti the Queen has sinned, but against all the ministers and against all the nations that are in all the provinces of King Achashverosh."

66. וַיֹּאמֶר מְמוּכָן: Memuchan is דניאל. His name ממוכן hints that he was מוכן-prepared for נסים. *–Midrash*

67. וַיֹּאמֶר מְמוּכָן: מְמוּכָן was דניאל who merited to set the stage for Esther.

68. וַיֹּאמֶר מְמוּכָן: דניאל used the שם המפורש, Hashem's name that cannot be pronounced, to cause the blemishes in Vashti.

As it says; "וַיֹּאמֶר מומכן מום כן." *–Midrash*

69. וַיֹּאמֶר מְמוּכָן: His name is spelled מום-כן– "here is a defect." Haman was a flawed person in many ways, including fooling Achashverosh into killing Vashti. Because of this, Achashverosh bore a grudge against Haman until Esther arranged for his death. *–Midrash*

70. Why did Haman advise Achashverosh to kill Vashti? Here are 3 reasons:

1. Vashti was mean to Haman and struck him in the face with her shoe.
2. Haman was upset that Vashti did not invite Haman's wife to the feast.
3. Haman wanted his daughter to marry Achashverosh.

–Midrash

יז. כִּי־יֵצֵא דְבַר־הַמַּלְכָּה עַל־כָּל־הַנָּשִׁים לְהַבְזוֹת בַּעְלֵיהֶן בְּעֵינֵיהֶן

17 "For word of the queen's deed will go out to all the women, to cause their husbands to be disgraced in their

71. יֵצֵא דְבַר הַמַּלְכָּה עַל כָּל הַנָּשִׁים: The women of the kingdom would learn from Vashti to disrespect their husbands. *–Rashi*

בְּאָמְרָם הַמֶּלֶךְ אֲחַשְׁוֵרוֹשׁ אָמַר לְהָבִיא אֶת־וַשְׁתִּי הַמַּלְכָּה לְפָנָיו וְלֹא־בָאָה׃

eyes. For they will say: 'The King Achashverosh said (commanded) to bring Queen Vashti before him, and [yet] she did not come!'

יח. וְהַיּוֹם הַזֶּה תֹּאמַרְנָה | שָׂרוֹת פָּרַס־וּמָדַי אֲשֶׁר שָׁמְעוּ אֶת־דְּבַר הַמַּלְכָּה לְכֹל שָׂרֵי הַמֶּלֶךְ וּכְדַי בִּזָּיוֹן וָקָצֶף׃

18 "And this day, the noblewomen of Persia and Media who have heard of the queen's deed will tell [about] it to all the king's nobles and there will be much disgrace and anger."

72. בִּזָּיוֹן: This word contains the letters "וי זנב!"– "Oy a tail"! Here is a hint that Vashti did not want to appear before the king because the Angel Gavriel planted a tail on her. *–Megillah 12b*

73. וּכְדַי בִּזָּיוֹן וָקָצֶף: This would cause so much disgrace and anger amongst the people of the kingdom, that Vashti deserves to be killed. *–Midrash/ Ibn Ezra*

יט. אִם־עַל־הַמֶּלֶךְ טוֹב יֵצֵא דְבַר־מַלְכוּת מִלְּפָנָיו וְיִכָּתֵב בְּדָתֵי פָרַס־וּמָדַי וְלֹא יַעֲבוֹר אֲשֶׁר לֹא־תָבוֹא וַשְׁתִּי לִפְנֵי הַמֶּלֶךְ אֲחַשְׁוֵרוֹשׁ וּמַלְכוּתָהּ יִתֵּן הַמֶּלֶךְ לִרְעוּתָהּ הַטּוֹבָה מִמֶּנָּה׃

19 "If it is good for (pleases) the king, a royal proclamation should go out from [before] him, and it should be written into the laws of Persia and Media and it will not be removed, that Vashti will never [again] come before King Achashverosh, and her reign - the king should give to her friend (another) who is better than she.

74. וְלֹא יַעֲבוֹר: This decree to not disgrace their husbands should apply to all women. *–Rashi*

75. אֲשֶׁר לֹא תָבוֹא וַשְׁתִּי: Since Vashti did not come when the king asked her to, she should not be allowed to come before him to plead her case. *–Rokeach*

76. וּמַלְכוּתָהּ יִתֵּן הַמֶּלֶךְ לִרְעוּתָהּ: Since there can be only one queen at a time, this means that Vashti should be killed. *–Ralbag/Da'as Mikra*

77. וּמַלְכוּתָהּ יִתֵּן הַמֶּלֶךְ לִרְעוּתָהּ: Haman advised Vashti's death because he wanted his daughter to marry Achashverosh.

כ. וְנִשְׁמַע פִּתְגָם הַמֶּלֶךְ אֲשֶׁר־יַעֲשֶׂה בְּכָל־מַלְכוּתוֹ כִּי רַבָּה הִיא וְכָל־הַנָּשִׁים יִתְּנוּ יְקָר לְבַעְלֵיהֶן לְמִגָּדוֹל וְעַד־קָטָן׃

20 "And it will be heard - the king's decree which he shall proclaim - in all of his kingdom, for it is great, and all the women will give respect to their husbands, from the great to the small (simple)."

78. כִּי רַבָּה הִיא: For the proclamation is very important. *–Targum*

79. כִּי רַבָּה הִיא: Even though the kingdom is great (big), it is still important that the word gets out to all. *–Ibn Ezra*

כא. וַיִּיטַב הַדָּבָר בְּעֵינֵי הַמֶּלֶךְ וְהַשָּׂרִים וַיַּעַשׂ הַמֶּלֶךְ כִּדְבַר מְמוּכָן׃

21 And the matter (idea) was good (pleasing) in the eyes of the king and the ministers, and the king did like the words (advice) of Memuchan.

80. בְּעֵינֵי הַמֶּלֶךְ וְהַשָּׂרִים: Notice it does not include the חכמים, the wise men of Persia, as they did not agree; but Achashverosh did not ask them their opinion. *–Alshich*

כב. וַיִּשְׁלַח סְפָרִים
אֶל־כָּל־מְדִינוֹת הַמֶּלֶךְ
אֶל־מְדִינָה וּמְדִינָה
כִּכְתָבָהּ וְאֶל־עַם וָעָם
כִּלְשׁוֹנוֹ לִהְיוֹת כָּל־אִישׁ
שֹׂרֵר בְּבֵיתוֹ וּמְדַבֵּר
כִּלְשׁוֹן עַמּוֹ׃

22 And he sent letters to all the king's provinces – to each province according to its script (writing) and to each nation according to its language, [ordering] that every man shall be master in his home and that he speak [like] the language of his nation.

81. לִהְיוֹת כָּל אִישׁ שֹׂרֵר בְּבֵיתוֹ: This can also be read שָׁרֵר with a shin, meaning singing. That each man should sing with joy in his household. –*Rokeach*

82. וּמְדַבֵּר כִּלְשׁוֹן עַמּוֹ: The husband could force his wife to speak his language if his wife spoke different one. – *Rashi*

83. לִהְיוֹת כָּל אִישׁ שֹׂרֵר בְּבֵיתוֹ וּמְדַבֵּר כִּלְשׁוֹן עַמּוֹ: This decree saved the Jews later on. How? The Persians would've begun making trouble for the Jews earlier than the next scheduled date decreed to kill the Jews. When the people saw that Achashverosh decreed that the man be the boss in his house, and the wife to speak the language of the husband, it made him look like a fool in their eyes. They all assumed that the man is the boss anyway and how could you command someone to speak a language that they don't know?! Therefore, they were worried that Achashverosh went mad, and when the next decree to kill the Jews arrived– they feared that he may change it– which he did... So they did not attack the Jews earlier than the scheduled time! – *Midrash*

פרק ב: א. אַחַר
הַדְּבָרִים הָאֵלֶּה כְּשֹׁךְ
חֲמַת הַמֶּלֶךְ אֲחַשְׁוֵרוֹשׁ
זָכַר אֶת־וַשְׁתִּי וְאֵת
אֲשֶׁר־עָשָׂתָה וְאֵת
אֲשֶׁר־נִגְזַר עָלֶיהָ׃

CHAPTER II 1 After these things (events), when the anger of King Achashverosh had calmed, he remembered Vashti and what she had done and [remembered] that which was decreed upon her.

84. כְּשֹׁךְ חֲמַת הַמֶּלֶךְ אֲחַשְׁוֵרוֹשׁ: During the seven years from when Vashti was killed until Haman was hanged, אֲחַשְׁוֵרוֹשׁ was depressed. After Haman's hanging, his anger subsided. – *Midrash Aba Guryon*

85. זָכַר אֶת וַשְׁתִּי: He remembered her beauty. – *Rashi*

86. זָכַר אֶת וַשְׁתִּי: Achashverosh had a portrait of Vashti hung over his bed until Esther became queen. He then hung up a portrait of Esther.

87. זָכַר אֶת וַשְׁתִּי וְאֵת אֲשֶׁר עָשָׂתָה וְאֵת אֲשֶׁר נִגְזַר עָלֶיהָ: He remembered what she did – that she acted correctly by not coming immodestly, and what was decreed – unjustly, that she was punished so severely, with death. –*Midrash*

88. זָכַר אֶת וַשְׁתִּי וְאֵת אֲשֶׁר עָשָׂתָה וְאֵת אֲשֶׁר נִגְזַר עָלֶיהָ: Vashti was punished in the same way she would punish the Jewish girls, as she would force them to work disrobed on שבת, so too, she was ordered to appear so – on שבת. –*Gra*

ב. וַיֹּאמְרוּ נַעֲרֵי־הַמֶּלֶךְ
מְשָׁרְתָיו יְבַקְשׁוּ לַמֶּלֶךְ
נְעָרוֹת בְּתוּלוֹת טוֹבוֹת
מַרְאֶה׃

2 And the king's young attendants said: "Let them seek for the king, young, unmarried girls, beautiful in appearance.

89. נַעֲרֵי הַמֶּלֶךְ: Realizing that he was upset for the loss of his beautiful queen, his servants suggested he find another beautiful queen. -*Ralbag*

ג. וְיַפְקֵד הַמֶּלֶךְ
פְּקִידִים בְּכָל־מְדִינוֹת
מַלְכוּתוֹ וְיִקְבְּצוּ
אֶת־כָּל־נַעֲרָה־בְתוּלָה
טוֹבַת מַרְאֶה אֶל־שׁוּשַׁן
הַבִּירָה אֶל־בֵּית הַנָּשִׁים
אֶל־יַד הֵגֶא סְרִיס
הַמֶּלֶךְ שֹׁמֵר הַנָּשִׁים
וְנָתוֹן תַּמְרֻקֵיהֶן׃

3 "And the king shall appoint officers in all the provinces of his kingdom, and they should gather every young, unmarried girl, beautiful in appearance to Shushan the capital, to the house of the women, [they should be given] into the charge of Heige, the king's chamberlain, the guard of the women, and their cosmetics should be given [to them].

90. וְיִקְבְּצוּ אֶת כָּל נַעֲרָה: Why should they bring so many beautiful girls to Achashverosh? Why not just choose one beautiful girl for the king? The girls who were chosen would disrespect Jewish girls, saying that they are not beautiful and no one cares for them. Now, they were all rejected by Achashverosh in return for their disrespect. –*Midrash*

91. תַּמְרוּקֵיהֶן: various cosmetics that cleanse, purify and smoothen the skin. -*Rashi*

ד. וְהַנַּעֲרָה אֲשֶׁר תִּיטַב
בְּעֵינֵי הַמֶּלֶךְ תִּמְלֹךְ
תַּחַת וַשְׁתִּי וַיִּיטַב
הַדָּבָר בְּעֵינֵי הַמֶּלֶךְ
וַיַּעַשׂ כֵּן׃

4 "And the young girl who will be good (pleasing) in the eyes of the king, shall rule instead of Vashti." And the thing (advice) was good (pleasing) in the eyes of the king and he did so.

92. בְּעֵינֵי הַמֶּלֶךְ: In the eyes of Hashem (as we learned earlier, when it says מלך alone, without the king's name – it refers to Hashem). –*Midrash*

ה. אִישׁ יְהוּדִי הָיָה בְּשׁוּשַׁן הַבִּירָה וּשְׁמוֹ מָרְדֳּכַי בֶּן יָאִיר בֶּן־שִׁמְעִי בֶּן־קִישׁ אִישׁ יְמִינִי:

5 A Jewish man was in Shushan the capital, and his name was Mordechai, the son of Yair, the son of Shim'i, the son of Kish, a man from the tribe of Binyamin -

93. אִישׁ יְהוּדִי: Originally, people were identified with their specific שבט. Ever since גלות בבל, all Jews – from all - שבטים were called יהודים. *–Rashi*

94. אִישׁ יְהוּדִי: He was called יהודי because he came from the kingdom of יהודה. *–Ibn Ezra*

95. אִישׁ יְהוּדִי... אִישׁ יְמִינִי: Although he was from שבט בנימין, he was called יהודי because he caused a קידוש ה' by not bowing to Haman('s little idol he wore) therefore ה' titled him "יהודי" as an honored representative of all the Jews. *-Midrash*

96. אִישׁ יְהוּדִי... אִישׁ יְמִינִי: מרדכי was originally the leader of שבט בנימין. After גלות בבל, when many of בני ישראל returned to ארץ ישראל, they joined מרדכי. שבט יהודה then led the people of יהודה. *– Gra*

97. אִישׁ יְהוּדִי... אִישׁ יְמִינִי: Mordechai's father was from שבט בנימין, while his mother was from שבט יהודה. Each שבט was proud to call מרדכי their own – so the מגילה mentions both. *–Megillah 12a 13b*

98. אִישׁ יְהוּדִי: If you drop the little final י into the ד, it turns into a - ה spelling ה"s holy name. Mordechai exceptional conduct earned him that special title. *–Midrash*

99. אִישׁ יְהוּדִי: The name יהודה contains within it all four letters of שם ה'. Every Jew who believes in 100 'ה% earns this holy title. *–Megillah 12a 13b*

100. אִישׁ יְהוּדִי... אִישׁ יְמִינִי: יהודה was מוסר נפש for בנימין while arguing with יוסף. For this ה' rewarded him that a later redeemer of the Jews - מרדכי – would be called by his name - יהודי. *–Midrash*

101. יְהוּדִי הָיָה: Roshei Teivos י"ה and Sofei Teivos י"ה. Mordechai was surrounded by 'ה. *–Rokeach*

102. הָיָה: Hashem had prepared Mordechai before Haman's decree – as it is Hashem's way to first arrange the solution – even before the challenge. *-Midrash*

103. וּשְׁמוֹ מָרְדֳּכַי: Wicked people "go before their names" like נבל שמו – גלית שמו – etc. Tzadikim's names go before them – ושמו מנוח – ושמו שאול – ושמו ישי – ושמו מרדכי, similar to ה' as it says 'ושמי ה'. *-Midrash*

104. וּשְׁמוֹ מָרְדֳּכַי: Just as מר is the leader (finest) of all spices, so too מרדכי was the leader of the all the צדיקים in his generation. *–Midrash*

105. וּשְׁמוֹ מָרְדֳּכַי: The finest spice of the קטורת was מר דרור, which the Targum translates as מירא דכיא – this is similar to מר-דכי, as מָרְדֳּכַי's tefillos were beloved to ה' like the קטורת. *–Midrash, Chulin 139b*

106. בֶּן יָאִיר בֶּן שִׁמְעִי בֶּן קִישׁ אִישׁ יְמִינִי: This list of מרדכי's ancestry skips a few generations in between each name, as קיש was שאול's father, and ימיני refers to בנימין, both of whom lived many generations earlier.
–Midrash

107. בֶּן קִישׁ: This is probably not the father of שאול, otherwise the מגילה would've mentioned שאול too, as his name would grace this list of מרדכי's ancestry. *–Ibn Ezra*

108. In response to the above: שאול's name was specifically not mentioned, as he was responsible for Haman being born, by saving King Agag. *–Megillah 12a 13b / Manos Halevy*

109. בֶּן יָאִיר בֶּן שִׁמְעִי בֶּן קִישׁ אִישׁ יְמִינִי: This is an actual list of immediate ancestors, not distant ones. *-Rambam*

110. בֶּן יָאִיר בֶּן שִׁמְעִי בֶּן קִישׁ: These names also describe מרדכי; - בן יאיר – he illuminated בני ישראל's eyes with his Torah (being from the סנהדרין and) בן שמעי – his תפילות were answered. בן קיש – he pounded on the gates of mercy, and they were opened for him. *-Megillah 12b (Midrash)*

111. NOTE: Haman came from Agag, while Mordechai came from Saul.

ו. אֲשֶׁר הָגְלָה מִירוּשָׁלַיִם עִם־הַגֹּלָה אֲשֶׁר הָגְלְתָה עִם יְכָנְיָה מֶלֶךְ־יְהוּדָה אֲשֶׁר הֶגְלָה נְבוּכַדְנֶאצַּר מֶלֶךְ בָּבֶל:

6 - Who was exiled from Yerushalayim with the exile[d group] that had been exiled with Yechoniah, the king of Yehudah, whom Nevuchanetzar the king of Bavel had exiled.

112. אֲשֶׁר הָגְלָה: Mordechai exiled himself, along with the others who were forcibly exiled. *–Megillah 12a*

113. אֲשֶׁר הָגְלָה... הַגֹּלָה... הָגְלְתָה... הֶגְלָה: all these repetitions teach us that מרדכי was exiled many times. *–Midrash*

114. Mordechai loved ארץ ישראל so much that he would return after each time he was exiled – and then he would be sent away again. *–Gra*

ז. וַיְהִי אֹמֵן אֶת־הֲדַסָּה הִיא אֶסְתֵּר בַּת־דֹּדוֹ כִּי אֵין לָהּ אָב וָאֵם וְהַנַּעֲרָה יְפַת־תֹּאַר וְטוֹבַת מַרְאֶה וּבְמוֹת אָבִיהָ וְאִמָּהּ לְקָחָהּ מָרְדֳּכַי לוֹ לְבַת:

7 And he had raised Hadassah – [she is] Esther, the daughter of his uncle, for she did not have a father and mother. And the young girl was beautiful in [her] features and beautiful in appearance, and when her father and mother died, Mordechai took her for himself - as a daughter.

115. הֲדַסָּה הִיא אֶסְתֵּר: Her name was אסתר but she was called הדסה because: צדיקים are described as הדסים (myrtles).

116. Her height was perfect, neither short or tall - like a הדס. She had a greenish complexion (color), and Hashem graced her with beauty. *-Megillah 13a*

117. She hid her identity as a Jew.

118. People compared her beauty to the moon – סהרה in Aramaic (or אסתר like star, in Persian). *-Megillah 13a*

119. Mordechai named her a Persian name – אסתר to hide her Jewish identity. *–Yalkut Shim'oni*

120. הֲדַסָּה: the הדס smells good, symbolizing אסתר's pleasant deeds.

121. אֵין לָהּ אָב וָאֵם... וּבְמוֹת אָבִיהָ וְאִמָּהּ: Why the repetition? To teach us that her father died after she was conceived, and her mother died at her birth, so she "never" had a father or mother. *–Megillah 12a*

122. לוֹ לְבַת: as a daughter; teaching us that whoever raises (adopts) an orphan, it's as if s/he gave birth to him/her. *–Midrash*

ח. וַיְהִי בְּהִשָּׁמַע
דְּבַר־הַמֶּלֶךְ וְדָתוֹ
וּבְהִקָּבֵץ נְעָרוֹת רַבּוֹת
אֶל־שׁוּשַׁן הַבִּירָה
אֶל־יַד הֵגָי וַתִּלָּקַח
אֶסְתֵּר אֶל־בֵּית הַמֶּלֶךְ
אֶל־יַד הֵגַי שֹׁמֵר
הַנָּשִׁים:

8 And it was, when the king's order and his decree were heard, and when many young girls were gathered to Shushan the capital, under the charge of Heigai; and Esther was taken to the palace under the charge of Heigai, the guard of the women.

123. וַתִּלָּקַח אֶסְתֵּר: She was taken by force. The other locals beautified themselves and made sure to be seen by the officers, so they would be taken to the palace. אסתר hid and was eventually found.

ט. וַתִּיטַב הַנַּעֲרָה
בְעֵינָיו וַתִּשָּׂא חֶסֶד
לְפָנָיו וַיְבַהֵל
אֶת־תַּמְרוּקֶיהָ
וְאֶת־מָנוֹתֶהָ לָתֵת לָהּ
וְאֵת שֶׁבַע הַנְּעָרוֹת
הָרְאֻיוֹת לָתֶת־לָהּ
מִבֵּית הַמֶּלֶךְ וַיְשַׁנֶּהָ
וְאֶת־נַעֲרוֹתֶיהָ לְטוֹב
בֵּית הַנָּשִׁים:

9 And the girl was good (pleasing) in his eyes, and she gained his kindness, and he hurried her cosmetics and meals - to give her, and the seven maids that were befitting to give to her from the palace. And he changed (moved) her and her maids to the best [area] of the women's house.

124. וְאֵת שֶׁבַע הַנְּעָרוֹת: אסתר assigned a different maid for each day of the week. *–Megillah 13a*

125. When the שבת maid appeared, she knew that it was שבת. *–Rashi*

126. She needed this reminder because the Persians did not have our regular 7 day week. *–Yalkut Shim'oni*

127. She arranged this so no one should find out that she is Jewish. Each maid did her daily work, and the Shabbos maid did not work at all. This way, only the Shabbos maid knew that she does not work – and thought this was "normal."

128. Esther would work all week, but not on Shabbos – and only the Shabbos maid knew that. *–Ya'aros D'vash.*

129. She named each of her 7 maids in connection to the 7 days of creation, to thank Hashem for each day, and to remember the day of Shabbos. *-Midrash/Manos HaLevi*

130. וַיְשַׁנֶּהָ: He gave her kosher food. Some say seeds. *–Megillah 13a*

131. וַיְשַׁנֶּהָ: Since she was (eating kosher) in a different place, no one realized that she was Jewish. *–Lekach Tov*

י. לֹא־הִגִּידָה אֶסְתֵּר
אֶת־עַמָּהּ
וְאֶת־מוֹלַדְתָּהּ כִּי
מָרְדֳּכַי צִוָּה עָלֶיהָ אֲשֶׁר
לֹא־תַגִּיד:

10 Esther did not tell [about] her nation or birthplace (heritage), for Mordechai had instructed her that she should not tell.

132. לֹא הִגִּידָה... כִּי מָרְדֳּכַי צִוָּה... לֹא תַגִּיד: If אחשורוש would find out her royal ancestry – that Esther came from King Shaul, he would want to keep her. Mordechai told her not to reveal this hoping אחשורוש would send her away thinking she is from a simple family. *–Rashi*

133. לֹא הִגִּידָה: So she could observe her Jewish way of life without disturbance. *–Ibn Ezra*

134. If the king would find out, he might get angry at her, and then he would take it out on her people. *–Targum*

135. כִּי מָרְדֳּכַי צִוָּה: Mordechai did not want to be recognized and honored in the kingdom as the one who raised Esther. He was humble and wanted to stay out of the public eye. *–Midrash*

יא. וּבְכָל־יוֹם וָיוֹם מָרְדֳּכַי מִתְהַלֵּךְ לִפְנֵי חֲצַר בֵּית־הַנָּשִׁים לָדַעַת אֶת־שְׁלוֹם אֶסְתֵּר וּמַה־יֵּעָשֶׂה בָּהּ׃

11 And every day Mordechai would walk about in front of the courtyard of the women's house, to know how Esther was faring and what would be done with her.

136. וּבְכָל יוֹם וָיוֹם מָרְדֳּכַי מִתְהַלֵּךְ... וּמַה יֵּעָשֶׂה בָּהּ: Mordechai knew that since אסתר was such a צדקת, yet ה' caused her to be married to a non-Jew - there must be a very important reason, one that would save all the Jewish people. So, he would walk about every day to see how this would play itself out. *–Rashi (from Mechilta)*

137. וּמַה יֵּעָשֶׂה בָּהּ: Mordechai would make sure that everything went well with her kosher food and other Jewish needs. *–Lekach Tov*

יב. וּבְהַגִּיעַ תֹּר נַעֲרָה וְנַעֲרָה לָבוֹא | אֶל־הַמֶּלֶךְ אֲחַשְׁוֵרוֹשׁ מִקֵּץ הֱיוֹת לָהּ כְּדָת הַנָּשִׁים שְׁנֵים עָשָׂר חֹדֶשׁ כִּי כֵּן יִמְלְאוּ יְמֵי מְרוּקֵיהֶן שִׁשָּׁה חֳדָשִׁים בְּשֶׁמֶן הַמֹּר וְשִׁשָּׁה חֳדָשִׁים בַּבְּשָׂמִים וּבְתַמְרוּקֵי הַנָּשִׁים׃

12 And when it arrived - the turn of each young girl - to come to [the] King Achashverosh, at the end of her having – [like] the law of the women - twelve months, for this is how the days of their cosmetics (beauty-care) would be completed; six months with oil of myrrh and six months with perfumes and women's cosmetics.

יג. וּבָזֶה הַנַּעֲרָה בָּאָה אֶל־הַמֶּלֶךְ אֵת כָּל־אֲשֶׁר תֹּאמַר יִנָּתֵן לָהּ לָבוֹא עִמָּהּ מִבֵּית הַנָּשִׁים עַד־בֵּית הַמֶּלֶךְ׃

13 And with this the young girl would come to the king; Whatever she would say (request) would be given to her, to come with her from the women's house to the king's palace.

138. וּבָזֶה הַנַּעֲרָה בָּאָה: (Could be read or referring to – and "like this" – like herself.) Every girl would bring in people of her type and looks to help and accompany her. If she was dark skinned, short etc., they would arrange dark skinned, short etc., helpers for her. *-Midrash*

139. כָּל אֲשֶׁר תֹּאמַר: She could bring with her any kind of entertainment or music. *–Rashi*

140. כָּל אֲשֶׁר תֹּאמַר יִנָּתֵן לָהּ: Some officers who wanted to be in the presence of the king during this time would pay her whatever she asked – to be allowed to join her. *–Lekach Tov*

יד. בָּעֶרֶב | הִיא בָאָה וּבַבֹּקֶר הִיא שָׁבָה

14 In the evening she would come [to the

141. בֵּית הַנָּשִׁים שֵׁנִי: If he did not want to marry her, she would remain in the "second" women's palace as a פלגש (secondary wife) to the

אֶל־בֵּית הַנָּשִׁים שֵׁנִי אֶל־יַד שַׁעַשְׁגַז סְרִיס הַמֶּלֶךְ שֹׁמֵר הַפִּילַגְשִׁים לֹא־תָבוֹא עוֹד אֶל־הַמֶּלֶךְ כִּי אִם־חָפֵץ בָּהּ הַמֶּלֶךְ וְנִקְרְאָה בְשֵׁם׃

king], and in the morning she would return to the second house of the women, under the charge of Shaashgaz, the king's chamberlain, the guard of the concubines. She would not go anymore to the king, unless the king desired her, and she was called [to come] by [her] name.

king. For no one else was allowed to marry one who is interviewed by the king. *-Ibn Ezra*

142. The first place the girls were taken to was the בית הנשים, under הגי's guard. Now they were placed under שעשגז's rule, who was the שמר הפלגשים. *–Lekach Tov*

143. כִּי אִם חָפֵץ בָּהּ הַמֶּלֶךְ: - The King of all Kings – ה'. Only the one that Hashem wanted to be queen, would be queen.

טו. וּבְהַגִּיעַ תֹּר־אֶסְתֵּר בַּת־אֲבִיחַיִל דֹּד מָרְדֳּכַי אֲשֶׁר לָקַח־לוֹ לְבַת לָבוֹא אֶל־הַמֶּלֶךְ לֹא בִקְשָׁה דָּבָר כִּי אִם אֶת־אֲשֶׁר יֹאמַר הֵגַי סְרִיס־הַמֶּלֶךְ שֹׁמֵר הַנָּשִׁים וַתְּהִי אֶסְתֵּר נֹשֵׂאת חֵן בְּעֵינֵי כָּל־רֹאֶיהָ׃

15 And when the turn came for Esther - daughter of Avichayil, the uncle of Mordechai, who took her as a daughter - to come to the king, she did not ask for a thing, aside from that which Heigai, the king's chamberlain, custodian of the women, had said (suggested her to bring). And Esther would find favor in the eyes of all who saw her.

144. לֹא בִקְשָׁה דָּבָר: She did not want to be chosen as queen. *–Manos HaLevi*

145. וַתְּהִי אֶסְתֵּר נֹשֵׂאת חֵן בְּעֵינֵי כָּל רֹאֶיהָ: This is surely written with רוח הקודש – otherwise, how could anyone know that she found favor in *absolutely everyone's* eyes? *–Megillah 7a*

146. וַתְּהִי אֶסְתֵּר נֹשֵׂאת חֵן בְּעֵינֵי כָּל רֹאֶיהָ: Every nationality claimed אסתר as their own. *–Megillah 13a*

147. וַתְּהִי אֶסְתֵּר נֹשֵׂאת חֵן בְּעֵינֵי כָּל רֹאֶיהָ: Whoever saw her said she is fitting to be the queen. *–Midrash*

148. וַתְּהִי אֶסְתֵּר נֹשֵׂאת חֵן בְּעֵינֵי כָּל רֹאֶיהָ: In the eyes of "all" who saw her, include all kinds of people; the intelligent and wise, who look for wisdom and good מדות, and the simple people to whom the external beauty is important. *–Midrash*

טז. וַתִּלָּקַח אֶסְתֵּר אֶל־הַמֶּלֶךְ אֲחַשְׁוֵרוֹשׁ אֶל־בֵּית מַלְכוּתוֹ בַּחֹדֶשׁ הָעֲשִׂירִי הוּא־חֹדֶשׁ טֵבֵת בִּשְׁנַת־שֶׁבַע לְמַלְכוּתוֹ׃

16 And Esther was taken to King Achashverosh, to his palace, in the tenth month, which is the month of Tevet, in the seventh year of his kingdom (rule).

149. בַּחֹדֶשׁ הָעֲשִׂירִי: During the cold season so Achashverosh would appreciate Esther helping him stay warm and would want to marry her. *–Rashi from Megillah 13.*

150. הוּא חֹדֶשׁ טֵבֵת: The names of the Jewish calendar months (as we know them now) came with the Jews from Bavel. (They are not Hebrew words or names – rather Babylonian names that we adopted.) *–Yerushalmi R"H 1:5*

יז. וַיֶּאֱהַב הַמֶּלֶךְ אֶת־אֶסְתֵּר מִכָּל־הַנָּשִׁים וַתִּשָּׂא־חֵן וָחֶסֶד לְפָנָיו מִכָּל־הַבְּתוּלֹת וַיָּשֶׂם כֶּתֶר־מַלְכוּת בְּרֹאשָׁהּ וַיַּמְלִיכֶהָ תַּחַת וַשְׁתִּי:

17 And the king loved Esther more than all the women and she "found" grace and kindness before him, more than all the [other] unmarried girls; And he placed the royal crown on her head and made her queen instead of Vashti.

151. וַיַּמְלִיכֶהָ תַּחַת וַשְׁתִּי: Ever since Vashti died, אחשורוש had a (painted) portrait of ושתי in his room. As each girl walked in – אחשורוש compared her to the portrait on the wall. When אסתר entered, אחשורוש removed ושתי's portrait and replaced it with a new painting of אסתר. – *Midrash AG*

152. וַיַּמְלִיכֶהָ תַּחַת וַשְׁתִּי: In the אשת חיל, the words "שקר החן והבל היופי" refer to ושתי. The next phrase, "אשה יראת ה' היא תתהלל" refer to אסתר. – *Midrash*

יח. וַיַּעַשׂ הַמֶּלֶךְ מִשְׁתֶּה גָדוֹל לְכָל־שָׂרָיו וַעֲבָדָיו אֵת מִשְׁתֵּה אֶסְתֵּר וַהֲנָחָה לַמְּדִינוֹת עָשָׂה וַיִּתֵּן מַשְׂאֵת כְּיַד הַמֶּלֶךְ:

18 And the king made a grand feast for all his ministers and servants, "The Feast of Esther." And he arranged a discount for [the taxes of] the provinces, and he gave presents as fitting for the king.

153. וַהֲנָחָה לַמְּדִינוֹת עָשָׂה: In attempt to influence אסתר to reveal her identity, אחשורוש lowered the taxes of her family. The problem was that he did not know who they were, so he lowered the taxes for all the people... *-Rashi*

154. That explains why later – at the end of the Megillah – after אחשורוש already found out who אסתר was – he assigned new taxes on all the provinces *–Gra*

יט. וּבְהִקָּבֵץ בְּתוּלוֹת שֵׁנִית וּמָרְדֳּכַי יֹשֵׁב בְּשַׁעַר־הַמֶּלֶךְ:

19 And when the unmarried girls were gathered a second time, [and] Mordechai was sitting at the king's gate.

155. וּבְהִקָּבֵץ בְּתוּלוֹת שֵׁנִית: Why was there a second gathering?

156. אחשורוש thought that if she would see that he is considering others to be queen, it would arouse her jealousy and she would reveal her identity. *–Midrash*

157. וּמָרְדֳּכַי יֹשֵׁב בְּשַׁעַר הַמֶּלֶךְ: Now that there was another competition for the queen's position, מרדכי was very concerned about אסתר's safety, worrying what may happen to אסתר if the king finds another candidate more beautiful than she. *- Midrash*

כ. אֵין אֶסְתֵּר מַגֶּדֶת מוֹלַדְתָּהּ וְאֶת־עַמָּהּ כַּאֲשֶׁר צִוָּה עָלֶיהָ מָרְדֳּכָי וְאֶת־מַאֲמַר מָרְדֳּכַי אֶסְתֵּר עֹשָׂה כַּאֲשֶׁר הָיְתָה בְאָמְנָה אִתּוֹ:

20 Esther was not telling [anyone about] her birthplace and nation, just as Mordechai had instructed her. And Esther followed Mordechai's instructions just like [she did] when she was raised by him.

158. אֵין אֶסְתֵּר מַגֶּדֶת מוֹלַדְתָּהּ: None of אחשורוש's tactics worked, although he tried by making a feast for her, giving presents to high officials in her honor and gathering the girls again to make her jealous *-Megillah 13a*

159. אֵין אֶסְתֵּר מַגֶּדֶת מוֹלַדְתָּהּ: What an amazing thing it is that not one Jew from all the countries came forward to tell the king who אסתר was! Surely they would've been generously rewarded! For this alone they deserved to be saved! *–Rambam*

160. אֵין אֶסְתֵּר מַגֶּדֶת מוֹלַדְתָּהּ: This is mentioned here and now, as an introduction to the following Possuk/story, that since Mordechai was not known, בגתן and תרש were not careful about discussing their plot in front of him. *–Me'am Lo'ez*

כא. בַּיָּמִים הָהֵם וּמָרְדֳּכַי יֹשֵׁב בְּשַׁעַר־הַמֶּלֶךְ קָצַף בִּגְתָן וָתֶרֶשׁ שְׁנֵי־סָרִיסֵי הַמֶּלֶךְ מִשֹּׁמְרֵי הַסַּף וַיְבַקְשׁוּ לִשְׁלֹחַ יָד בַּמֶּלֶךְ אֲחַשְׁוֵרֹשׁ׃

21 In those days, [while] Mordechai sat at the king's gate, Bigsan and Seresh - two of the king's chamberlains from the guards of the threshold (entrance) - became angry, and sought (planned) to send a hand against (assassinate) King Achashverosh.

161. וּמָרְדֳּכַי יֹשֵׁב בְּשַׁעַר הַמֶּלֶךְ: Esther convinced Achashverosh to appoint Mordechai as an advisor. When אחשורוש kept asking אסתר about her family, she said: "I'm concerned that you are asking me all these questions so you can find something wrong with me and then you will kill me like you killed Vashti." Achashverosh answered, "It wasn't my idea – it was the idea of the advisors of פרס and מדי." She responded, "Why do you have such advisors? Your predecessors – The really great kings before you like Nevuchanetzar and Belshatzar had the Jewish prophet Daniel as their advisor." Achashverosh asked, "Are there still Jews like him today?" To which she responded, "Yes – Mordechai". That is how Mordechai was appointed. *-Midrash*

162. קָצַף: They were angry at אחשורוש for removing them from their position, and appointing מרדכי in their stead. *–Midrash*

163. וַיְבַקְשׁוּ לִשְׁלֹחַ יָד: They planned to poison his drink. *–Rashi*

164. וַיְבַקְשׁוּ לִשְׁלֹחַ יָד: They prepared knives in their shoes, a rope to strangle him and a poisonous snake for his drink – and all these plans were foiled by מרדכי. *–Midrash*

כב. וַיִּוָּדַע הַדָּבָר לְמָרְדֳּכַי וַיַּגֵּד לְאֶסְתֵּר הַמַּלְכָּה וַתֹּאמֶר אֶסְתֵּר לַמֶּלֶךְ בְּשֵׁם מָרְדֳּכָי׃

22 And the matter became known to Mordechai and he told [it] to Esther the Queen. And Esther told [it] to the king in the name of Mordechai.

165. וַיִּוָּדַע הַדָּבָר לְמָרְדֳּכַי: As a member of the Sanhedrin, מרדכי was required to be fluent in all 70 languages. They did not suspect Mordechai of understanding their native tongue (language). *–Rashi*

166. וַיִּוָּדַע הַדָּבָר לְמָרְדֳּכַי: through רוח הקודש. (רבי מאיר) *–Megillah 7a*

167. וַיַּגֵּד לְאֶסְתֵּר הַמַּלְכָּה: Why did מרדכי want to save the king? A few reasons:

168. Mordechai was the guard, and he didn't want to cause a חילול ה' by not doing his job well.

169. This would give him a chance to help the Jews, should an evil decree arise.

170. People shouldn't say that he was killed because the Jewess he married brought him bad luck.

171. He hoped that through this favor, Achashverosh would allow the Jews to rebuild the B"H. *-Midrash*

172. וַתֹּאמֶר אֶסְתֵּר לַמֶּלֶךְ בְּשֵׁם מָרְדֳּכָי: From here we learn, "כל האומר דבר בשם אמרו מביא גאולה לעולם" – Whoever says something in the name of the one who said it, brings redemption to the world. *–Megillah 15a / Pirkei Avos*

173. Hashem always prepares the solution before the challenge. We can see here how Hashem set the stage to save the Jews later on. 1. Esther became queen. 2. Mordechai was appointed to be

gatekeeper, which angered בגתן and תרש. 3. Mordechai found out about their plot. 4. The king did not reward Mordechai at this time. *-Malbim*

כג. וַיְבֻקַּשׁ הַדָּבָר וַיִּמָּצֵא וַיִּתָּלוּ שְׁנֵיהֶם עַל־עֵץ וַיִּכָּתֵב בְּסֵפֶר דִּבְרֵי הַיָּמִים לִפְנֵי הַמֶּלֶךְ׃

23 And the matter was investigated and found (to be true), and they were hanged - both of them - on a gallows. And it was written in the Book of Chronicles before the king.

174. וַיְבֻקַּשׁ הַדָּבָר וַיִּמָּצֵא: When Bigsan and Seresh came to serve Achashverosh a jug of water, he ordered them to pour out the contents (in a manner that he could clearly see what's inside). They responded, "Our master the king, this water is wonderful, good, cold and clear – why pour it out?" "Just do it" was the swift reply. The poison was found in the jug and the rest is history. *–Midrash*

175. בְּסֵפֶר דִּבְרֵי הַיָּמִים לִפְנֵי הַמֶּלֶךְ: This was the king's personal diary. *- Malbim:*

פרק ג: א. אַחַר | הַדְּבָרִים הָאֵלֶּה גִּדַּל° הַמֶּלֶךְ אֲחַשְׁוֵרוֹשׁ אֶת־הָמָן בֶּן־הַמְּדָתָא הָאֲגָגִי וַיְנַשְּׂאֵהוּ וַיָּשֶׂם אֶת־כִּסְאוֹ מֵעַל כָּל־הַשָּׂרִים אֲשֶׁר אִתּוֹ׃

CHAPTER III 1 After these events, King Achashverosh promoted Haman, the son of Hamdasa, the Agagi and raised him (his position); He placed his seat (position) above all the ministers who were with him.

176. אַחַר הַדְּבָרִים הָאֵלֶּה: Rava says, "אין הקב"ה מכה את ישראל אלא אם כן בורא רפואה תחילה" – Hashem always first prepares the cure before the "strike" for the Jews. Hashem has arranged all these previous events to prepare the world – to set the stage for the Jews to be saved. *– Megillah 13b*

177. גִּדַּל: Hashem arranged for Haman's position to be raised before he fell – so he fell from a higher place. Ouch. *– Midrash*

178. An interesting conversation was overheard between a young donkey and an older, more experienced one. "Look at this, we work so hard every day, all day, and get just a bit of food, while that fat pig there sits around lazing all day long and gets so much food! Shouldn't it be the opposite?" "Good question my little donkey, it seems like it should be the reverse. However, know that all the food the pig is getting and eating – is not for her own good. The fatter she gets, the closer she is to becoming a meal herself..."

179. Here too – Haman was elevated to a high position – so that his fall would be greater. *– Midrash*

180. הָאֲגָגִי: He was a descendant of Agag, the king of Amalek. While Mordechai was a descendant of Shaul, who battled Amalek. History was repeating itself.

181. וַיָּשֶׂם אֶת כִּסְאוֹ מֵעַל כָּל הַשָּׂרִים: Each officer had an assigned seat. Haman's was now elevated. *– Ibn Ezra*

ב. וְכָל־עַבְדֵי הַמֶּלֶךְ אֲשֶׁר־בְּשַׁעַר הַמֶּלֶךְ כֹּרְעִים וּמִשְׁתַּחֲוִים לְהָמָן כִּי־כֵן צִוָּה־לוֹ הַמֶּלֶךְ וּמָרְדֳּכַי לֹא יִכְרַע וְלֹא יִשְׁתַּחֲוֶה׃

2 And all the King's servants who were at the king's gate, would kneel and bow to Haman, for so had the king commanded about him. And Mordechai would not kneel nor bow.

182. כִּי כֵן צִוָּה לוֹ הַמֶּלֶךְ: It was the custom for all to bow to high ranking officials in those days and places. Why did the king need to order that people bow to Haman? Since his family was not a royal, noble family, rather a very simple one, the nobles did not want to lower themselves to him. *- Rokeach*

183. וּמָרְדֳּכַי לֹא יִכְרַע וְלֹא יִשְׁתַּחֲוֶה: Haman considered himself a god and wanted people to bow to him. That's why Mordechai did not bow. *– Rashi*

184. Haman wore an image of an idol on his clothing in order to get Mordechai to bow and sin! *– Midrash*

185. Mordechai and Haman were generals in the king's army. Haman ran out of food while Mordechai planned ahead carefully and had enough. Haman begged him to share of his food. Mordechai agreed on the condition that Haman sell himself as a slave to Mordechai – which he did, and they wrote the contract on Mordechai's shoe (assuming they ran out of paper ;). Now, when Mordechai would pass Haman, instead of bowing he would waive the contract shoe. *– Midrash*

186. Haman said to Mordechai, "You can get into big trouble by not following the king's order, and anyway, your ancestors bowed to mine. Didn't Yaakov (your ancestor) bow to Eisav (my ancestor)? Mordechai replied, "Binyomin was not born yet, and he did not bow, and I come from Binyomin – as you see I am called "איש ימיני". – *Midrash*

187. וּמָרְדֳּכַי לֹא יִכְרַע וְלֹא יִשְׁתַּחֲוֶה: Mordechai endangered himself and all the Jews by not bowing to Haman. One of the reasons he was so determined is because Mordechai was a גלגול of יעקב while Haman was a גלגול of עשו. Mordechai needed to fix the two things that יעקב did; he bowed to עשו and called him "אדוני" – my master. Therefore, מרדכי "bought" המן as a slave, and did not bow to him. – *Sha'ar HaGilgulim*

ג. וַיֹּאמְרוּ עַבְדֵי הַמֶּלֶךְ אֲשֶׁר־בְּשַׁעַר הַמֶּלֶךְ לְמָרְדֳּכָי מַדּוּעַ אַתָּה עוֹבֵר אֵת מִצְוַת הַמֶּלֶךְ:

3 And the king's servants who were at the king's gate said to Mordechai, "Why do you transgress the command of the king?"

188. מַדּוּעַ אַתָּה עוֹבֵר אֵת מִצְוַת הַמֶּלֶךְ: When the kings servants saw that Mordechai would not bow, they thought he may just be an unmannered person, and tried to convince him to bow, as this was the king's order. Mordechai answered them, "I am a Jew, always deeply connected to Hashem. It is not becoming of someone connected to Hashem to bow to a human." – *Midrash*

189. Mordechai did not even need to bow to Haman as his position was above the עַבְדֵי הַמֶּלֶךְ that were ordered to bow. Nevertheless, when they asked him why he did not bow, instead of telling them that he did not need to – he told them it was because he was a Jew and proud to be part of Hashem's chosen nation who does not bow.

190. מַדּוּעַ אַתָּה עוֹבֵר אֵת מִצְוַת הַמֶּלֶךְ: Even though Haman himself is certainly not worthy of the respect – why are you not following the king's order? – *Eshkol HaKofer*

ד. וַיְהִי באמרם (כְּאָמְרָם) אֵלָיו יוֹם וָיוֹם וְלֹא שָׁמַע אֲלֵיהֶם וַיַּגִּידוּ לְהָמָן לִרְאוֹת הַיַעַמְדוּ דִּבְרֵי מָרְדֳּכַי כִּי־הִגִּיד לָהֶם אֲשֶׁר־הוּא יְהוּדִי:

4 And it was, when they said this to him every day and he did not listen to them; [and] they told [this] to Haman to see if Mordechai's words would stand, for he had told them that he is a Jew.

191. [כְּאָמְרָם] וַיְהִי בְּאָמְרָם: This word is written וַיְהִי בְּאָמְרָם in the Megillah, but is pronounced וַיְהִי כְּאָמְרָם. The first letters of each version are כ-ב = 22, hinting to the תורה which was written with the 22 letters of the א-ב. – *Midrash*

192. הֲיַעַמְדוּ דִּבְרֵי מָרְדֳּכַי: They wanted to find out if what Mordechai had told them - that Haman had sold himself to Mordechai as a slave for food – was true. – *Midrash*

ה. וַיַּרְא הָמָן כִּי־אֵין מָרְדֳּכַי כֹּרֵעַ וּמִשְׁתַּחֲוֶה לוֹ וַיִּמָּלֵא הָמָן חֵמָה:

5 And Haman saw that Mordechai is not kneeling or bowing to him, and Haman became filled with anger.

193. וַיַּרְא הָמָן ... וַיִּמָּלֵא הָמָן חֵמָה: When Haman passed Mordechai and he did not bow, Haman walked around and approached Mordechai from a different direction, to see if this was really true. Haman greeted Mordechai with "שלום" – Mordechai answered "אין שלום לרשעים" - says Hashem, "There is no peace for the wicked!" Quoting a Possuk in ישעיה נז: כא. This is when Haman was filled with anger... - *Midrash AG.*

ו. וַיִּבֶז בְּעֵינָיו לִשְׁלֹחַ יָד בְּמָרְדֳּכַי לְבַדּוֹ כִּי־הִגִּידוּ לוֹ אֶת־עַם מָרְדֳּכָי וַיְבַקֵּשׁ הָמָן לְהַשְׁמִיד אֶת־כָּל־הַיְּהוּדִים אֲשֶׁר בְּכָל־מַלְכוּת אֲחַשְׁוֵרוֹשׁ עַם מָרְדֳּכָי:

6 And it was disgraceful in his eyes to send his hand (kill) Mordechai alone, for they had told him of Mordechai's nation. And Haman sought (wanted) to destroy all the Jews who were in Achashverosh's entire kingdom; [he wanted to destroy] Mordechai's nation.

194. וַיִּבֶז בְּעֵינָיו: Haman was following his ancestor Eisav's footsteps, as it says regarding Eisav: "וַיִּבֶז עשו". – *Midrash ER 7:10*

195. בְּמָרְדֳּכַי לְבַדּוֹ... עַם מָרְדֳּכָי... אֶת כָּל הַיְּהוּדִים: At first Haman wanted to kill just מרדכי, then all the "people like מרדכי" – the חכמים, then – all the Jews. – *Megillah 13b*

ז. בַּחֹדֶשׁ הָרִאשׁוֹן הוּא־חֹדֶשׁ נִיסָן בִּשְׁנַת שְׁתֵּים עֶשְׂרֵה לַמֶּלֶךְ אֲחַשְׁוֵרוֹשׁ הִפִּיל פּוּר הוּא הַגּוֹרָל לִפְנֵי הָמָן מִיּוֹם | לְיוֹם וּמֵחֹדֶשׁ לְחֹדֶשׁ שְׁנֵים־עָשָׂר הוּא־חֹדֶשׁ אֲדָר:

7 In the first month, which is the month of Nissan, in the twelfth year of the King Achashverosh['s rule], he cast a "Pur," this is a lot, before Haman, for every day and every month, until [it fell on] the 12th month, which is the month of Adar.

196. הִפִּיל פּוּר הוּא הַגּוֹרָל לִפְנֵי הָמָן מִיּוֹם: Haman first cast a lot to choose the day of the week that would be best suited for his evil plan. Each of the days argued to ה' that their day was not suitable for Haman's plan. This is a summary of what happened for each day of the week:

יום ראשון said: רבונו של עולם! You created the heavens and earth on this day - for the Jewish People! This wicked man wants to wipe them out (ח"ו)! Before you allow this to happen, You must first get rid of the heavens and earth!

יום שני said: רבונו של עולם! On this day You separated the higher waters from the lower waters. So too the Jewish people are separated from the nations of the world. Before You allow this evil decree to happen, You must first mix the heavenly waters with those from below!

יום שלישי said: רבונו של עולם! On this day the fruits and vegetables were created, from which the Jewish People separate תרומות ומעשרות. The Trees were created, from which the Jewish People praise You with the special four species on סוכות. The waters of the ocean were set in place – which divided for the Jews into twelve paths. Now, how can we all exist without the Jews?!

יום רביעי said: רבונו של עולם! On this day the great lights of the heavens were created to serve the Jewish People. The stars were created, and Your children are compared to stars. We have no reason to exist without them!

יום חמישי said: רבונו של עולם! On this day the birds were created, from which You commanded בני ישראל to offer קרבנות which cause You to forgive all the people of their wrongdoings. Who will offer the קרבנות if not they?

יום שישי said: רבונו של עולם! On this day Adam (mankind) was created, and Your children בני ישראל represent Adam. If You want to destroy them – You must destroy all mankind.

יום שבת קודש said: רבונו של עולם! On this day Your creation was completed, and שבת was given as an *everlasting covenant* - ברית עולם to בני ישראל. Before You allow this evil decree to happen, You must first get rid of שבת.

After failing with the days of the week, Haman went on to search for a month that had no merits - זכויות.

These are the months – and the reasons they did not work:

Nissan: Pesach!

Iyar: פסח שני and the זכות of the מן that began falling during this month.

Sivan: מתן תורה!

Tammuz & Av: Both these months claimed that they had more than enough terrible things happen in them already (Destruction of the B"H)!

Elul: The walls of ירושלים were completed on כה אלול and מעשר בהמה is separated during אלול.

(The Midrash doesn't say this but perhaps another זכות of אלול is that it contains the first five days of creation.)

Tishrei: ראש השנה (שופר), יום כיפור, סוכות.

Cheshvan: זכות of רחל אמנו who passed away in this month.

Kislev: חנוכה! (Even though the story of Chanukah had not yet happened, it was still considered as a merit for the בני ישראל).

Teiveis: In the זכות of עזרא הסופר (who did something special for all of ישראל during this month).

Sh'vat: In the זכות of אנשי כנסת הגדולה (same as above). Adar: Haman could not find a merit / זכות for this month, and began rejoicing. - *Midrash Esther Rabba, 7-11.*

197. חֹדֶשׁ נִיסָן: This is the month when many נסים happened to ישראל. - *Midrash LT*

198. הִפִּיל פּוּר הוּא הַגּוֹרָל: Pur is a Persian word for גורל. – *Ibn Ezra*

199. מִיּוֹם לְיוֹם וּמֵחֹדֶשׁ לְחֹדֶשׁ: Haman cast a lot for every day of the year, to determine which day would be best suited to harm the Jews (ח"ו). - *Midrash*חֹדֶשׁ אֲדָר: The lot "chose" the month of Adar. Haman was happy about that thinking that since this was the month that Moshe Rabeinu passed away, it was not a good month for בני ישראל. He did not know that Moshe was also born in this month, therefore it is a lucky month for us. - *Megillah 13b*

ח. וַיֹּאמֶר הָמָן לַמֶּלֶךְ אֲחַשְׁוֵרוֹשׁ יֶשְׁנוֹ עַם־אֶחָד מְפֻזָּר וּמְפֹרָד בֵּין הָעַמִּים בְּכֹל מְדִינוֹת מַלְכוּתֶךָ וְדָתֵיהֶם שֹׁנוֹת מִכָּל־עָם וְאֶת־דָּתֵי הַמֶּלֶךְ אֵינָם עֹשִׂים וְלַמֶּלֶךְ אֵין־שֹׁוֶה לְהַנִּיחָם׃

8 And Haman said to King Achashverosh, "There is one nation, scattered and dispersed among the nations, in all the provinces of your kingdom, and their laws are different from any other nation and the laws of the king – they do not do (obey), and for the king there is no value to let them be.

200. וַיֹּאמֶר הָמָן: The conversation between Haman and Achashverosh went something like this:

Haman: Let us kill the Jews (ח"ו).

Achashverosh: I'm afraid of their G-d, lest He do to me what he did to my predecessors.

201. Haman: יֶשְׁנוֹ עַם אֶחָד – they are sleeping – not keeping the Torah and Mitzvos, no need to worry, their G-d won't save them (ח"ו).

Achashverosh: But they have the רבנן – the holy rabbis who are awake - keeping all the מצוות!

202. Haman: They are עם אחד – one nation. The rabbis are responsible for the rest of the Jews.

Achashverosh: If they all suddenly disappear – there will be this "empty space" in my kingdom!

Haman: Don't worry about a "missing gap" in your nation when they are gone: they are מפוזר ומפורד בין העמים – scattered and dispersed amongst the nations.

Achashverosh: What about all the benefit I can get from them?

203. Haman: ומפורד – like פרד – a mule. They are like the mule, who is not able to reproduce.

Achashverosh: Perhaps we just gather them together into one small area?

204. Haman: No chance! They are בְּכֹל מְדִינוֹת מַלְכוּתֶךָ – all over the world!

205. And...Listen to this! וְדָתֵיהֶם שֹׁנוֹת מִכָּל עָם – They don't eat our food nor would they marry someone who is not Jewish. And...

206. וְאֶת דָּתֵי הַמֶּלֶךְ אֵינָם עֹשִׂים – All year long they have so many excuses not to work! They have so many holidays, Shabbos, Pesach, [Sukkos, Shavuos, Rosh Hashanah, Yom Kippur, Sh'mini Atzeres, (Chanukah, Purim – oops – those didn't happen yet!) and so many more...] Therefore...

207. וְלַמֶּלֶךְ אֵין שֹׁוֶה לְהַנִּיחָם: "It is not worth letting them live! Not only that, but even in their ways of eating and drinking – they disrespect the kingdom! If one of them finds a fly in his drink, he removes the fly and drinks the contents. If you, O King Achashverosh, would touch a cup of wine – the Jew would spill the wine on the ground and not drink it! -?

208. וְדָתֵיהֶם שֹׁנוֹת מִכָּל עָם: They have such strange ways! They rest every 7th day, they recite the שמע – stating that there is only their One G-d, they then stand and pray for our destruction! *– Midrash PA*

209. שְׁנוֹת מִכָּל עָם = ר"ת שמע – which is also שחרית – מנחה – ערבית - and the שמע is said when שאו מרום עיניכם – when one can look up and see the stars! – *Sha'arei Bina*

210. וְלַמֶּלֶךְ אֵין שֹׁוֶה לְהַנִּיחָם: While Haman was prosecuting (accusing the Jews of doing wrong things) below, מלאך מכאל was defending above (in the heavenly court, to Hashem). He said, "Master of the universe, look and see how Your children are not being accused of worshiping idols, conducting themselves immorally (not keeping the proper laws of marriage and tznius) or killing – they are only being accused of observing Your Mitzvos!" Hashem replied; "I swear that just as I did not forsake them until now – I will not forsake them in the future." – *Midrash ER*

ט. אִם-עַל-הַמֶּלֶךְ טוֹב יִכָּתֵב לְאַבְּדָם וַעֲשֶׂרֶת אֲלָפִים כִּכַּר-כֶּסֶף אֶשְׁקוֹל עַל-יְדֵי עֹשֵׂי הַמְּלָאכָה לְהָבִיא אֶל-גִּנְזֵי הַמֶּלֶךְ:

9 "If it is good for (pleases) the king, let it be written (decreed) to destroy them, and ten thousand silver talents I will weigh - through the people who will do the job - to bring to the king's treasuries."

211. יִכָּתֵב לְאַבְּדָם: Haman is compared to a bird, whose nest was swept away by the waves of the ocean. Angry at the water, the bird said: I will dry up the whole ocean! And the bird began to fill its beak with water and pour it on the dry land. Over and over again. The bird is still working at it now. – (? - Not sure what this means!) - *Midrash*

212. וַעֲשֶׂרֶת אֲלָפִים כִּכַּר כֶּסֶף: Resh Lakish said; "Haman was now weighing his Shekalim to destroy the Jews, but Hashem had already prevented the disaster by having the Jews give their Shekalim to the Mishkan – the Machatzis Hashekel – which saved them." – *Megillah 13b*

213. וַעֲשֶׂרֶת אֲלָפִים כִּכַּר כֶּסֶף: Achashverosh said to Haman; Are you referring to the nation that wakes up early every morning and says "שמע ה' אלוקנו ה' אחד"?! Don't you know what happened to all the previous kings who caused trouble to the Jews? Remember what happened to פרעה – סיחון – עוג – סיסרא – יבין – סנחריב – נבוכדנצר – בלשצר and many more!? I'm afraid that their G-d will harm me if I harm them!" Answered Haman: You would have reason to fear if their G-d was pleased with them, but now, look! The Beis Hamikdash - His holy home was destroyed and He is angry with them! Also – remember the Shekalim the Jews donated to the Mishkan - בֶּקַע לַגֻּלְגֹּלֶת – that all equaled up to 10,000 silver talents – which I am giving you now – in exchange – and to combat – any good that they did with their donation. – *Midrash PA*

214. כִּכַּר כֶּסֶף: There were four galuyos by four kingdoms, represented by four kinds of materials which the בני ישראל brought to the Mishkan.

215. זהב – gold refers to בבל, who is described as having a golden head.

216. כסף – silver refers to מדי – our story – with the silver talents that Haman offered.

217. נחושת – copper refers to יון – the lowest of these kingdoms.

218. עורות אלים מאדמים – the red ram skins, refers to גלות אדום in which we are until משיח comes.

219. After these materials, the Torah lists שמן למאור – oil for the illuminator – this refers to מלך המשיח who will redeem us eternally from all our גלויות. – *Midrash Tanchuma*

י. וַיָּסַר הַמֶּלֶךְ
אֶת־טַבַּעְתּוֹ מֵעַל יָדוֹ
וַיִּתְּנָהּ לְהָמָן
בֶּן־הַמְּדָתָא הָאֲגָגִי צֹרֵר
הַיְּהוּדִים׃

10 And the king removed his [signet] ring from his hand and he gave it to Haman, the son of Hamdasa, the Agagi, oppressor of the Jews.

220. טַבַּעְתּוֹ: His signet ring. This is the ring that would have the king's signature engraved on it, and it would be used as the stamp of approval for his decrees and laws. – *Soncino pg. 155 / cf. v111 2*

221. וַיָּסַר הַמֶּלֶךְ אֶת טַבַּעְתּוֹ: The one with the ring is the boss. – *Rashi*

222. וַיָּסַר הַמֶּלֶךְ אֶת טַבַּעְתּוֹ: Rabbi Abba bar Kahana said, "The removal of the ring caused more good than 48 נביאים and 7 נביאות who all tried – but did not completely succeed in returning all the Jews to Hashem, while this ring did." – *Megillah 14a*

223. וַיָּסַר הַמֶּלֶךְ אֶת טַבַּעְתּוֹ: Achashverosh hated the Jews more than Haman did, so he was so quick in giving him the signet ring – even before he got his money! – *Midrash ER*

יא. וַיֹּאמֶר הַמֶּלֶךְ לְהָמָן
הַכֶּסֶף נָתוּן לָךְ וְהָעָם
לַעֲשׂוֹת בּוֹ כַּטּוֹב
בְּעֵינֶיךָ׃

11 And the king said to Haman, "The money is given to you (yours to keep), and the nation [is yours] to do with it, as is good in your eyes (as you please.)"

224. הַכֶּסֶף נָתוּן לָךְ: Achashverosh said he did not want to get rid of the Jews for the money – and even offered to pay for the work to be done – because he believed it was the right thing to do. – *Malbim*

225. הַכֶּסֶף: The גמטריא for הַכֶּסֶף is the same as העץ. (Hinting that Haman was now earning his own gallows...) – *Midrash ER*

יב. וַיִּקָּרְאוּ סֹפְרֵי הַמֶּלֶךְ
בַּחֹדֶשׁ הָרִאשׁוֹן
בִּשְׁלוֹשָׁה עָשָׂר יוֹם בּוֹ
וַיִּכָּתֵב כְּכָל־אֲשֶׁר־צִוָּה
הָמָן אֶל
אֲחַשְׁדַּרְפְּנֵי־הַמֶּלֶךְ
וְאֶל־הַפַּחוֹת אֲשֶׁר |
עַל־מְדִינָה וּמְדִינָה
וְאֶל־שָׂרֵי עַם וָעָם
מְדִינָה וּמְדִינָה כִּכְתָבָהּ
וְעַם וָעָם כִּלְשׁוֹנוֹ בְּשֵׁם
הַמֶּלֶךְ אֲחַשְׁוֵרֹשׁ נִכְתָּב
וְנֶחְתָּם בְּטַבַּעַת הַמֶּלֶךְ׃

12 And the king's scribes were called on the first month, on its thirteenth day, and it was written, just as Haman commanded to the king's messengers and the governors of every province and to the officials of each nation; [It was written] to each province according to its script and each nation according to its language. It was written in the name of King Achashverosh and sealed with the king's [signet] ring.

226. וְאֶל־שָׂרֵי עַם וָעָם מְדִינָה וּמְדִינָה כִּכְתָבָהּ: There were a few nationalities in each of the 127 provinces. Each nationality (even within the same province) spoke their own unique language, but used the same script / writing / letters as its province. - *Malbim*

227. בַּחֹדֶשׁ הָרִאשׁוֹן בִּשְׁלוֹשָׁה עָשָׂר יוֹם בּוֹ: Bad choice for Haman. This is the day when they offered the קרבן פסח in ירושלים! - *Midrash PA*

228. וַיִּכָּתֵב כְּכָל אֲשֶׁר צִוָּה הָמָן: see Torah Temima pg. קכ-א & Me'am Loeiz for the letter.

יג. וְנִשְׁלוֹחַ סְפָרִים בְּיַד הָרָצִים אֶל־כָּל־מְדִינוֹת הַמֶּלֶךְ לְהַשְׁמִיד לַהֲרֹג וּלְאַבֵּד אֶת־כָּל־הַיְּהוּדִים מִנַּעַר וְעַד־זָקֵן טַף וְנָשִׁים בְּיוֹם אֶחָד בִּשְׁלוֹשָׁה עָשָׂר לְחֹדֶשׁ שְׁנֵים־עָשָׂר הוּא־חֹדֶשׁ אֲדָר וּשְׁלָלָם לָבוֹז׃

13 And letters were sent by runners (couriers) to all the provinces of the king: to annihilate, to kill and cause to perish - all the Jews, from young to old, children and women, on one day – on the thirteenth day of the twelfth month, which is the month of Adar, and their possessions [were] for plunder (free to all to take).

229. טַף: After the decree was sealed, Haman and his friends saw Mordechai approaching 3 school children. They came near to hear the conversation, and this is what they learned:

230. Mordechai said to the children: "פסוק לי פסוקיך" – recite for me a Possuk you learned in school today! This is what the kids replied:

231. Child #1: "אל תירא מפחד פתאום ומשואת רשעים כי תבוא" (משלי ג:כה). Have no fear of sudden terror... the destruction of the wicked is on its way!

232. Child #2: (ישעי'ה ח:י) "עוצו עצה". They can make plans – they will not succeed! Plan a plot – and it will not happen – because Hashem is with US!

233. Child #3: (שם מו:ד) "ועד זקנה" When you are old – I will be with you. When you turn white – I will sustain you, I made you, I will "carry" you, and I will sustain you and rescue you!

234. Mordechai rejoiced when he heard these encouraging words! Haman was very upset, and promised to deal (in his evil decree) with the children first! – *Midrash ER 7:13*

235. וְנָשִׁים: Women are obligated to hear the Megillah on Purim – just as men are, as they, too, were saved by the miracle. – *Megillah 4a*

236. וּשְׁלָלָם לָבוֹז: Haman was (also) very interested in the Jews' money. When the Jews fought against their enemies, it says, "ובביזה לא שלחו את ידם". The Jews did not touch the possessions of their enemies. – *Midrash*

יד. פַּתְשֶׁגֶן הַכְּתָב לְהִנָּתֵן דָּת בְּכָל־מְדִינָה וּמְדִינָה גָּלוּי לְכָל־הָעַמִּים לִהְיוֹת עֲתִדִים לַיּוֹם הַזֶּה׃

14 Copies of the writing (decree) were to be given as law in every province, revealed [clearly] to all the nations, to be ready for this day.

237. פַּתְשֶׁגֶן: - The content / theme / main idea. – *Midrash Esther Rabba 6:24*

238. גָּלוּי לְכָל־הָעַמִּים לִהְיוֹת עֲתִדִים לַיּוֹם הַזֶּה: Actually, there were two decrees sent out to all of the nations. The first one simply said to be ready for the 13th of Adar. The second one, which was sent with instructions that it shouldn't be opened until the 13th of Adar, included all of the details of the decree.

טו. הָרָצִים יָצְאוּ דְחוּפִים בִּדְבַר הַמֶּלֶךְ וְהַדָּת נִתְּנָה בְּשׁוּשַׁן הַבִּירָה וְהַמֶּלֶךְ וְהָמָן יָשְׁבוּ לִשְׁתּוֹת וְהָעִיר שׁוּשָׁן נָבוֹכָה׃

15 The runners (couriers) went out – rushed by order of the king and the law was given in Shushan the capital. And the king and Haman sat to drink, and the city of Shushan was bewildered.

239. הָרָצִים יָצְאוּ דְחוּפִים: Some people run to do good things, and some for the opposite. About those who run do to good it says והעיר שושן שמחה. About the others it says והעיר שושן נבוכה. – *Zohar*

240. וְהָעִיר שׁוּשָׁן: The Jews of the city. – *Rashi*

241. וְהָעִיר שׁוּשָׁן נָבוֹכָה: The date for the decree was set to the 13th of Adar. Once they heard of the plan, the enemies wanted to steal from the Jews right away. The officials didn't want to losc "their share" so they forbade any such stealing. Because of this, there was constant tension and fighting amongst the Shushanites. – *Midrash Esther Rabba 7:25*

242. Strange, tragic things suddenly began happening (to our enemies) after the decree went out: women would tend to their rooftop gardens and fall off, and men would dig pits and fall in! - *Midrash PA*

פרק ד: א. וּמָרְדֳּכַי יָדַע אֶת־כׇּל־אֲשֶׁר נַעֲשָׂה וַיִּקְרַע מָרְדֳּכַי אֶת־בְּגָדָיו וַיִּלְבַּשׁ שַׂק וָאֵפֶר וַיֵּצֵא בְּתוֹךְ הָעִיר וַיִּזְעַק זְעָקָה גְדוֹלָה וּמָרָה:

CHAPTER IV 1 And Mordechai knew [about] all that happened, and Mordechai tore his clothes and put on sackcloth and ash. And he went out into the midst of the city and he cried a great bitter cry.

243. וּמָרְדֳּכַי יָדַע אֶת כָּל אֲשֶׁר נַעֲשָׂה: Mordechai was informed in a dream that בני ישראל were being punished for bowing to an idol in the times of ,נבוכדנצר and for enjoying themselves from the feast of אחשורוש. – *Rashi*

244. וּמָרְדֳּכַי יָדַע: In a dream, מרדכי saw a large serpent-like creature flying over בני ישראל aiming to hurt us, and suddenly a strong wind came from all directions and shredded the snake to many pieces. From this מרדכי knew that בני ישראל would suffer for a while and be redeemed.

245. וּמָרְדֳּכַי יָדַע: בי ישמעאל related: 18,500 people ate and drank etc. from the feast. The Satan approached 'ה: "Why are You keeping בני ישראל when they are not following Your ways, nor doing תשובה?!"

ה' asked: "What about my precious Torah?"

"We, in the heavens enjoy Your Torah!" responded the Satan.

Hashem responded: "Why should I keep a nation for whom I'd done so many miracles and wonders (and they do not follow and appreciate My Torah)? Bring me a scroll on which to write the decree."

The תורה and מלאכים cried before 'ה: If בני ישראל are destroyed (ח"ו) what purpose do we have?!

The sun and moon, planets and stars also cried out to 'ה.

אליהו הנביא rushed to our forefathers and משה רבנו crying out "Until when will the fathers of the world slumber and not notice the troubles of their children?! All of creation is crying and objecting to Hashem's plan and you are quiet?!"

They asked אליהו הנביא – What is happening to בני ישראל? He answered: 'ה is threatening their destruction because they enjoyed themselves at the סעודה of אחשורוש.

Our forefathers אברהם, יצחק and יעקב responded: If they transgressed ה"s laws and the decree was signed – what could we do?

אליהו ran to משה רבנו: You are the faithful shepherd of בני ישראל! You've saved them many times from destruction! Please help them now!"

Moshe answered: "Is there any צדיק in the world below?"

"מרדכי הצדיק is there."

"Go tell him to daven from below and I will daven from above and together we will ask for רחמים from 'ה".

"Faithful shepherd! The decree was already written!"

"If it was written in cement, our prayers will be answered, if it was written in blood... what will be, will be..."

"It was written in cement!"

"Quick, go tell מרדכי!"

This is how – "...וּמָרְדֳּכַי יָדַע " - *Esther Rabba 6:13*

246. וַיִּלְבַּשׁ שַׂק וָאֵפֶר: After a צדיק's suffering come blessings, as it later says: ומרדכי יצא... בלבוש מלכות.

247. וַיִּזְעַק/וַיִּלְבַּשׁ: After donning his own sackcloth as a sign of mourning, מרדכי gathered all the Jewish Children and put sacks on them too, while they cried with him. – *Midrash Abba Guryon*

248. וַיִּזְעַק: Why did מרדכי shout? Why did he not daven silently like חנה did - and her תפילות were answered? מרדכי said to himself: when עשו shouted to יצחק, his request was answered and יצחק blessed him. Now that בני ישראל are in trouble מרדכי was going to do what he knew works!

---

249. וַיָּבוֹא עַד לִפְנֵי שַׁעַר הַמֶּלֶךְ: So that אסתר would hear about him being there [and inquire further]. – *Lekach Tov*

250. וַיָּבוֹא.. שַׁעַר הַמֶּלֶךְ... שַׁעַר הַמֶּלֶךְ: - Twice. The first time it means that מרדכי reached the שער of the real king – 'ה – the מלך מלכי המלכים. The second time refers to אחשוורוש's gate, where it was not proper to enter in sackclot. – *Agadas Esther*

251. כִּי אֵין לָבוֹא... שָׂק: When it was time for יוסף to bury his father יעקב in ארץ כנען, יוסף sent messengers to פרעה to ask his permission to leave מצרים for this purpose. Why did יוסף not go himself to פרעה? For the same reason as we see here: יוסף was mourning – and it is not "proper" to enter the king's gate while mourning. – *Megillah 15a.*

2 And he came until before the king's gate, because it is not [proper] to enter the king's gate clothed in sackcloth.

ב. וַיָּבוֹא עַד לִפְנֵי שַׁעַר־הַמֶּלֶךְ כִּי אֵין לָבוֹא אֶל־שַׁעַר הַמֶּלֶךְ בִּלְבוּשׁ שָׂק:

---

252. אֵבֶל גָּדוֹל לַיְּהוּדִים: A mourner's pain usually diminishes as time goes by. This mourning increased as time progressed, as the time for the decree was nearing. – *Esther Rabba 8:2*

253. שַׂק וָאֵפֶר יֻצַּע לָרַבִּים: All the Jews slept in sackcloth as they were mourning. - *Midrash Panim Acheirim*

3 And in every province, each place that the word of the king and his law reaches, [there was] great mourning for the Jews, and fasting and crying and lamenting; sackcloth and ash were offered to the public.

ג. וּבְכָל־מְדִינָה וּמְדִינָה מְקוֹם אֲשֶׁר דְּבַר־הַמֶּלֶךְ וְדָתוֹ מַגִּיעַ אֵבֶל גָּדוֹל לַיְּהוּדִים וְצוֹם וּבְכִי וּמִסְפֵּד שַׂק וָאֵפֶר יֻצַּע לָרַבִּים:

---

254. וַתְּשְׁלַח בְּגָדִים: אסתר wanted מרדכי to come and tell her what the Jews were mourning about, so she sent appropriate clothing for him to dress in and come to the palace. מרדכי refused the clothing, not wanting to stop davening and pleading to 'ה even for a short while, demonstrating his complete אמונה in 'ה rather than in בני אדם. – *Malbim*

4 And Esther's girls (maidens) and chamberlains came and told her [about it] and the queen was very

ד. ותבואינה (וַתָּבוֹאנָה) נַעֲרוֹת אֶסְתֵּר וְסָרִיסֶיהָ וַיַּגִּידוּ לָהּ וַתִּתְחַלְחַל הַמַּלְכָּה

מְאֹד וַתִּשְׁלַח בְּגָדִים לְהַלְבִּישׁ אֶת־מָרְדֳּכַי וּלְהָסִיר שַׂקּוֹ מֵעָלָיו וְלֹא קִבֵּל׃

afraid (terrified). And she sent clothing - to dress Mordechai, and to remove his sackcloth from upon him, but he did not accept [them].

255. וּלְהָסִיר שַׂקּוֹ מֵעָלָיו וְלֹא קִבֵּל: One who separates himself from a community that is suffering, and does not participate in their pain, loses the merit to be saved with them. One who participates in their suffering, merits to be redeemed with them. One might think that he can do what he wants in the privacy of his home, yet the walls of his house will testify about his activities. Here too, מרדכי refused to remove his sackcloth, as he participated in the suffering of בני ישראל. - *Agadas Esther*

ה. וַתִּקְרָא אֶסְתֵּר לַהֲתָךְ מִסָּרִיסֵי הַמֶּלֶךְ אֲשֶׁר הֶעֱמִיד לְפָנֶיהָ וַתְּצַוֵּהוּ עַל־מָרְדֳּכָי לָדַעַת מַה־זֶּה וְעַל־מַה־זֶּה׃

5 And Esther called Hasach, [one] of the king's chamberlains whom he had placed before her (to serve her), and she commanded him regarding Mordechai, to find out what is this and for what [reason] is [he doing] this.

256. וַתִּקְרָא אֶסְתֵּר לַהֲתָךְ: דניאל was called התך (relating to the word חתך – which means "cutting") for a few reasons. Some of them:

He was "cut off" from his greatness in the times of אחשורוש. All the laws were "cut" (decided) by his advice. - *Megillah 15a / Midrash Megillah*

257. וַתִּקְרָא אֶסְתֵּר לַהֲתָךְ: אסתר trusted התך with her confidential information (secrets). – *Malbim*

258. לָדַעַת מַה־זֶּה וְעַל־מַה־זֶּה: She wanted to find out 2 things: 1) why מרדכי was crying 2) why he refused the royal clothing. – *Targum*

259. מַה־זֶּה וְעַל־מַה־זֶּה: Were בני ישראל not being careful with the תורה which was written מזה ומזה ...? – *Megillah 15a*

260. מַה־זֶּה: Were בני ישראל not being careful with the 100 ברכות per day – which we learn from "מה ה' אלקיך שואל מעמך"? – *Rokeach (from Menachos 43b:)*

ו. וַיֵּצֵא הֲתָךְ אֶל־מָרְדֳּכָי אֶל־רְחוֹב הָעִיר אֲשֶׁר לִפְנֵי שַׁעַר־הַמֶּלֶךְ׃

6 And Hasach went out to Mordechai, to the city square that was in front of the king's gate.

261. אֶל־רְחוֹב הָעִיר: When you need to speak with another privately, make sure to meet him in a (wide) public place, like יעקב when he called רחל and לאה to the field. – *Agadas Esther*

ז. וַיַּגֶּד־לוֹ מָרְדֳּכַי אֵת כָּל־אֲשֶׁר קָרָהוּ וְאֵת ׀ פָּרָשַׁת הַכֶּסֶף אֲשֶׁר אָמַר הָמָן לִשְׁקוֹל עַל־גִּנְזֵי הַמֶּלֶךְ ביהודיים (בַּיְּהוּדִים) לְאַבְּדָם׃

7 And Mordechai told him all that had happened to him, and the explanation of the silver that Haman said (ordered) to weigh (and deposit) to the king's treasuries for the Jews - to destroy them.

262. אֵת כָּל־אֲשֶׁר קָרָהוּ: מרדכי told התך to inform אסתר that the grandson of "אֲשֶׁר קָרְךָ" the one who "chanced upon us" right after מתן תורה (and tried to "cool us off" from our inspiration from Hashem) – referring to עמלק about whom it says: אשר קרך בדרך - he is causing the trouble. - *Esther Rabba 8:5*

ח. וְאֶת־פַּתְשֶׁגֶן כְּתָב־הַדָּת אֲשֶׁר־נִתַּן בְּשׁוּשָׁן לְהַשְׁמִידָם נָתַן לוֹ לְהַרְאוֹת אֶת־אֶסְתֵּר וּלְהַגִּיד לָהּ וּלְצַוּוֹת עָלֶיהָ לָבוֹא אֶל־הַמֶּלֶךְ לְהִתְחַנֶּן־לוֹ וּלְבַקֵּשׁ מִלְּפָנָיו עַל־עַמָּהּ׃

8 And the copy of the written law (decree) that was given in Shushan to destroy them, he gave him to show Esther and to tell her [about it], and to order her to go to the king to plea to him and to request before him for her nation.

263. וּלְבַקֵּשׁ מִלְּפָנָיו עַל־עַמָּהּ: At this time, מרדכי gave אסתר permission to disclose her Jewish identity, as she had kept it secret until now. – *Lekach Tov.*

ט. וַיָּבוֹא הֲתָךְ וַיַּגֵּד לְאֶסְתֵּר אֵת דִּבְרֵי מָרְדֳּכָי׃

9 And Hasach came and told to Esther the words of Mordechai.

י. וַתֹּאמֶר אֶסְתֵּר לַהֲתָךְ וַתְּצַוֵּהוּ אֶל־מָרְדֳּכָי׃

10 And Esther said [this] to Hasach; and she ordered him to [tell] Mordechai:

יא. כָּל־עַבְדֵי הַמֶּלֶךְ וְעַם־מְדִינוֹת הַמֶּלֶךְ יֹדְעִים אֲשֶׁר כָּל־אִישׁ וְאִשָּׁה אֲשֶׁר יָבוֹא־אֶל־הַמֶּלֶךְ אֶל־הֶחָצֵר הַפְּנִימִית אֲשֶׁר לֹא־יִקָּרֵא אַחַת דָּתוֹ לְהָמִית לְבַד מֵאֲשֶׁר יוֹשִׁיט־לוֹ הַמֶּלֶךְ אֶת־שַׁרְבִיט הַזָּהָב וְחָיָה וַאֲנִי לֹא נִקְרֵאתִי לָבוֹא אֶל־הַמֶּלֶךְ זֶה שְׁלוֹשִׁים יוֹם׃

11 "All the king's servants and the people of the king's provinces know, that any man and woman who will come to the king, into the inner courtyard – who was not called [to come], his law is one; to be killed; except for whom the king extends his golden scepter, [only] he shall live. And I have not been called to come to the king for these [past] thirty days."

264. מֵאֲשֶׁר יוֹשִׁיט־לוֹ הַמֶּלֶךְ אֶת־שַׁרְבִיט הַזָּהָב וְחָיָה: 'ה saves us, בני ישראל, from our enemies in the merits of שבת and מילה. This is hinted in the posuk: "או אז יכנע לבבם הערל". Through או and אז the enemies will be subdued. או is 7 בגמטריא – hinting to שבת, and אז is בגמטריא 8 – referring to מילה. In the ראשי תבות of this פסוק we see a reference to מילה and אשה: "מֵאֲשֶׁר יוֹשִׁיט־לוֹ הַמֶּלֶךְ אֶת־שַׁרְבִיט הַזָּהָב וְחָיָה" (showing how men and women are saved through this special מצוה – even though it is only a מצוה for men). – *Midrash*

265. (The אשה here may also be referring to אסתר המלכה through whom the נס occurred – cba)

יב. וַיַּגִּידוּ לְמָרְדֳּכָי אֵת דִּבְרֵי אֶסְתֵּר׃

12 And they told [to] Mordechai the words of Esther.

266. וַיַּגִּידוּ לְמָרְדֳּכָי: Where did התך go? See next פסוק!

יג. וַיֹּאמֶר מָרְדֳּכַי לְהָשִׁיב אֶל־אֶסְתֵּר אַל־תְּדַמִּי בְנַפְשֵׁךְ לְהִמָּלֵט בֵּית־הַמֶּלֶךְ מִכָּל־הַיְּהוּדִים׃

13 And Mordechai said to reply to Esther, "Do not imagine (think to yourself) to escape in[side] the king's palace from [the fate of] all the Jews.

267. וַיֹּאמֶר מָרְדֳּכַי לְהָשִׁיב אֶל־אֶסְתֵּר: Where did התך go? When המן saw התך going back and forth (transmitting messages between מרדכי and אסתר) he killed him! From now on, the messages between מרדכי and אסתר were transmitted through רוח הקודש. *–Midrash Abba Guryon.*

יד. כִּי אִם־הַחֲרֵשׁ תַּחֲרִישִׁי בָּעֵת הַזֹּאת רֶוַח וְהַצָּלָה יַעֲמוֹד לַיְּהוּדִים מִמָּקוֹם אַחֵר

14 "For if you will be [completely] silent at this time, relief and rescue will arise for the Jews from another

268. כִּי אִם־הַחֲרֵשׁ תַּחֲרִישִׁי... מִמָּקוֹם אַחֵר: If you will be silent now, you will be silent later – in עולם הבא, without an excuse about why you didn't help save the Jewish People. Either way 'ה will save His people, the question is whether you will have the opportunity to play a role and do your part in this. *–Midrash Esther Rabba 8:6*

וְאַתְּ וּבֵית־אָבִיךְ תֹּאבֵדוּ וּמִי יוֹדֵעַ אִם־לָעֵת כָּזֹאת הִגַּעַתְּ לַמַּלְכוּת:

place, and you and your father's house will perish. And who knows if for [just such] a time like this, you reached this [position of] royalty."

269. וּמִי יוֹדֵעַ אִם־לָעֵת כָּזֹאת: Who knows if the king will even be interested in (keeping) you (as his queen – or even alive -) at this time next year – when the time of the decree arrives? – *Rashi*

270. מִמָּקוֹם אַחֵר: Their salvation will come from 'ה- Who is called "מקום". Yet the מגילה doesn't mention 'ה's Name because it was written in the kingdom of מדי ופרס and included in their royal libraries, and the חכמים were concerned that when they copy and share the story in the future, they may replace ה"s Name with a name of ע"ז. *-Lekach Tov and many others.*

271. ה"s Name is hinted in a few places like: **י**בוא **ה**מלך **ו**המן **ה**יום / כי **ה**ינוּ **ז**ה איננ**ו** שו**ה** לי / וכל **ז**ה אינני שו**ה** לי – Midrash.

272. וְאַתְּ וּבֵית־אָבִיךְ תֹּאבֵדוּ וּמִי יוֹדֵעַ אִם־לָעֵת כָּזֹאת הִגַּעַתְּ לַמַּלְכוּת: We learn from מרדכי to use both ימין מקרבת and שמאל דוחה. First מרדכי threatened harshly employing the "דוחה בשתי ידים" method, then מרדכי softened and used ימין מקרבת in saying ומי יודע...

273. וְאַתְּ וּבֵית־אָבִיךְ תֹּאבֵדוּ: Being that Mordechai was a descendant of Shaul and Esther was his cousin, she was also Shaul's descendant. Mordechai was telling her that here was her chance to correct his sin of keeping Agag alive. If she wouldn't act now, his sin could never again be corrected – and he would be "lost" forever.

טו. וַתֹּאמֶר אֶסְתֵּר לְהָשִׁיב אֶל־מָרְדֳּכָי:

15 And Esther said to reply to Mordechai:

טז. לֵךְ כְּנוֹס אֶת־כָּל־הַיְּהוּדִים הַנִּמְצְאִים בְּשׁוּשָׁן וְצוּמוּ עָלַי וְאַל־תֹּאכְלוּ וְאַל־תִּשְׁתּוּ שְׁלֹשֶׁת יָמִים לַיְלָה וָיוֹם גַּם־אֲנִי וְנַעֲרֹתַי אָצוּם כֵּן וּבְכֵן אָבוֹא אֶל־הַמֶּלֶךְ אֲשֶׁר לֹא־כַדָּת וְכַאֲשֶׁר אָבַדְתִּי אָבָדְתִּי:

16 "Go, gather all the Jews who are in Shushan, and fast for my sake, and do not eat nor drink for three days, night and day. Also I and my maidens shall fast so. And thus I shall come to the king – which is not according to the law, and if I perish, I perish."

274. לֵךְ כְּנוֹס: The main idea of a fast day is the gathering (of Jewish people to daven together to 'ה. *-Midrash Tehillim 22:5*

275. וְצוּמוּ עָלַי - וְאַל־תֹּאכְלוּ וְאַל־תִּשְׁתּוּ: Why the double expression? אסתר instructed בני ישראל of שושן too fast for her sake, that she find favor in the eyes of the king, and not eat or drink to atone for the food and drink they enjoyed at the royal feast. – *Lekach Tov*

276. שְׁלֹשֶׁת יָמִים: to cancel/nullify/counteract the three decrees; להשמיד להרוג ולאבד. – *Rokeach*

277. וְאַל־תֹּאכְלוּ וְאַל־תִּשְׁתּוּ שְׁלֹשֶׁת יָמִים לַיְלָה וָיוֹם: Some people may not survive without food and drink for 3 days straight, so this could not be what אסתר was requesting. This fast was like the יום כיפור and תשעה באב fast days in that we eat just before nightfall, and fast the rest of the night and day. – *Midrash Tehillim 22:5 & more.*

278. וּבְכֵן אָבוֹא אֶל־הַמֶּלֶךְ אֲשֶׁר לֹא־כַדָּת: The law doesn't permit me to enter. *–Rashi*

279. Until now I entered against my will, now I will go to the king willingly. *–Rashi from Midrash*

280. וְכַאֲשֶׁר אָבַדְתִּי אָבָדְתִּי: Just as I was lost (separated) from father's household, so too I will be lost to you, מרדכי, as until now I was forced to meet with אחשורוש and this time I am going willingly. *–Megillah 15a*

281. וְכַאֲשֶׁר אָבַדְתִּי אָבָדְתִּי: Just as I've been lost and separated from you מרדכי, so too I am prepared to lose my life for בני ישראל. *–Lekach Tov.*

282. לֵךְ כְּנוֹס... שְׁלֹשֶׁת יָמִים... וַיַּעֲבֹר מָרְדֳּכָי: The three days אסתר requested were the 14th, 15th and 16th of ניסן. (some say 13, 14 & 15). מרדכי responded to אסתר that this includes the first day of פסח – to which אסתר responded: (My dear elderly cousin) What use is פסח without the Jews?! That is when "וַיַּעֲבֹר מָרְדֳּכָי" – that מרדכי "exchanged/replaced – העביר" the first day of פסח with a fast day! מרדכי gathered all the little ones, had them fast, cry out to 'ה and learn תורה.

283. At the same time אסתר was so concerned with the decree, she wore clothing of mourning, fasted and davened to 'ה: ...Eternal Master of the universe, please help Your orphaned servant, wandering from home to home. Here I am pleading with You from window to window of אחשורוש's palace. Now, please help Your poor servant and save Your flock from these threatening enemies. We have no hope aside from You, Father of orphans, please help this orphan – me – who trusts in You - to find mercy before this fearful man and subdue him before me... *–Esther Rabba 8:7*

---

17 So Mordecai passed and did according to all that Esther had commanded him.

יז. וַיַּעֲבֹר מָרְדֳּכָי וַיַּעַשׂ כְּכֹל אֲשֶׁר צִוְּתָה עָלָיו אֶסְתֵּר:

פרק ה: א. וַיְהִי | בַּיּוֹם הַשְּׁלִישִׁי וַתִּלְבַּשׁ אֶסְתֵּר מַלְכוּת וַתַּעֲמֹד בַּחֲצַר בֵּית הַמֶּלֶךְ הַפְּנִימִית נֹכַח בֵּית הַמֶּלֶךְ וְהַמֶּלֶךְ יוֹשֵׁב עַל כִּסֵּא מַלְכוּתוֹ בְּבֵית הַמַּלְכוּת נֹכַח פֶּתַח הַבָּיִת:

CHAPTER V: 1. Now it came to pass on the third day that Esther clothed herself regally, and she stood in the inner court of the king's house, opposite the king's house, and the king was sitting on his royal throne in the royal palace, opposite the entrance of the house.

284. וַיְהִי בַּיּוֹם הַשְּׁלִישִׁי: The 3rd day was the 16th day of ניסן. –*Rashi*

285. The 3rd day was the 15th of ניסן, because the 3 days began on the 13th of ניסן, when the decrees were sent out. –*Megillah 16a, Midrash*

286. How did Rashi come up with a different calculation for the 3 days than the Gemara and the Midrash? They all agreed that the decrees were sent out on the 13th of ניסן, but their opinions differ on how Mordechai found out about it. Rashi believes that all of the information was given over to Mordechai in a dream that night. Therefore, the count could not have started until the next day (the 14th). The other opinions state that Mordechai was told about the decree through Ruach Hakodesh as soon as it was sent out (on the 13th), so the 3 days began that day. –*The Rebbe*

287. She was successful on the third day in the merit of the third day that the Jews were camped out by Har Sinai and received the Torah, and the third day in Avraham's travels when he spotted the mountain for Akeidas Yitzchak. –Bereishis Rabba 56:1

288. וַתִּלְבַּשׁ אֶסְתֵּר מַלְכוּת: She wore royal clothing. –*Rashi*

289. She was completely surrounded by רוח הקודש. –*Megillah 15a*

290. וַתַּעֲמֹד: Hashem orchestrated that at that moment, Achashverosh wasn't busy and was just watching who was coming and going in the inner court. –*Alshich*

ב. וַיְהִי כִרְאוֹת הַמֶּלֶךְ אֶת אֶסְתֵּר הַמַּלְכָּה עֹמֶדֶת בֶּחָצֵר נָשְׂאָה חֵן בְּעֵינָיו וַיּוֹשֶׁט הַמֶּלֶךְ לְאֶסְתֵּר אֶת שַׁרְבִיט הַזָּהָב אֲשֶׁר בְּיָדוֹ וַתִּקְרַב אֶסְתֵּר וַתִּגַּע בְּרֹאשׁ הַשַּׁרְבִיט:

2. And it came to pass when the king saw Queen Esther standing in the court that she won favor in his eyes, and the king extended to Esther the golden scepter that was in his hand, and Esther approached and touched the end of the scepter.

291. וַיְהִי: What came to pass? That the king saw Esther and forgot about the decree of not coming in unannounced. - *Malbim*

292. וַיּוֹשֶׁט הַמֶּלֶךְ: Hashem sent an angel to stretch out the scepter, so Esther wasn't under Achashverosh's control anymore. –*Eshkol Hasofer*

293. This was the beginning of the redemption of the Jewish people; the heavenly decree had been annulled. –*The Rebbe*

294. וַתִּגַּע בְּרֹאשׁ הַשַּׁרְבִיט: Esther didn't have the strength to go forward and touch the scepter, so the Angel Michael helped her. –*Midrash Panim Acheirim 56b*

ג. וַיֹּאמֶר לָהּ הַמֶּלֶךְ מַה לָּךְ אֶסְתֵּר הַמַּלְכָּה וּמַה בַּקָּשָׁתֵךְ עַד חֲצִי הַמַּלְכוּת וְיִנָּתֵן לָךְ:

3. And the king said to her, "What concerns you, Queen Esther, and what is your petition? Even to half the kingdom, it will be given to you."

295. וַיֹּאמֶר לָהּ הַמֶּלֶךְ מַה לָּךְ: Achashverosh knew her request must be something big because she had just risked her life to come. That's why he offers her to be ruler over half of his kingdom. – *Alshich*

296. עַד חֲצִי הַמַּלְכוּת: He was willing to give her everything up to a certain point in the middle of his kingdom, which was the בית המקדש. -*Rashi*

297. יָבוֹא הַמֶּלֶךְ וְהָמָן הַיּוֹם: Why did Esther also invite Haman to this feast? She wanted to make the king and the officers jealous of him – she wanted the king to think that Haman wanted to marry her, so he would want to kill him. *– Rashi*

298. Haman was invited to Esther's feast so that he would be caught by surprise and would not have the opportunity to think of a conspiracy. Another reason is because she wanted Achashverosh to act immediately when he got angry, and not give him the chance to change his mind. *– Megilla 15b*

299. יָבוֹא הַמֶּלֶךְ וְהָמָן הַיּוֹם: The first letters of these four words spell out Hashem's name yud-hei-vav-hei.
–Rabbeinu Bachyai ben Asher

300. Why didn't Esther just ask right then and there to punish Haman? She wanted to make him "greater" before she brought him down, so she invited him to two banquets. By the second one, she had treated him as an equal to the king, and now his downfall would be more powerful and a bigger deal than it would have been before. *– The Rebbe*

4. And Esther said, "If it pleases the king, let the king and Haman come today to the banquet that I have prepared for him."

ד. וַתֹּאמֶר אֶסְתֵּר אִם עַל הַמֶּלֶךְ טוֹב יָבוֹא הַמֶּלֶךְ וְהָמָן הַיּוֹם אֶל הַמִּשְׁתֶּה אֲשֶׁר עָשִׂיתִי לוֹ:

---

301. מַהֲרוּ אֶת הָמָן: The king thought Haman might leave, so he said to hurry. The words וַיָּבֹא הַמֶּלֶךְ וְהָמָן are still part of this possuk to show how fast they came to the party. *–Megillas Sesarim*

5 And the king said, "Rush Haman to do Esther's bidding," and the king and Haman came to the banquet that Esther had prepared.

ה. וַיֹּאמֶר הַמֶּלֶךְ מַהֲרוּ אֶת הָמָן לַעֲשׂוֹת אֶת דְּבַר אֶסְתֵּר וַיָּבֹא הַמֶּלֶךְ וְהָמָן אֶל הַמִּשְׁתֶּה אֲשֶׁר עָשְׂתָה אֶסְתֵּר:

---

302. בְּמִשְׁתֵּה הַיַּיִן: Why was a key factor in the miracle of Purim brought about through wine and why do we celebrate with wine? Wine represents something that comes froms squeezing. Sometimes a Jew goes through a quick squeeze right before the greatest moment is about the come. *– The Rebbe*

303. מַה־שְּׁאֵלָתֵךְ..וּמַה־בַּקָּשָׁתֵךְ: "What is your request... and what is your petition?" Request refers to something personal, and petition to something on behalf of others. *– Vilna Goan*

6 And the king said to Esther during the wine banquet, "What is your petition? It shall be granted you. And what is your request? Even up to half the kingdom, it shall be fulfilled."

ו. וַיֹּאמֶר הַמֶּלֶךְ לְאֶסְתֵּר בְּמִשְׁתֵּה הַיַּיִן מַה שְּׁאֵלָתֵךְ וְיִנָּתֵן לָךְ וּמַה בַּקָּשָׁתֵךְ עַד חֲצִי הַמַּלְכוּת וְתֵעָשׂ:

---

304. שְׁאֵלָתִי וּבַקָּשָׁתִי: "It is not for half the kingdom, nor money, nor the rebuilding of the Bais Hamikdash..." *–Targum*

7. Esther replied and said, "My petition and my request [are as follows]:

ז. וַתַּעַן אֶסְתֵּר וַתֹּאמַר שְׁאֵלָתִי וּבַקָּשָׁתִי:

ח. אִם מָצָאתִי חֵן בְּעֵינֵי הַמֶּלֶךְ וְאִם עַל הַמֶּלֶךְ טוֹב לָתֵת אֶת שְׁאֵלָתִי וְלַעֲשׂוֹת אֶת בַּקָּשָׁתִי יָבוֹא הַמֶּלֶךְ וְהָמָן אֶל הַמִּשְׁתֶּה אֲשֶׁר אֶעֱשֶׂה לָהֶם וּמָחָר אֶעֱשֶׂה כִּדְבַר הַמֶּלֶךְ:

8. If I have found favor in the king's eyes, and if it pleases the king to grant my petition and to fulfill my request, let the king and Haman come to the banquet that I will make for them, and tomorrow I will do the king's bidding."

305. אֲשֶׁר אֶעֱשֶׂה לָהֶם: Esther made Achashverosh and Haman sound equal by saying "them" and not saying their names separately, to make Achashverosh jealous. – *M'nos Halevi*

306. וּמָחָר אֶעֱשֶׂה כִּדְבַר הַמֶּלֶךְ: Tomorrow, I will do what you have been asking me to do the whole time- I will reveal my lineage to you. – *Rashi*

ט. וַיֵּצֵא הָמָן בַּיּוֹם הַהוּא שָׂמֵחַ וְטוֹב לֵב וְכִרְאוֹת הָמָן אֶת מָרְדֳּכַי בְּשַׁעַר הַמֶּלֶךְ וְלֹא קָם וְלֹא זָע מִמֶּנּוּ וַיִּמָּלֵא הָמָן עַל מָרְדֳּכַי חֵמָה:

9. And Haman went out on that day, happy and with a cheerful heart, but when Haman saw Mordechai in the king's gate, and he neither rose nor stirred because of him, Haman was filled with wrath against Mordechai.

307. שָׂמֵחַ וְטוֹב לֵב: Happy, because of the honor he was given, and with a cheerful heart, because of the good food. Until then, Haman had been uncertain about his friendship with Queen Esther. After this party, however, he was very confident and happy, and therefore not suspecting of anything against him. – *M'nos Halevi*

308. עַל מָרְדֳּכַי חֵמָה: This was the first time Haman saw Mordechai since the decree against the Jews. And this time, "וְלֹא זָע מִמֶּנּוּ" – Mordechai didn't even move, let alone bow. He completely ignored Haman. This was too much for him to swallow, and he was ready to kill Mordechai then. – *Malbim, Alshich.*

י. וַיִּתְאַפַּק הָמָן וַיָּבוֹא אֶל בֵּיתוֹ וַיִּשְׁלַח וַיָּבֵא אֶת אֹהֲבָיו וְאֶת זֶרֶשׁ אִשְׁתּוֹ:

10. But Haman restrained himself, and he came home, and he sent and brought his friends and Zeresh his wife.

309. וַיִּתְאַפַּק הָמָן: He was afraid to take revenge without the king's permission. – *Rashi*

310. וְאֶת זֶרֶשׁ אִשְׁתּוֹ: Zeresh was the only one able to give him cruel enough advice. She said that the way to get rid of Mordechai was by punishing him in a way no Jew was punished before. Chananya was sawved from a fire, Daniel was saved from lions, Yosef was saved from prison, etc... Hanging Mordechai would be the only way it would work, because no Jew had been saved from the gallows yet. – *Midrash*

יא. וַיְסַפֵּר לָהֶם הָמָן אֶת כְּבוֹד עָשְׁרוֹ וְרֹב בָּנָיו וְאֵת כָּל אֲשֶׁר גִּדְּלוֹ הַמֶּלֶךְ וְאֵת אֲשֶׁר נִשְּׂאוֹ עַל הַשָּׂרִים וְעַבְדֵי הַמֶּלֶךְ:

11. And Haman recounted to them the glory of his riches and the multitude of his sons, and all [the ways] that the king had promoted him and that he had exalted him over the princes and the king's servants.

311. אֶת כְּבוֹד עָשְׁרוֹ: Three things make a man happy: wealth, children, and honor. Haman wanted to prove he had these three things – glory of his riches, ten sons, and the honor the king and queen had given him. All these things went away soon after: his money went to honor Mordechai, his ten sons were hanged with him, and the king and queen turned against him. – *Alshich*

312. Mordechai's good name was more valuable than Haman's riches. –*Shemos Rabba 33:5*

יב. וַיֹּאמֶר הָמָן אַף לֹא הֵבִיאָה אֶסְתֵּר הַמַּלְכָּה עִם הַמֶּלֶךְ אֶל הַמִּשְׁתֶּה אֲשֶׁר עָשָׂתָה כִּי אִם אוֹתִי וְגַם לְמָחָר אֲנִי קָרוּא לָהּ עִם הַמֶּלֶךְ:

12. And Haman said, "Esther did not even bring [anyone] to the party that she made, except me, and tomorrow, too, I am invited to her with the king.

313. אַף: Also means anger. Four biblical characters began in anger and ended in anger: The נחש, Pharoah's baker, Korach's followers, and Haman. -

314. כִּי אִם אוֹתִי: The main reason for his pride was that Esther invited him to her party and not Mordechai. – *Alshich*

יג. וְכָל זֶה אֵינֶנּוּ שֹׁוֶה לִי בְּכָל עֵת אֲשֶׁר אֲנִי רֹאֶה אֶת מָרְדֳּכַי הַיְּהוּדִי יוֹשֵׁב בְּשַׁעַר הַמֶּלֶךְ:

13. But all this is worth nothing to me, every time I see Mordechai the Jew sitting in the king's gate."

315. בְּכָל עֵת: Whenever Mordechai would see Haman, Mordechai would show Haman his shoe, on which it was written that Haman had sold himself as a slave to Mordechai – *Rashi*

316. יוֹשֵׁב בְּשַׁעַר הַמֶּלֶךְ: Haman wanted to make it seem he was bothered by Mordechai sitting by the palace. It was a place of honor he thought Mordechai was unworthy of. Really though, he was just bothered by Mordechai's existence. – *Me'am Loez*

יד. וַתֹּאמֶר לוֹ זֶרֶשׁ אִשְׁתּוֹ וְכָל אֹהֲבָיו יַעֲשׂוּ עֵץ גָּבֹהַּ חֲמִשִּׁים אַמָּה וּבַבֹּקֶר | אֱמֹר לַמֶּלֶךְ וְיִתְלוּ אֶת מָרְדֳּכַי עָלָיו וּבֹא עִם הַמֶּלֶךְ אֶל הַמִּשְׁתֶּה שָׂמֵחַ וַיִּיטַב הַדָּבָר לִפְנֵי הָמָן וַיַּעַשׂ הָעֵץ:

14 And Zeresh his wife and all his friends said, "Let them make a gallows fifty cubits high, and in the morning say to the king that they should hang Mordechai on it, and go to the king to the banquet joyfully." The matter pleased Haman, and he made the gallows.

317. עֵץ גָּבֹהַּ חֲמִשִּׁים אַמָּה: Haman raised himself to be able to receive influence from the 50th level of purity. The miracle was that even though this level is higher than nature, he was still hung regardless. – *The Rebbe*

318. עֵץ גָּבֹהַּ חֲמִשִּׁים אַמָּה: Haman looked all over for a 50 gallow(feet) tree, but couldn't find one. His son was a governor of the Mt. Ararat area, the mountain that Noach's Ark rested on, and got him a 50-foot wooden board from the boat. *-Midrash Abba Gorion*

319. יַעֲשׂוּ עֵץ: If Haman would kill Mordechai because of their private fight it wouldn't have been good for Haman's reputation. Instead, his wife suggested hanging him, as they used to punish people who rebelled against the king. This way it would seem that Mordechai had been punished by King Achashverosh as state law, and Haman would keep his honor intact. *-Malbim*

320. וַיַּעַשׂ הָעֵץ: What kind of tree was the gallows made from? All the trees offered themselves for Haman to be hanged on them– the fig tree because of the first fruits, bikkurim. The pomegranate tree because the Jewish nation is full of good deeds like the seeds of pomegranates. The citron tree because of the esrog. The fir trees, because the Mishkan was built from them. And it went on... until the thorn offered itself: "I don't have anything special, except that a thorn should be hanged on a thorn. And so it was. *-Midrash*

321. וַיַּעַשׂ הָעֵץ: After Haman built the tree he went to Mordechai and found him with his students studying and crying. Haman counted 22,000. He threw chains on top of them, appointed guards to watch them and said, "Tomorrow these children will die before I hang Mordechai." The mothers of the children came and begged their kids to eat and drink so they wouldn't die of hunger. The kids put their hands on their holy books and said "By the life of Mordechai our teacher, we won't eat or drink!" They then broke out into thunderous cries. Their cries reached the heavens and Hashem asked, "What's the sound... coming from earth?" Moshe answered Hashem, ...They're your children whom the enemy is about to destroy." Hashem took the decree and smashed it and disturbed Achashverosh's sleep. So continues the Megilla, בַּלַּיְלָה הַהוּא.

פרק ו: א. בַּלַּיְלָה הַהוּא נָדְדָה שְׁנַת הַמֶּלֶךְ וַיֹּאמֶר לְהָבִיא אֶת־סֵפֶר הַזִּכְרֹנוֹת דִּבְרֵי הַיָּמִים וַיִּהְיוּ נִקְרָאִים לִפְנֵי הַמֶּלֶךְ׃

CHAPTER VI 1. On that night, the king's sleep was disturbed. And he said (ordered) to bring the book of records, the chronicles, and they were (would be) read before the king.

322. בַּלַּיְלָה הַהוּא: The reader of the Megilla raises his voice during these words to represent what Hashem did at that time, calling out to the most distant Jews to return. –*The Rebbe*

323. נָדְדָה שְׁנַת הַמֶּלֶךְ: Hashem, the King of all Kings, could not sleep. But when does Hashem sleep? He doesn't. Sleep represents a level of not being fully aware, or not present. When the Jews are in a time of *golut*, exile, it's considered as if Hashem is sleeping; because we are not fully aware of Hashem in our lives. Now, Hashem's sleep was being disturbed – this was the beginning of the *geula*, redemption, for the Jewish people. -*Midrash* and *Chassidus*

324. Achashverosh was worried because Esther invited Haman to her party. He thought they were ganging up against him and would try to overthrow the throne. Thinking of his friends, Achashverosh was sure someone would tell him of the plan, if there was one... but, if someone was upset at him, they might help them, not him! So he ordered to have the chronicles read to see if he owed anyone a favor who might want revenge. -*Rashi*

325. The Angel Gavriel picked Achashverosh up and threw him on the ground in middle of his sleep and screamed at him, "Get up and reward the one who deserves reward!" –*Midrash Abba Gurion*

326. Achashverosh had a dream that Haman was about to kill him. He woke up in fright, and asked his scribes to read him the book of chronicles. They read him the story of Mordechai saving the king from a plot to poison him, and then he was informed that Haman was standing in the courtyard. Achashverosh thought his dream was coming true! –*Esther Rabba*

327. The sleep of our forefathers in Me'aras Hamachpeila was disturbed. -*Midrash*

ב. וַיִּמָּצֵא כָתוּב אֲשֶׁר הִגִּיד מָרְדֳּכַי עַל־בִּגְתָנָא וָתֶרֶשׁ שְׁנֵי סָרִיסֵי הַמֶּלֶךְ מִשֹּׁמְרֵי הַסַּף אֲשֶׁר בִּקְשׁוּ לִשְׁלֹחַ יָד בַּמֶּלֶךְ אֲחַשְׁוֵרוֹשׁ׃

2. And it was found written that Mordechai had informed on Bigsan and Seresh, two chamberlains of the king, from the guards of the threshold (entrance), who had sought (planned) to send their hand against (assassinate) the King Achashverosh.

328. וַיִּמָּצֵא כָתוּב: "It was found written" can be understood as it was written itself, or in a miraculous way. -*Meam Lo'ez*

329. Right when Haman was coming to ask Achashverosh to hang Mordechai, Hashem caused the servants to read the story of Mordechai saving the king's life. -*Malbim*

330. עַל־בִּגְתָנָא וָתֶרֶשׁ: Why does Bigsan have an א at the end of his name here, unlike before, in Perek Beis? Haman's sons were the scribes who recorded the event with Mordechai, and they wanted to make it seem less significant. They wrote: בִּגְתָן או תֶרֶשׁ, Bigsan *or* Seresh, implying that Mordechai suspected an innocent man. When the attendants read it out to Achashverosh, however, the word או seperated, now reading Bigsan *and* Seresh. -*Alshich, M'nos Halevi*

ג. וַיֹּאמֶר הַמֶּלֶךְ מַה־נַּעֲשָׂה יְקָר וּגְדוּלָּה לְמָרְדֳּכַי עַל־זֶה וַיֹּאמְרוּ נַעֲרֵי הַמֶּלֶךְ מְשָׁרְתָיו

3. And the king said; "What honor and greatness has been done (rewarded) to

331. מַה־נַּעֲשָׂה יְקָר וּגְדוּלָּה: What honor- to make known that Mordechai saved my life, and what dignity- did I make him higher than all other ministers? -*Malbim*

332. לֹא־נַעֲשָׂה עִמּוֹ דָּבָר: His servants said this not because they liked Mordechai, but because they hated Haman. *-Talmud*	Mordechai for this?" And the king's young servants said "Nothing was done with (for) him."	לֹא־נַעֲשָׂה עִמּוֹ דָּבָר׃
333. מִי בֶחָצֵר: Achashverosh had just woken up from his dream, that Haman was about to kill him. When he heard Haman himself was in his courtyard, he screamed out, "My dream is coming true!" *-Midrash Abba Gorion*	4 And the king said; "Who is in the courtyard?" And Haman had come to the outer courtyard of the king's palace to tell the king to hang Mordechai on the gallows that he had prepared for him.	ד. וַיֹּאמֶר הַמֶּלֶךְ מִי בֶחָצֵר וְהָמָן בָּא לַחֲצַר בֵּית־הַמֶּלֶךְ הַחִיצוֹנָה לֵאמֹר לַמֶּלֶךְ לִתְלוֹת אֶת־מָרְדֳּכַי עַל־הָעֵץ אֲשֶׁר־הֵכִין לוֹ׃
	5 And the king's servants said to him; "Behold Haman is standing in the courtyard." And the king said, "Let him come."	ה. וַיֹּאמְרוּ נַעֲרֵי הַמֶּלֶךְ אֵלָיו הִנֵּה הָמָן עֹמֵד בֶּחָצֵר וַיֹּאמֶר הַמֶּלֶךְ יָבוֹא׃
334. בִּיקָרוֹ: In possuk ג Achashverosh says - יְקָר וּגְדוּלָּה "the man whom he wants to give honor and greatness", and in this possuk he tells Haman "the man whom he wishes to honor." Why did he leave out the greatness? Because Haman knew he already had all the greatness possible, but honor there is no limit to. This way Haman will think the man whom the king is talking about is he. *-Vilna Gaon*	6 And Haman came, and the king said to him, "What [do you recommend] to do, for a man whom the king desires his honor (- for him to have honor). And Haman said in his heart (to himself), "To whom would the king wish to [cause] honor more than me?"	ו. וַיָּבוֹא הָמָן וַיֹּאמֶר לוֹ הַמֶּלֶךְ מַה־לַּעֲשׂוֹת בָּאִישׁ אֲשֶׁר הַמֶּלֶךְ חָפֵץ בִּיקָרוֹ וַיֹּאמֶר הָמָן בְּלִבּוֹ לְמִי יַחְפֹּץ הַמֶּלֶךְ לַעֲשׂוֹת יְקָר יוֹתֵר מִמֶּנִּי׃
	7 And Haman said to the king, "[For] a man whom the king wishes his honor;	ז. וַיֹּאמֶר הָמָן אֶל־הַמֶּלֶךְ אִישׁ אֲשֶׁר הַמֶּלֶךְ חָפֵץ בִּיקָרוֹ׃
	8 "Let them bring a royal garment that the king has worn, and a horse that the king rode upon, and on whose head the royal crown has been placed.	ח. יָבִיאוּ לְבוּשׁ מַלְכוּת אֲשֶׁר לָבַשׁ־בּוֹ הַמֶּלֶךְ וְסוּס אֲשֶׁר רָכַב עָלָיו הַמֶּלֶךְ וַאֲשֶׁר נִתַּן כֶּתֶר מַלְכוּת בְּרֹאשׁוֹ׃

ט. וְנָתוֹן הַלְּבוּשׁ וְהַסּוּס עַל־יַד־אִישׁ מִשָּׂרֵי הַמֶּלֶךְ הַפַּרְתְּמִים וְהִלְבִּישׁוּ אֶת־הָאִישׁ אֲשֶׁר הַמֶּלֶךְ חָפֵץ בִּיקָרוֹ וְהִרְכִּיבֻהוּ עַל־הַסּוּס בִּרְחוֹב הָעִיר וְקָרְאוּ לְפָנָיו כָּכָה יֵעָשֶׂה לָאִישׁ אֲשֶׁר הַמֶּלֶךְ חָפֵץ בִּיקָרוֹ:

9 "And the garment and the horse shall be given into the hands of one of the king's noble ministers, and they shall dress the man whom the king wishes to honor, and they shall lead him on the horse in the city square, and they shall call out (proclaim) before him, 'So shall be done for the man whom the king desires his honor."

335. וְהִלְבִּישׁוּ אֶת הָאִישׁ אֲשֶׁר הַמֶּלֶךְ חָפֵץ בִּיקָרוֹ: Haman left out the crown, because he saw that Achashverosh became jealous when he said it the first time. *-Rashi*

336. וְקָרְאוּ לְפָנָיו: Haman suggested this to calm the king's jealousy – that this man, royally robed and riding the king's horse, should call out that all the honor is due to the king. *-Rav Amara*

י. וַיֹּאמֶר הַמֶּלֶךְ לְהָמָן מַהֵר קַח אֶת־הַלְּבוּשׁ וְאֶת־הַסּוּס כַּאֲשֶׁר דִּבַּרְתָּ וַעֲשֵׂה־כֵן לְמָרְדֳּכַי הַיְּהוּדִי הַיּוֹשֵׁב בְּשַׁעַר הַמֶּלֶךְ אַל־תַּפֵּל דָּבָר מִכֹּל אֲשֶׁר דִּבַּרְתָּ:

10 And The king said to Haman, "Hurry! Take the garment and the horse just as you spoke, and do so for Mordechai the Jew who sits at the king's gate. Do not leave out a thing from all that you spoke."

337. מַהֵר: Achashverosh wanted Haman to carry out the plan quickly, before his dinner party with Esther. If she'll ask him why Mordechai wasn't rightly rewarded, he'd be able to tell her the mistake was fixed. *-Yosef Lekach*

338. לְמָרְדֳּכַי הַיְּהוּדִי הַיּוֹשֵׁב בְּשַׁעַר הַמֶּלֶךְ: "For Mordechai" – and Haman said, which one? "The Jew" – and Haman said there are many Jews named Mordechai. "Who sits at the king's gate" – and Haman had no choice but to listen.

339. אַל־תַּפֵּל דָּבָר: Human nature is that when we do something we don't want to, we tend to "forget" some details. Achashverosh wanted to make sure Haman wouldn't do that. *-Me'am Loez*

יא. וַיִּקַּח הָמָן אֶת־הַלְּבוּשׁ וְאֶת־הַסּוּס וַיַּלְבֵּשׁ אֶת־מָרְדֳּכָי וַיַּרְכִּיבֵהוּ בִּרְחוֹב הָעִיר וַיִּקְרָא לְפָנָיו כָּכָה יֵעָשֶׂה לָאִישׁ אֲשֶׁר הַמֶּלֶךְ חָפֵץ בִּיקָרוֹ:

11 And Haman took the garment and the horse and he dressed Mordechai, and he led him in the city square and he called out (proclaimed) before him: 'So shall be done for the man whom the king desires his honor.

340. וַיִּקַּח הָמָן אֶת־הַלְּבוּשׁ וְאֶת־הַסּוּס: When Haman came to get Mordechai, Mordechai was afraid. He told his students to run away because Haman was coming to destroy him. His students replied: "If you die, we die with you." Mordechai said, "If so, daven and we'll be saved." When they finished davening they sat down to learn the laws of sefiras ha'omer because that day was the first day of the Omer had the Bais Hamikdash been standing. When Haman came to them he asked what they were learning, and they told him and showed him how small the Omer would be. Haman asked, "Was this sacrifice made of gold or silver?" And they replied, "Neither gold or silver. It was a tenth of an ephah (a measurement) of barley." Haman then told the children, "Your tenth was victorious over my ten thousand talents of silver!" The children learning a part of Torah that wasn't relevant at the time because the Bais Hamikdash wasn't standing, showed that Torah is timeless and not limited to whatever situation we are in. This proved that the Jewish nation is eternal, and brought about the miracle for them at that time.

341. וַיַּרְכִּיבֵהוּ בִּרְחוֹב הָעִיר: Haman's daughter, watching the parade from her window way above, thought the man leading the horse was Mordechai and the rider was her father. So when the procession passed by she tossed smelly garbage at who she thought was Mordechai. Haman looked up, when she saw what she did, she jumped out of the high window. *-Megilla 16a*

---

342. וַיָּשָׁב מָרְדֳּכַי אֶל־שַׁעַר הַמֶּלֶךְ: Mordechai returned to mourning, in sackcloth and ashes. *-Midrash*

343. He went back to the children and told them he had wanted to ask Achashverosh to save the Jews as a reward for saving his life. Now that he had just been rewarded, there was no one to rely on except for Hashem. *-Me'am Loez*

344. אָבֵל וַחֲפוּי רֹאשׁ: Mourning, because his daughter had just committed suicide, and with a covered head, the shame he had just been through. *-Megilla 16a*

12 And Mordechai returned to the king's gate and Haman was rushed to his house, mourning and with a covered head.

יב. וַיָּשָׁב מָרְדֳּכַי אֶל־שַׁעַר הַמֶּלֶךְ וְהָמָן נִדְחַף אֶל־בֵּיתוֹ אָבֵל וַחֲפוּי רֹאשׁ:

חֲכָמָיו: His advisors. First they are called his friends, and then they are called his wise men. When he started consulting them they considered themselves his friends, but as soon as he lost some of his power their friendship also went down. *-Sfas Emes*

Zeresh said: "This nation is compared to the stars and the sand. When they fall, they fall all the way to the sand. And when they rise, they rise all the way to the sky and the stars." *-Rashi*

לֹא־תוּכַל לוֹ: Why are they telling him that he won't succeed? Doesn't seem like encouraging or helpful advice. His advisors were smart - they knew that once Mordechai was rewarded it only was the start of more good for him. Haman's only hope, then, would be to tear down the gallows and beg forgiveness from Mordechai – "you will certainly fall before him." *-Yosef Lekach, Vilna Gaon*

13 And Haman told to Zeresh his wife and to all his friends [about] all that happened to him. And his wise men and Zeresh his wife said to him, "If Mordechai - before whom you have begun to fall - is of Jewish seed (descent) - you will not overcome (succeed against) him, but you will certainly fall before him."

יג. וַיְסַפֵּר הָמָן לְזֶרֶשׁ אִשְׁתּוֹ וּלְכָל־אֹהֲבָיו אֵת כָּל־אֲשֶׁר קָרָהוּ וַיֹּאמְרוּ לוֹ חֲכָמָיו וְזֶרֶשׁ אִשְׁתּוֹ אִם מִזֶּרַע הַיְּהוּדִים מָרְדֳּכַי אֲשֶׁר הַחִלּוֹתָ לִנְפֹּל לְפָנָיו לֹא־תוּכַל לוֹ כִּי־נָפוֹל תִּפּוֹל לְפָנָיו:

---

345. עוֹדָם מְדַבְּרִים עִמּוֹ: Haman was thinking about taking down the gallows when the gaurds came to take him to the party. This was because Haman was meant to be hanged on his own gallows. *-Vilna Gaon*

14. [While] they were still speaking with him - the chamberlains of the king arrived, and they rushed to bring Haman to the feast that Esther had made.

יד. עוֹדָם מְדַבְּרִים עִמּוֹ וְסָרִיסֵי הַמֶּלֶךְ הִגִּיעוּ וַיַּבְהִלוּ לְהָבִיא אֶת־הָמָן אֶל־הַמִּשְׁתֶּה אֲשֶׁר־עָשְׂתָה אֶסְתֵּר:

פרק ז: א. וַיָּבֹא הַמֶּלֶךְ וְהָמָן לִשְׁתּוֹת עִם־אֶסְתֵּר הַמַּלְכָּה:

CHAPTER VII: 1. And the king and Haman came to drink with Esther the Queen.

346. לִשְׁתּוֹת עִם־אֶסְתֵּר הַמַּלְכָּה: "To drink with the Queen.": Earlier, the Megilla stated "to the feast." Why does it say to drink with the Queen here? The first party was more general, a sit down meal. But once Haman was invited to the second party it became personal. Drinking is different than eating – drinking together shows on closeness. Both the king and Haman felt special being invited, and a bit jealous of the other's relationship with Esther. This was what Esther wanted to prepare for Haman's downfall. *-Ohr Chadash*

347. Now that Esther's three days of fasting were over she joined them in eating and drinking. *-Alshich*

348. Hashem made a miracle that even though Achashverosh was disturbed by his dream, the wine cheered him up, and he was ready to fulfill Esther's every wish. *-Rav Galico*

ב. וַיֹּאמֶר הַמֶּלֶךְ לְאֶסְתֵּר גַּם בַּיּוֹם הַשֵּׁנִי בְּמִשְׁתֵּה הַיַּיִן מַה־שְּׁאֵלָתֵךְ אֶסְתֵּר הַמַּלְכָּה וְתִנָּתֵן לָךְ וּמַה־בַּקָּשָׁתֵךְ עַד־חֲצִי הַמַּלְכוּת וְתֵעָשׂ:

2 And the king said to Esther also on the second day at the wine feast, "What is your plea, Queen Esther - it will be given to you. And what is your request? Until half the kingdom - it will be done."

349. גַּם בַּיּוֹם הַשֵּׁנִי: The king was in a good mood just as he was at the first banquet. *–Rav Galico*

350. מַה־שְּׁאֵלָתֵךְ..וּמַה־בַּקָּשָׁתֵךְ: Achashverosh was told Esther was happy about Haman's downfall so he knew he didn't have to be jealous anymore, and it was just that her request required Haman's presence. *-Alshich*

ג. וַתַּעַן אֶסְתֵּר הַמַּלְכָּה וַתֹּאמַר אִם־מָצָאתִי חֵן בְּעֵינֶיךָ הַמֶּלֶךְ וְאִם־עַל־הַמֶּלֶךְ טוֹב תִּנָּתֶן־לִי נַפְשִׁי בִּשְׁאֵלָתִי וְעַמִּי בְּבַקָּשָׁתִי:

3 And Queen Esther replied and said: "If I have found favor in your eyes, O King, and if it is good for (pleases) the King, let my soul (life) be given to me for my plea, and my people for my request.

351. בְּעֵינֶיךָ הַמֶּלֶךְ: The first "King" is referring to Hashem – Esther sent up a prayer before she asked for Achashverosh's help. *–Targum*

352. וְעַמִּי בְּבַקָּשָׁתִי: I desire no gift, only my life and the lives of my people. *–Alshich*

353. וְעַמִּי בְּבַקָּשָׁתִי: When Achashverosh heard Esther's plea, her personal request, was for her own life to be spared, he immediately said he'd do anything to save her life. She replied that her life was secondary to her request (petition), which was to save her nation. For if they were destroyed, her life wouldn't mean anything to her and she would die from despair. *–Yosef Lekach*

ד. כִּי נִמְכַּרְנוּ אֲנִי וְעַמִּי לְהַשְׁמִיד לַהֲרוֹג וּלְאַבֵּד וְאִלּוּ לַעֲבָדִים וְלִשְׁפָחוֹת נִמְכַּרְנוּ הֶחֱרַשְׁתִּי כִּי אֵין הַצָּר שֹׁוֶה בְּנֵזֶק הַמֶּלֶךְ:

4 "For we have been sold – I and my people - to be annihilated, to be killed and to perish! And if we had been sold as slaves and maidservants I would have kept silent. But the oppressor is not (calculating, valuing or) bothered by the King's loss."

354. כִּי אֵין הַצָּר שֹׁוֶה בְּנֵזֶק הַמֶּלֶךְ: He (Haman) does not care for the king's loss, for if he sought your benefit, he should have said, "Sell them for slaves and bondswomen and receive the money, or keep them to be your slaves, they and their descendants." *-Rashi*

ה. וַיֹּאמֶר֙ הַמֶּ֣לֶךְ
אֲחַשְׁוֵר֔וֹשׁ וַיֹּ֖אמֶר
לְאֶסְתֵּ֣ר הַמַּלְכָּ֑ה מִ֣י
ה֥וּא זֶה֙ וְאֵי־זֶ֣ה ה֔וּא
אֲשֶׁר־מְלָא֥וֹ לִבּ֖וֹ
לַעֲשׂ֥וֹת כֵּֽן׃

5 And King Achashverosh said [-and he said] to Queen Esther, "Who is this, and which one is he, whose heart fills him (with the chutzpa) to do so?"

355. וַיֹּאמֶר: Originally, he would speak to her by messenger, but now that he knew that she was of a royal family, he spoke to her personally. *-Rashi*

356. מִי הוּא זֶה וְאֵי־זֶה הוּא אֲשֶׁר־מְלָאוֹ לִבּוֹ לַעֲשׂוֹת כֵּן: "Who is this man and where is he right now?" He was sure it wasn't Haman. *–Lekach Tov*

357. "Who dared to do this?" This could not be something planned quickly, rather it requires much thought. *-Eshkol Hakofer*

ו. וַתֹּ֣אמֶר אֶסְתֵּ֔ר אִ֚ישׁ
צַ֣ר וְאוֹיֵ֔ב הָמָ֥ן הָרָ֖ע
הַזֶּ֑ה וְהָמָ֣ן נִבְעַ֔ת מִלִּפְנֵ֖י
הַמֶּ֥לֶךְ וְהַמַּלְכָּֽה׃

6 "And Esther said, "A man [who is] an oppressor and an enemy: This evil Haman!" And Haman was terrified before the king and the queen.

358. וְהָמָן נִבְעַת מִלִּפְנֵי הַמֶּלֶךְ וְהַמַּלְכָּה: If it was just one of them, the king or queen, Haman could have talked his way out. He could explain to the queen that he didn't know she was Jewish, and if he knew he would never had made the decree. To the king he could claim that even though Esther was Jewish, the nation was still worthless and should be killed... But before both of them, Haman couldn't excuse himself!

ז. וְהַמֶּ֜לֶךְ קָ֤ם בַּחֲמָתוֹ֙
מִמִּשְׁתֵּ֣ה הַיַּ֔יִן אֶל־גִּנַּ֖ת
הַבִּיתָ֑ן וְהָמָ֣ן עָמַ֗ד
לְבַקֵּ֤שׁ עַל־נַפְשׁוֹ֙
מֵֽאֶסְתֵּ֣ר הַמַּלְכָּ֔ה כִּ֣י
רָאָ֔ה כִּֽי־כָלְתָ֥ה אֵלָ֛יו
הָרָעָ֖ה מֵאֵ֥ת הַמֶּֽלֶךְ׃

7 And the king arose in anger from the wine feast [and went] to the palace garden. And Haman stood up to request (beg) for his life from Esther the Queen, for he saw, that the [intent to cause him] evil was decided against him – by the king.

359. בַּחֲמָתוֹ: This was part of the Master Plan - that the king left to cool down and Haman looked even worse by seemingly "attacking" the queen. *-Rav Galico*

360. מֵאֵת הַמֶּלֶךְ: From the King of the Universe. *-Midrash*

ח. וְהַמֶּ֡לֶךְ שָׁ֠ב מִגִּנַּ֨ת
הַבִּיתָ֜ן אֶל־בֵּ֣ית ׀
מִשְׁתֵּ֣ה הַיַּ֗יִן וְהָמָן֙ נֹפֵ֔ל
עַל־הַמִּטָּה֙ אֲשֶׁ֣ר אֶסְתֵּ֣ר
עָלֶ֔יהָ וַיֹּ֣אמֶר הַמֶּ֔לֶךְ
הֲ֠גַם לִכְבּ֧וֹשׁ
אֶת־הַמַּלְכָּ֛ה עִמִּ֖י בַּבָּ֑יִת
הַדָּבָ֗ר יָצָא֙ מִפִּ֣י הַמֶּ֔לֶךְ
וּפְנֵ֥י הָמָ֖ן חָפֽוּ׃

8 And the king returned from the palace garden to the wine-feast house, and Haman was falling on the couch upon which Esther was. And the king said, "[Are you] also [trying] to conquer the queen with me in the palace?!" [As soon as] the words left the king's mouth - the face of Haman was covered.

361. וְהַמֶּלֶךְ שָׁב מִגִּנַּת: Walking around the garden, Achashverosh was reminded of something else that happened in the same place - Vashti's execution! And now Haman, the same evil man who wanted to get rid of both his queens - is alone with Esther! The king rushed back. *-M'nos Halevi*

362. וּפְנֵי הָמָן חָפוּ: The servants quickly covered Haman's face so the king wouldn't have to look at his enemy. *-Ibn Ezra*

363. It was common practice in Persia to cover the face of a prisoner who was going to be killed. *-Alshich*

ט. וַיֹּ֣אמֶר חַ֠רְבוֹנָה אֶחָ֨ד
מִן־הַסָּרִיסִ֜ים לִפְנֵ֣י
הַמֶּ֗לֶךְ גַּ֣ם הִנֵּה־הָעֵ֣ץ
אֲשֶׁר־עָשָׂ֣ה הָמָ֡ן

9 And Charvonah, one of the chamberlains before the king, said, "Also, behold [there is] the gallows that Haman

364. חַרְבוֹנָה: "May Charvonah also be remembered favorably": Rabbis established this in a prayer, because it is thanks to Charvonah's quick thinking and words that Haman didn't have a chance to excuse himself. *- Purim prayer*

365. גַּם: He also committed another evil, that he prepared the gallows to hang the king's friend, who saved the king from poison. -*Rashi*	made for Mordechai, who spoke well for the King, standing at Haman's house, fifty cubits high!" And the king said "Hang him on it!"	לְמָרְדֳּכַ֞י אֲשֶׁ֧ר דִּבֶּר־ט֣וֹב עַל־הַמֶּ֗לֶךְ עֹמֵד֙ בְּבֵ֣ית הָמָ֔ן גָּבֹ֖הַּ חֲמִשִּׁ֣ים אַמָּ֑ה וַיֹּ֥אמֶר הַמֶּ֖לֶךְ תְּלֻ֥הוּ עָלָֽיו׃
366. וַחֲמַת הַמֶּלֶךְ שָׁכָכָה: Why is שָׁכָכָה spelled with two "chs" when it's usually spelled with one in the Torah? Because there were two angers calmed with Haman's hanging: The King of all Kings, Hashem's, and King Achashverosh's. -*Talmud*	10 And they hanged Haman on the gallows that he prepared for Mordechai, and the king's anger calmed.	י. וַיִּתְלוּ֙ אֶת־הָמָ֔ן עַל־הָעֵ֖ץ אֲשֶׁר־הֵכִ֣ין לְמָרְדֳּכָ֑י וַחֲמַ֥ת הַמֶּ֖לֶךְ שָׁכָֽכָה׃

פרק ח: א. בַּיּוֹם הַהוּא נָתַן הַמֶּלֶךְ אֲחַשְׁוֵרוֹשׁ לְאֶסְתֵּר הַמַּלְכָּה אֶת־בֵּית הָמָן צֹרֵר היהודיים (הַיְּהוּדִים) וּמָרְדֳּכַי בָּא לִפְנֵי הַמֶּלֶךְ כִּי־הִגִּידָה אֶסְתֵּר מַה הוּא־לָהּ:

CHAPTER VIII 1. On that day, King Achashverosh gave [to] Esther the Queen the house of Haman, oppressor of the Jews. And Mordechai came before the king, for Esther had told [the king] what he was to her (how he was related).

367. נָתַן הַמֶּלֶךְ אֲחַשְׁוֵרוֹשׁ לְאֶסְתֵּר הַמַּלְכָּה: The decree had not been taken away yet and was still in effect because the king wanted to show Mordechai and Esther that they were excluded from it. -*Alshich*

368. וּמָרְדֳּכַי בָּא לִפְנֵי הַמֶּלֶךְ: Mordechai became a prime minister to the king. - *Midrash*

ב. וַיָּסַר הַמֶּלֶךְ אֶת־טַבַּעְתּוֹ אֲשֶׁר הֶעֱבִיר מֵהָמָן וַיִּתְּנָהּ לְמָרְדֳּכָי וַתָּשֶׂם אֶסְתֵּר אֶת־מָרְדֳּכַי עַל־בֵּית הָמָן:

2 And the king removed his ring, which he had transferred from Haman - and gave it to Mordechai. And Esther put Mordechai in charge of Haman's house.

369. וַתָּשֶׂם אֶסְתֵּר אֶת־מָרְדֳּכָי: Esther appointed Mordechai as administrator over Haman's estate. She had just received it as a gift from Achashverosh so didn't want to make it obvious she wanted to give it to Mordechai. –*M'nos Halevi*

ג. וַתּוֹסֶף אֶסְתֵּר וַתְּדַבֵּר לִפְנֵי הַמֶּלֶךְ וַתִּפֹּל לִפְנֵי רַגְלָיו וַתֵּבְךְּ וַתִּתְחַנֶּן־לוֹ לְהַעֲבִיר אֶת־רָעַת הָמָן הָאֲגָגִי וְאֵת מַחֲשַׁבְתּוֹ אֲשֶׁר חָשַׁב עַל־הַיְּהוּדִים:

3 And Esther continued and she spoke [again] before the king, and she fell before his feet, and she cried and begged him to avert (remove) the evil decree of Haman the Agagi, and his thought (plot) that he had plotted against the Jews.

370. וַתּוֹסֶף אֶסְתֵּר: Mordechai was appointed as Prime Minister, but the king still didn't say anything about the decree against the Jews. This is the second time Esther risks her life and pleads for mercy. *-M'nos Halevi, Rav Galico, Yosef Lekach*

ד. וַיּוֹשֶׁט הַמֶּלֶךְ לְאֶסְתֵּר אֵת שַׁרְבִט הַזָּהָב וַתָּקָם אֶסְתֵּר וַתַּעֲמֹד לִפְנֵי הַמֶּלֶךְ:

4 And the king extended to Esther the golden scepter. And Esther arose and she stood before the king.

371. וַיּוֹשֶׁט הַמֶּלֶךְ: This was a sign of encouragement for her to speak. *-M'nos Halevi, Rav Galico, Yosef Lekach*

ה. וַתֹּאמֶר אִם־עַל־הַמֶּלֶךְ טוֹב וְאִם־מָצָאתִי חֵן לְפָנָיו וְכָשֵׁר הַדָּבָר לִפְנֵי הַמֶּלֶךְ וְטוֹבָה אֲנִי בְּעֵינָיו יִכָּתֵב לְהָשִׁיב אֶת־הַסְּפָרִים מַחֲשֶׁבֶת

5 And she said, " If it is good for (pleases) the King, and if I have found favor before him, and the matter is fitting (proper) before the King, and I am good (pleasing) in his eyes, let it be written

372. יִכָּתֵב: Let it be written - because a verbal decree would not be permanent enough. -*Maamer Mordechai*

373. לְהָשִׁיב: One opinion: to return. Esther suggested collecting all the papers Haman had sent out so it wouldn't be embarrassing to have contradicting decrees from the king. -*Malbim*

374. Another opinion: to nullify - even though it was Persian law that a decree couldn't be taken away, Esther phrased it as the law from

הָמָן בֶּן־הַמְּדָתָא הָאֲגָגִי אֲשֶׁר כָּתַב לְאַבֵּד אֶת־הַיְּהוּדִים אֲשֶׁר בְּכָל־מְדִינוֹת הַמֶּלֶךְ׃

(ordered) to return the letters [- the books containing] the plot of Haman, son of Hamdasa, the Agagi, [in] which he wrote (ordered) to cause to perish - the Jews that are in all the King's provinces.

Haman - not the king's - and then be able to be nullified. -*Yosef Lekach, M'nos Halevi*

ו. כִּי אֵיכָכָה אוּכַל וְרָאִיתִי בָּרָעָה אֲשֶׁר־יִמְצָא אֶת־עַמִּי וְאֵיכָכָה אוּכַל וְרָאִיתִי בְּאָבְדַן מוֹלַדְתִּי׃

6 "For how will I able to [tolerate and] see the evil that will find (befall) my nation? And how will I able to [tolerate and] see the destruction of my heritage?"

375. כִּי אֵיכָכָה אוּכַל וְרָאִיתִי: Esther was telling Achashverosh that her personal wellbeing was dependent on removing the decree against her nation and letting them live in peace. -*M'nos Halevi, Rav Galico, Yosef Lekach*

ז. וַיֹּאמֶר הַמֶּלֶךְ אֲחַשְׁוֵרֹשׁ לְאֶסְתֵּר הַמַּלְכָּה וּלְמָרְדֳּכַי הַיְּהוּדִי הִנֵּה בֵית־הָמָן נָתַתִּי לְאֶסְתֵּר וְאֹתוֹ תָּלוּ עַל־הָעֵץ עַל אֲשֶׁר־שָׁלַח יָדוֹ ביהודיים (בַּיְּהוּדִים)׃

7 And the King Achashverosh said to Esther the Queen and to Mordechai the Jew, "Behold, Haman's house - I have given to Esther, and they hung him on the gallows because he sent his hand against the Jews.

376. הִנֵּה בֵית־הָמָן: Behold the house of Haman, etc.: And from now on everyone will see that I desire you, and whatever you say, everyone will believe that it comes from me; therefore, you do not have to rescind them, but write other letters as you see fit. -*Rashi*

377. Don't worry about the citizens of Shushan, the word is out that Mordechai has power now. The faraway cities need to be told. -*Alshich, D'na Pashra*

ח. וְאַתֶּם כִּתְבוּ עַל־הַיְּהוּדִים כַּטּוֹב בְּעֵינֵיכֶם בְּשֵׁם הַמֶּלֶךְ וְחִתְמוּ בְּטַבַּעַת הַמֶּלֶךְ כִּי־כְתָב אֲשֶׁר־נִכְתָּב בְּשֵׁם־הַמֶּלֶךְ וְנַחְתּוֹם בְּטַבַּעַת הַמֶּלֶךְ אֵין לְהָשִׁיב׃

8 "And you write concerning the Jews as is good in your eyes (as you please) in the name of the king, and seal it with the king's ring. For a writing (order) that was written in the name of the King and was sealed with the king's ring – it is not [able] to be returned."

378. כַּטּוֹב בְּעֵינֵיכֶם: This was an amazing miracle - for the first time in history, Jews were given official permission to do what they wanted with their enemies! -*Midrash*

379. אֵין לְהָשִׁיב: It is not fitting to return a king's decree. -*Rashi*

ט. וַיִּקָּרְאוּ סֹפְרֵי־הַמֶּלֶךְ בָּעֵת־הַהִיא בַּחֹדֶשׁ הַשְּׁלִישִׁי הוּא־חֹדֶשׁ סִיוָן בִּשְׁלוֹשָׁה וְעֶשְׂרִים בּוֹ וַיִּכָּתֵב כְּכָל־אֲשֶׁר־צִוָּה מָרְדֳּכַי

9 And the king's scribes were called at that time, in the third month, which is the month of Sivan, on its twenty-third day. And it was

380. This verse describes the reversal of that which is described in 3:12, where the issuing of the decree to kill the Jews is described in almost identical words. This verse, however, contains 3 more words than its counterpart, hinting to the three days of fasting which countered the decree. -*Rokeach*

אֶל־הַיְּהוּדִים וְאֶל
הָאֲחַשְׁדַּרְפְּנִים־וְהַפַּחוֹת
וְשָׂרֵי הַמְּדִינוֹת אֲשֶׁר |
מֵהֹדּוּ וְעַד־כּוּשׁ שֶׁבַע
וְעֶשְׂרִים וּמֵאָה מְדִינָה
מְדִינָה וּמְדִינָה כִּכְתָבָהּ
וְעַם וָעָם כִּלְשֹׁנוֹ
וְאֶל־הַיְּהוּדִים כִּכְתָבָם
וְכִלְשׁוֹנָם׃

written according to all that Mordechai instructed the Jews, and the satraps, and the governors, and the ministers of the provinces [who were] from Hodu to Cush, one hundred twenty-seven provinces. [It was written to] each province according to its script and each nation according to its language, and to the Jews according to their script and their language.

381. The second decree allowing the Jews to fight back was sent two months after Haman's death. One reason is because Mordechai waited for the same messengers Haman had sent with his first decree. This was to show that even though it's contradicting the first, it's legitimate and from the king. -*Yosef Lekach*

י. וַיִּכְתֹּב בְּשֵׁם הַמֶּלֶךְ
אֲחַשְׁוֵרֹשׁ וַיַּחְתֹּם
בְּטַבַּעַת הַמֶּלֶךְ וַיִּשְׁלַח
סְפָרִים בְּיַד הָרָצִים
בַּסּוּסִים רֹכְבֵי הָרֶכֶשׁ
הָאֲחַשְׁתְּרָנִים בְּנֵי
הָרַמָּכִים׃

10 And he wrote in the name of King Achashverosh and he sealed it with the king's ring.

And he sent the letters by the runners (couriers) on horseback, riders of the swift, royal camels (?):

382. בְּיַד הָרָצִים בַּסּוּסִים: The messengers had just returned from their first mission and were tired. Mordechai therefore sent them with horses, the fastest animals, so it would reach Jews' faster. -*Vilna Gaon*

יא. אֲשֶׁר נָתַן הַמֶּלֶךְ
לַיְּהוּדִים | אֲשֶׁר
בְּכָל־עִיר־וָעִיר לְהִקָּהֵל
וְלַעֲמֹד עַל־נַפְשָׁם
לְהַשְׁמִיד וְלַהֲרֹג וּלְאַבֵּד
אֶת־כָּל־חֵיל עַם
וּמְדִינָה הַצָּרִים אֹתָם
טַף וְנָשִׁים וּשְׁלָלָם לָבוֹז׃

11 That the king had given [permission to] the Jews of every city to gather and stand up for their lives; to annihilate, kill and cause to perish, every army (force) of a nation and province that is oppressing them, [including their] children and women, and their possessions [are for the Jews] to plunder.

383. לְהִקָּהֵל: Through unity the Jews can win despite being outnumbered. -*Yosef Lekach*

384. צָרִים אֹתָם: The Jews were allowed to fight in self-defense - except for the descendants of Amalek, whom they could kill without being threatened by them.

385. וּשְׁלָלָם לָבוֹז: The Jews were given permission to take their spoils for plunder, as was written in the first letters, but "upon the spoils they did not lay their hands," for they showed everyone that it was not done for the sake of money. -*Rashi*

יב. בְּיוֹם אֶחָד
בְּכָל־מְדִינוֹת הַמֶּלֶךְ
אֲחַשְׁוֵרוֹשׁ בִּשְׁלוֹשָׁה
עָשָׂר לְחֹדֶשׁ
שְׁנֵים־עָשָׂר הוּא־חֹדֶשׁ
אֲדָר׃

12 On one day in all the provinces of King Achashverosh, on the thirteenth of the twelfth month- this is the month of Adar.

386. בְּיוֹם אֶחָד: Unlike Haman's decree, which allowed for looting the next day, Mordechai stated the self-defense, killing, and looting should be done in one day. This was showing that the Jews' fighting was only for self-defense. -*Malbim*

יג. פַּתְשֶׁגֶן הַכְּתָב לְהִנָּתֵן דָּת בְּכָל־מְדִינָה וּמְדִינָה גָּלוּי לְכָל־הָעַמִּים וְלִהְיוֹת היהודיים (הַיְּהוּדִים) עתודים (עֲתִידִים) לַיּוֹם הַזֶּה לְהִנָּקֵם מֵאֹיְבֵיהֶם׃

13 A copy of the writing (order) was to be given (proclaimed) as law in every province, clearly, to all the nations, and that the Jews be ready for that day, to exact revenge from their enemies.

יד. הָרָצִים רֹכְבֵי הָרֶכֶשׁ הָאֲחַשְׁתְּרָנִים יָצְאוּ מְבֹהָלִים וּדְחוּפִים בִּדְבַר הַמֶּלֶךְ וְהַדָּת נִתְּנָה בְּשׁוּשַׁן הַבִּירָה׃

14 The runners (couriers), riders of the royal swift camels (?), went out rushed and pressed by the king's order, and the law was given (proclaimed) in Shushan the capital.

387. מְבֹהָלִים: Can also mean confused. Everyone was confused by the turn of event, that the Jews were now being saved. *-M'nos Halevi*

טו. וּמָרְדֳּכַי יָצָא | מִלִּפְנֵי הַמֶּלֶךְ בִּלְבוּשׁ מַלְכוּת תְּכֵלֶת וָחוּר וַעֲטֶרֶת זָהָב גְּדוֹלָה וְתַכְרִיךְ בּוּץ וְאַרְגָּמָן וְהָעִיר שׁוּשָׁן צָהֲלָה וְשָׂמֵחָה׃

15 And Mordechai went out from before the king ['s presence, dressed] in a royal garment of blue and white, and a large golden crown, and a cloak of fine linen and purple wool. And the city of Shushan cheered in delight and rejoiced.

388. וּמָרְדֳּכַי יָצָא: Mordechai only went out in royal clothing after he was sure the decree was sent around.

389. וְהָעִיר...וְשָׂמֵחָה: The joy was so complete that even the stones rejoiced. *- D'na Parsha*

טז. לַיְּהוּדִים הָיְתָה אוֹרָה וְשִׂמְחָה וְשָׂשֹׂן וִיקָר׃

16 For the Jews there was light and happiness, joy and honor.

390. לַיְּהוּדִים הָיְתָה אוֹרָה: Just like when someone is in the dark for a long time, the light will seem brighter - for the Jewish people, they had been through a very dark time. Now with this good news, the rejoicing and light was that much greater. *-Ibn Ezra*

391. "Light" refers to Torah, "happiness" to the festivals, "joy" to circumcision, and "prestige" to Tefillin. Haman had prohibited observing these four mitzvot, and now that he was gone the Jews were again able to perform them. *-Rashi*

392. Why didn't the Megilla just write out the above mentioned four mitzvos? It's showing that with this redemption the Jews realized what true happiness is - that true light and joy and honor is really learning Torah and fulfilling mitzvot.

יז. וּבְכָל־מְדִינָה וּמְדִינָה וּבְכָל־עִיר וָעִיר מְקוֹם אֲשֶׁר דְּבַר־הַמֶּלֶךְ וְדָתוֹ מַגִּיעַ שִׂמְחָה וְשָׂשׂוֹן לַיְּהוּדִים מִשְׁתֶּה וְיוֹם טוֹב וְרַבִּים מֵעַמֵּי הָאָרֶץ מִתְיַהֲדִים כִּי־נָפַל פַּחַד־הַיְּהוּדִים עֲלֵיהֶם׃

17 And in every province and in every city – every place to which the king's order and law reached, [there was] happiness and joy for the Jews, feasting and a holiday.
And many of the people of the land converted to Judaism, for fear of the Jews had fallen on them.

393. כִּי־נָפַל פַּחַד־הַיְּהוּדִים: The Jews' Fear of Heaven, Yirat Shamayim, was so strong that it even influenced non-Jews around them to convert and serve Hashem. *-R' Moshe Isserles*

פרק ט: א. וּבִשְׁנֵים עָשָׂר חֹדֶשׁ הוּא־חֹדֶשׁ אֲדָר בִּשְׁלוֹשָׁה עָשָׂר יוֹם בּוֹ אֲשֶׁר הִגִּיעַ דְּבַר־הַמֶּלֶךְ וְדָתוֹ לְהֵעָשׂוֹת בַּיּוֹם אֲשֶׁר שִׂבְּרוּ אֹיְבֵי הַיְּהוּדִים לִשְׁלוֹט בָּהֶם וְנַהֲפוֹךְ הוּא אֲשֶׁר יִשְׁלְטוּ הַיְּהוּדִים הֵמָּה בְּשֹׂנְאֵיהֶם:

CHAPTER IX 1 And in the twelfth month, which is the month of Adar, on its thirteenth day, when the time arrived for the king's order and law to be done (executed), on the day that the enemies of the Jews had hoped to rule over them, [instead –] it was overturned (reversed): that the Jews ruled; they over their enemies.

394. וְנַהֲפוֹךְ הוּא: The enemies started on top and fell really low, and the Jews started out in a very bad situation and came out on top! *-Alshich*

ב. נִקְהֲלוּ הַיְּהוּדִים בְּעָרֵיהֶם בְּכָל־מְדִינוֹת הַמֶּלֶךְ אֲחַשְׁוֵרוֹשׁ לִשְׁלֹחַ יָד בִּמְבַקְשֵׁי רָעָתָם וְאִישׁ לֹא־עָמַד לִפְנֵיהֶם כִּי־נָפַל פַּחְדָּם עַל־כָּל־הָעַמִּים:

2 The Jews gathered in their cities in all the provinces of King Achashverosh to send a hand against (attack) those who sought their evil. And no man stood before them (in their way), for the fear of them (of the Jews) had fallen on all the nations.

395. נִקְהֲלוּ הַיְּהוּדִים: Many Jews had run away to smaller towns where Haman's decree wasn't as well-known, hoping they would survive. Now these Jews came back to their cities to fight. *-Rav Arama*

ג. וְכָל־שָׂרֵי הַמְּדִינוֹת וְהָאֲחַשְׁדַּרְפְּנִים וְהַפַּחוֹת וְעֹשֵׂי הַמְּלָאכָה אֲשֶׁר לַמֶּלֶךְ מְנַשְּׂאִים אֶת־הַיְּהוּדִים כִּי־נָפַל פַּחַד־מָרְדֳּכַי עֲלֵיהֶם:

3 And all the ministers of the provinces, and the satraps, and the governors and the king's staff elevated (respected) the Jews, for the fear of Mordechai had fallen on them.

396. כִּי־נָפַל פַּחַד־מָרְדֳּכַי עֲלֵיהֶם: The common folk didn't fight back because they were afraid of the Jews, while the princes and ministers respected the greatness of Mordechai, and passed that down to their people. *– Vilna Gaon*

ד. כִּי־גָדוֹל מָרְדֳּכַי בְּבֵית הַמֶּלֶךְ וְשָׁמְעוֹ הוֹלֵךְ בְּכָל־הַמְּדִינוֹת כִּי־הָאִישׁ מָרְדֳּכַי הוֹלֵךְ וְגָדוֹל:

4 For Mordechai was great in the palace of the king and his fame was spreading in all the provinces, for the man Mordechai was growing (in power).

397. כִּי־גָדוֹל מָרְדֳּכַי: At first, people assumed Mordechai got promoted because he saved the king's life. Now they saw he was a great man in his own right.

ה. וַיַּכּוּ הַיְּהוּדִים בְּכָל־אֹיְבֵיהֶם

5 And the Jews struck at all their enemies [with the] strike of the

398. מַכַּת־חֶרֶב וְהֶרֶג וְאַבְדָן: The swords were used in the streets and the "killing and destruction" refers to in the houses. *-Midrash*

מַכַּת־חֶרֶב וְהֶרֶג וְאַבְדָן
וַיַּעֲשׂוּ בְשֹׂנְאֵיהֶם
כִּרְצוֹנָם:

sword and killing and destruction, and they did with their enemies as was their wish.

ו. וּבְשׁוּשַׁן הַבִּירָה הָרְגוּ
הַיְּהוּדִים וְאַבֵּד חֲמֵשׁ
מֵאוֹת אִישׁ:

6 And in Shushan the capital, the Jews killed and destroyed five hundred men.

399. חֲמֵשׁ מֵאוֹת אִישׁ: They were all Amaleki dignitaries. -*Targum*

ז. וְאֵת | פַּרְשַׁנְדָּתָא
וְאֵת | דַּלְפוֹן וְאֵת |
אַסְפָּתָא:

7 And Parshandasa, and Dalfon, and Aspasa;

400. All ten of Haman's sons were killed that day, and each one was as important as five hundred men! In the Megillah their names are written in a way that each name is on its own line - first on top of second, second on top of third, etc. This is so they will never rise up again. -*Megilla 16a*

ח. וְאֵת | פּוֹרָתָא וְאֵת |
אֲדַלְיָא וְאֵת |
אֲרִידָתָא:

8 and Porasa and Adalya and Aridasa;

ט. וְאֵת | פַּרְמַשְׁתָּא
וְאֵת | אֲרִיסַי וְאֵת |
אֲרִידַי וְאֵת | וַיְזָתָא:

9 and Parmashta and Arisai and Aridai and Vaizasa,

י. עֲשֶׂרֶת בְּנֵי הָמָן
בֶּן־הַמְּדָתָא צֹרֵר
הַיְּהוּדִים הָרָגוּ וּבַבִּזָּה
לֹא שָׁלְחוּ אֶת־יָדָם:

10 -- the ten sons of Haman, son of Hamdasa, oppressor of the Jews, they killed; but in the spoils (enemy's possessions) - they did not send their hands (take anything).

401. לֹא שָׁלְחוּ אֶת־יָדָם: Even though Mordechai permitted taking spoils, the Jews held themselves back so Achashverosh wouldn't be jealous. Instead, they collected the loot and sent it to the palace. -*Rashi, Ibn Ezra*

402. Not taking the spoils was to rectify another time in history when Jews fought their enemies. In the times of King Shaul, the Jews were commanded not to loot and they ignored the command. Here, they were allowed to, and held back. -*Nachal Eshkol*

403. As reward for the Jews restraining themselves from taking their enemies money and possessions, it was established that Purim is a day to give gifts to the poor without restraint. *Gcrrcr Rebbe*

404. Mordechai was a descendant of King Shaul who mistakenly left the Amalek king, Agag, alive - and Haman descended from Agag. The story of Purim was a fixing for that mishap.

יא. בַּיּוֹם הַהוּא בָּא
מִסְפַּר הַהֲרוּגִים בְּשׁוּשַׁן
הַבִּירָה לִפְנֵי הַמֶּלֶךְ:

11 On that day, the number of those killed in Shushan the capital came (was reported) before the king.

405. מִסְפַּר הַהֲרוּגִים: The only Jews that fought were ones who lived in Shushan the capital. –*Me'am Loaz*

יב. וַיֹּאמֶר הַמֶּלֶךְ לְאֶסְתֵּר הַמַּלְכָּה בְּשׁוּשַׁן הַבִּירָה הָרְגוּ הַיְּהוּדִים וְאַבֵּד חֲמֵשׁ מֵאוֹת אִישׁ וְאֵת עֲשֶׂרֶת בְּנֵי־הָמָן בִּשְׁאָר מְדִינוֹת הַמֶּלֶךְ מֶה עָשׂוּ וּמַה־שְּׁאֵלָתֵךְ וְיִנָּתֵן לָךְ וּמַה־בַּקָּשָׁתֵךְ עוֹד וְתֵעָשׂ׃

12 And the king said to Esther the Queen, "In Shushan the capital, the Jews killed and destroyed five hundred men and the ten sons of Haman; in the rest of the provinces of the king - what have they done?

"What is your plea - it will be given to you; And what else is your request - it shall be done."

406. בִּשְׁאָר מְדִינוֹת הַמֶּלֶךְ: Achashverosh said, "If the Jews killed five hundred enemies just in the capital city of Shushan, there must be many more enemies in the other cities. I now see what kind of danger the Jews were in. What else can I do for you? -*Malbim*

יג. וַתֹּאמֶר אֶסְתֵּר אִם־עַל־הַמֶּלֶךְ טוֹב יִנָּתֵן גַּם־מָחָר לַיְּהוּדִים אֲשֶׁר בְּשׁוּשָׁן לַעֲשׂוֹת כְּדָת הַיּוֹם וְאֵת עֲשֶׂרֶת בְּנֵי־הָמָן יִתְלוּ עַל־הָעֵץ׃

13 And Esther said, "If it is good for (pleases) the King, tomorrow should also be given to the Jews who are in Shushan, to do according to the law (decree) of today, and the ten sons of Haman – they should hang on the gallows."

407. וַתֹּאמֶר אֶסְתֵּר: Esther asked that strong example be set in Shushan so the enemies won't start up with the Jews in the rest of the empire. -*Malbim*

יד. וַיֹּאמֶר הַמֶּלֶךְ לְהֵעָשׂוֹת כֵּן וַתִּנָּתֵן דָּת בְּשׁוּשָׁן וְאֵת עֲשֶׂרֶת בְּנֵי־הָמָן תָּלוּ׃

14 And the king ordered that this be done, and the law was given (proclaimed) in Shushan, and the ten sons of Haman were hanged.

408. וַתִּנָּתֵן דָּת בְּשׁוּשָׁן: Achashverosh issued a decree of Esther's request, so that Jews wouldn't be afraid to get together the next day. -*Alshich*

טו. וַיִּקָּהֲלוּ היהודיים (הַיְּהוּדִים) אֲשֶׁר־בְּשׁוּשָׁן גַּם בְּיוֹם אַרְבָּעָה עָשָׂר לְחֹדֶשׁ אֲדָר וַיַּהַרְגוּ בְשׁוּשָׁן שְׁלֹשׁ מֵאוֹת אִישׁ וּבַבִּזָּה לֹא שָׁלְחוּ אֶת־יָדָם׃

15 And the Jews of Shushan gathered [again] also on the fourteenth day of the month of Adar, and they killed three hundred men in Shushan, but in the spoils (enemy's possessions) - they did not send their hands (take anything).

409. שְׁלֹשׁ מֵאוֹת אִישׁ: Three hundred men - after the first day of fighting, the enemies were afraid to show up to the fight. Therefore, on the second day, the Jews killed two hundred less men from the whole city than they had killed in the capitol earlier. -*Yad Hamelech*

טז. וּשְׁאָר הַיְּהוּדִים אֲשֶׁר בִּמְדִינוֹת הַמֶּלֶךְ

16 And the rest of the Jews who were in the king's provinces; they

410. It seems a bit repetitive to say again that the Jews fought their enemies, etc., but here it's talking about the specific case of the Jews who lived outside of the cities in the little villages. They too were

נִקְהֲלוּ | וְעָמֹד
עַל־נַפְשָׁם וְנוֹחַ
מֵאֹיְבֵיהֶם וְהָרוֹג
בְּשֹׂנְאֵיהֶם חֲמִשָּׁה
וְשִׁבְעִים אָלֶף וּבַבִּזָּה
לֹא שָׁלְחוּ אֶת־יָדָם:

gathered and stood up for their lives and rested from their enemies and killed of those who hated them; seventy-five thousand, but in the spoils (enemy's possessions) - they did not send their hands (take anything).

able to stand up for themselves even though they didn't have any of the king's officers to protect them or make sure that the new decree was followed. -*Malbim*

יז. בְּיוֹם־שְׁלוֹשָׁה עָשָׂר
לְחֹדֶשׁ אֲדָר וְנוֹחַ
בְּאַרְבָּעָה עָשָׂר בּוֹ
וְעָשֹׂה אֹתוֹ יוֹם מִשְׁתֶּה
וְשִׂמְחָה:

17 On the thirteenth day of the month of Adar, and they rested on its fourteenth day and made it a day of feasting and joy.

411. Chanukah celebrates the triumph of the Jewish soul. The Greeks did not seek to kill the Jew; they sought to destroy him spiritually by indoctrinating him with Hellenism. Thus Chanukah is celebrated with the kindling of lights, a symbol of spirituality. In contrast, Purim celebrates the deliverance of the Jew's bodily existence from the plot of Haman who sought to destroy the Jews physically. Thus Purim is celebrated with physical feasting. -*Levush Mordechai*

412. There are four levels of happiness - 1) serving Hashem with joy, which should be a constant goal. 2) Moadim - holidays - our joy is connected with something specific, a yom tov. 3) The month of Adar generally increases happiness, not only for something holy like a holiday, but all regular things too. And the 4) Purim. Which is the source of joy. It's beyond reason - "Ad Lo Yadah." And this is the level expressed by the days of Mordechai and Esther, which we can tap into today. -*The Rebbe*

יח. והיהודיים (וְהַיְּהוּדִים)
אֲשֶׁר־בְּשׁוּשָׁן נִקְהֲלוּ
בִּשְׁלוֹשָׁה עָשָׂר בּוֹ
וּבְאַרְבָּעָה עָשָׂר בּוֹ
וְנוֹחַ בַּחֲמִשָּׁה עָשָׂר בּוֹ
וְעָשֹׂה אֹתוֹ יוֹם מִשְׁתֶּה
וְשִׂמְחָה:

18 And the Jews who were in Shushan gathered on its thirteenth and fourteenth [day], and rested on its fifteenth [day] and made it a day of feasting and happiness.

יט. עַל־כֵּן הַיְּהוּדִים
הפרוזים (הַפְּרָזִים)
הַיֹּשְׁבִים בְּעָרֵי הַפְּרָזוֹת
עֹשִׂים אֵת יוֹם אַרְבָּעָה
עָשָׂר לְחֹדֶשׁ אֲדָר
שִׂמְחָה וּמִשְׁתֶּה וְיוֹם
טוֹב וּמִשְׁלֹחַ מָנוֹת אִישׁ
לְרֵעֵהוּ:

19 Therefore, the Jews of the villages, who dwell in un-walled cities, make the fourteenth day of the month of Adar [a day of] joy and feasting and a holiday, and [a day of] sending portions [of food] each man to his friend.

413. וּמִשְׁלֹחַ מָנוֹת אִישׁ לְרֵעֵהוּ: Portions - in plural form. Our Rabbis learn from here that Mishloach Manot must consist of two different kinds of food.

414. We celebrate Purim by giving Mishloach Manot to others, an act of kindness, because Hashem took care of us with His Kindness. –*Midrash Hagadol Devarim*

כ. וַיִּכְתֹּב מָרְדֳּכַי אֶת־הַדְּבָרִים הָאֵלֶּה וַיִּשְׁלַח סְפָרִים אֶל־כָּל־הַיְּהוּדִים אֲשֶׁר בְּכָל־מְדִינוֹת הַמֶּלֶךְ אֲחַשְׁוֵרוֹשׁ הַקְּרוֹבִים וְהָרְחוֹקִים׃

20 And Mordechai wrote these things (events) and sent letters [books] to all the Jews who were in all the provinces of King Achashverosh, the near and far ones.

415. וַיִּכְתֹּב מָרְדֳּכַי: And Mordechai wrote: Exactly how we have it in the Megilla. -*Rashi*

כא. לְקַיֵּם עֲלֵיהֶם לִהְיוֹת עֹשִׂים אֵת יוֹם אַרְבָּעָה עָשָׂר לְחֹדֶשׁ אֲדָר וְאֵת יוֹם־חֲמִשָּׁה עָשָׂר בּוֹ בְּכָל־שָׁנָה וְשָׁנָה׃

21 To [have them] establish (accept) upon themselves) to make (celebrate) the fourteenth day of the month of Adar and its fifteenth day, every year.

416. Mordechai's goal was to unite the entire Jewish nation through celebrating Purim. -*D'na Pashra*

417. Every year - The holiday of Purim will never be abolished - even in the days of Mashiach!

כב. כַּיָּמִים אֲשֶׁר־נָחוּ בָהֶם הַיְּהוּדִים מֵאֹיְבֵיהֶם וְהַחֹדֶשׁ אֲשֶׁר נֶהְפַּךְ לָהֶם מִיָּגוֹן לְשִׂמְחָה וּמֵאֵבֶל לְיוֹם טוֹב לַעֲשׂוֹת אוֹתָם יְמֵי מִשְׁתֶּה וְשִׂמְחָה וּמִשְׁלֹחַ מָנוֹת אִישׁ לְרֵעֵהוּ וּמַתָּנוֹת לָאֶבְיוֹנִים׃

22 Like the days upon which the Jews rested from their enemies, and the month which had been overturned (transformed) for them from sorrow to joy, and from mourning to holiday, to make them days of feasting and joy, and sending portions [of food] to one another and [giving] gifts to the poor.

418. וּמַתָּנוֹת לָאֶבְיוֹנִים: The possuk states "gifts to the poor" and not "charity". The word charity implies one giving out of pity. A gift, on the other hand, is what two friends exchange, where the one who gives is equal to the one getting. This shows the truth about giving tzedaka: it's not a one-way action. When we give, we get in return. -*The Rebbe*

419. It's better to spend more money on giving tzedaka on Purim than on Mishloach Manot and the festive meal. -*Rambam*

כג. וְקִבֵּל הַיְּהוּדִים אֵת אֲשֶׁר־הֵחֵלּוּ לַעֲשׂוֹת וְאֵת אֲשֶׁר־כָּתַב מָרְדֳּכַי אֲלֵיהֶם׃

23 And the Jews accepted [upon themselves to continue] that which they had begun to do, and that about which Mordechai wrote to them.

420. וְקִבֵּל הַיְּהוּדִים: It says accepted in the singular form because they were united as one man. –*Lekach Tov*

כד. כִּי הָמָן בֶּן־הַמְּדָתָא הָאֲגָגִי צֹרֵר כָּל־הַיְּהוּדִים חָשַׁב

24 For Haman, son of Hamdasa, the Agagi, oppressor of all the Jews, thought (plotted) against the Jews to

421. צֹרֵר כָּל־הַיְּהוּדִים: Haman was even worse than Pharoah. Pharoah's evil decree was against the Jewish boys, whereas Haman's plan was against every man, woman, and child. -*Alshich*

עַל־הַיְּהוּדִים לְאַבְּדָם וְהִפִּל פּוּר הוּא הַגּוֹרָל לְהֻמָּם וּלְאַבְּדָם:	cause them to perish, and he cast a Pur, which is a lot, to stun (cause chaos and terrify) them and to cause them to perish.	
כה. וּבְבֹאָהּ לִפְנֵי הַמֶּלֶךְ אָמַר עִם־הַסֵּפֶר יָשׁוּב מַחֲשַׁבְתּוֹ הָרָעָה אֲשֶׁר־חָשַׁב עַל־הַיְּהוּדִים עַל־רֹאשׁוֹ וְתָלוּ אֹתוֹ וְאֶת־בָּנָיו עַל־הָעֵץ:	25 And when she came before the king, he commanded through the letter (decree) that [Haman's] evil thought which he plotted against the Jews - be returned upon his [own] head, and they hanged him and his sons upon the gallows.	422. וּבְבֹאָהּ לִפְנֵי הַמֶּלֶךְ: When she came: When Esther came to plead before Achashverosh. -*Rashi*
כו. עַל־כֵּן קָרְאוּ לַיָּמִים הָאֵלֶּה פוּרִים עַל־שֵׁם הַפּוּר עַל־כֵּן עַל־כָּל־דִּבְרֵי הָאִגֶּרֶת הַזֹּאת וּמָה־רָאוּ עַל־כָּכָה וּמָה הִגִּיעַ אֲלֵיהֶם:	26 Therefore, they called these days "Purim," named after "the Pur". Therefore, because of all of the events of this letter, and what they saw about this matter – and what happened to them – [because of this -]	423. פּוּרִים: One reason for calling the holiday Purim is that it means "lots". Haman threw the lots and picked the month of Adar which was eleven months later. This gave Mordechai time to daven, gather the children, and take away the decree.
כז. קִיְּמוּ וקבל (וְקִבְּלוּ) הַיְּהוּדִים ׀ עֲלֵיהֶם ׀ וְעַל־זַרְעָם וְעַל כָּל־הַנִּלְוִים עֲלֵיהֶם וְלֹא יַעֲבוֹר לִהְיוֹת עֹשִׂים אֵת שְׁנֵי הַיָּמִים הָאֵלֶּה כִּכְתָבָם וְכִזְמַנָּם בְּכָל־שָׁנָה וְשָׁנָה:	27 - The Jews established and accepted upon themselves, and upon their descendants, and upon all who joined with them, - and it will not be removed (end) - to make (celebrate) these two days according to their script and according to their dates, every year.	424. קִיְּמוּ וְקִבְּלוּ: What had they begun to do? By Matan Torah, the Jewish nation were forced to accept the Torah - Hashem held the mountain over them like a barrel over their heads. Now by the Purim story, the Jews wholeheartedly accepted the Torah with their own free choice. -*Talmud* 425. What does it mean Hashem forced them to take the Torah? He forced them with His great love - overwhelmed them with miracles and wonders, so that they couldn't not accept His Torah. By Purim there weren't any miracles or revelations. In fact, the situation seemed horrible for the Jews. And they still chose to keep the Torah. -*Maharal*

כח. וְהַיָּמִים הָאֵלֶּה נִזְכָּרִים וְנַעֲשִׂים בְּכָל־דּוֹר וָדוֹר מִשְׁפָּחָה וּמִשְׁפָּחָה מְדִינָה וּמְדִינָה וְעִיר וָעִיר וִימֵי הַפּוּרִים הָאֵלֶּה לֹא יַעַבְרוּ מִתּוֹךְ הַיְּהוּדִים וְזִכְרָם לֹא־יָסוּף מִזַּרְעָם׃

28 And these days are remembered and observed in every generation, by every family, in every province and every city. And these days of Purim will never pass from among the Jews, and their memory will not end from their descendants.

426. נִזְכָּרִים וְנַעֲשִׂים: "..remembered and observed" One of the laws of reading the Megilla is that one can't hear it backwards. First chapter one, then two, three, etc.

The deeper meaning of this halacha is that when the Megilla is being read, we can't think of it as backwards - something that happened a long time ago, a nice story, a piece of history. We have to relate the Purim story to our lives today, take it seriously and apply the lessons we learn. *-Ba'al Shem Tov*

Purim - Yom Kippur is called like Purim - showing that the holiness of Purim is even greater than Yom Kippur. *-Zohar*

How could that be? It seems like those two days are complete opposites - Yom Kippur is full of fasting, praying, wearing white - and Purim is all about eating, drinking, having fun and dressing up. But, both are about reaching a high level of serving Hashem, of not being limited by nature. And while Yom Kippur achieves this by staying away from physicality, Purim accomplishes this through it - showing that the physical world we live in can be holy itself. *-The Rebbe*

כט. וַתִּכְתֹּב אֶסְתֵּר הַמַּלְכָּה בַת־אֲבִיחַיִל וּמָרְדֳּכַי הַיְּהוּדִי אֶת־כָּל־תֹּקֶף לְקַיֵּם אֵת אִגֶּרֶת הַפֻּרִים הַזֹּאת הַשֵּׁנִית׃

29 And Esther the Queen, daughter of Avichayil, and Mordechai the Jew, wrote about all the acts of power (the miracles), to establish [the holiday with] this second Purim letter.

427. תִּכְתֹּב: The letter תּ is enlarged in the Megilla to show that just like תּ is the last letter in the Aleph-Bet, Megillas Esther is the last book of miracles to be added to Torah. *-Me'am Loez*

428. בַת־אֲבִיחַיִל: Esther had to hide her Jewish identity for so long. Now she is proud to state her father's name. *-Me'am Loez*

429. This shows us that under Mordechai, the Persian Empire grew stronger.	CHAPTER X 1 And King Achashverosh placed a tax upon the land and the islands of the sea.	פרק י: א. וַיָּשֶׂם֩ הַמֶּ֨לֶךְ אחשרש (אֲחַשְׁוֵ֧רֹשׁ ׀) מַ֛ס עַל־הָאָ֖רֶץ וְאִיֵּ֥י הַיָּֽם׃
	2 And all his mighty and powerful acts, and the description of Mordechai's greatness - to which the king had promoted him; are they not recorded in the Book of Chronicles of the kings of Media and Persia?	ב. וְכָל־מַעֲשֵׂ֤ה תָקְפּוֹ֙ וּגְב֣וּרָת֔וֹ וּפָרָשַׁת֙ גְּדֻלַּ֣ת מָרְדֳּכַ֔י אֲשֶׁ֥ר גִּדְּל֖וֹ הַמֶּ֑לֶךְ הֲלוֹא־הֵ֣ם כְּתוּבִ֗ים עַל־סֵ֙פֶר֙ דִּבְרֵ֣י הַיָּמִ֔ים לְמַלְכֵ֖י מָדַ֥י וּפָרָֽס׃
430. דֹּרֵ֥שׁ טוֹב֙ לְעַמּ֔וֹ: All the money Mordechai took from Haman's house he donated it to the rebuilding of the Bais Hamikdash. – *Lekach Tov* 431. Mordechai is considered equal to Moshe in his generation in the way he took care of the Jewish people. –*Esther Rabba 6:2*	3 For Mordechai the Jew – [was] second to King Achashverosh, and great amongst the Jews, and accepted by most of his brethren; Seeking goodness for his nation and speaking (arranging) peace for all their descendants.	ג. כִּ֣י ׀ מָרְדֳּכַ֣י הַיְּהוּדִ֗י מִשְׁנֶה֙ לַמֶּ֣לֶךְ אֲחַשְׁוֵר֔וֹשׁ וְגָדוֹל֙ לַיְּהוּדִ֔ים וְרָצ֖וּי לְרֹ֣ב אֶחָ֑יו דֹּרֵ֥שׁ טוֹב֙ לְעַמּ֔וֹ וְדֹבֵ֥ר שָׁל֖וֹם לְכָל־זַרְעֽוֹ׃

More Mefarshim in the next edition,
B'ezras Hashem!

בס"ד

שְׁמִי _____
יוֹם ____ לְחוֹדֶשׁ _____

הִלְכוֹת פּוּרִים
סִי' קמא סְעִיפִים א - ה

קִיצוּר שׁוּלְחָן עָרוּךְ

1. Translate: משנכנס אדר... _____ _____ _____
2. What should a person try to schedule in the month of אדר? _____
_____
3. What happened on the 13th of אדר in the year 3404? _____
_____
4. Who does *not* have to fast on תענית אסתר? (5) _____
_____
5. If they don't fast on *this* day, what *should* they do? _____
6. If פורים falls on a Sunday, we fast on _____
7. Rabbi Schmidt's baby had a ברית today. Of those who participated in the ברית, who does not have to "make up" their fast on another day? _____
8. How should one prepare for the מגילה reading at night? (Similar to שבת and יום טוב) _____
_____
9. What תפילה is said both before and after the מגילה reading? _____
10. On (day, time) _____ we give 1/2 a שקל to remember: _____
_____
11. How many coins should the equivalent of 1/2 שקל be given in, and why? _____
_____
12. When is a father מחוייב to give a 1/2 שקל for his son? _____
13. Who is considered a קטן in this case? _____

בס"ד   קִיצוּר שׁוּלְחָן עָרוּךְ   הִלְכוֹת פּוּרִים   סִי׳ קמא סְעִיפִים ו - ט   שמי _____   יום ___ לְחוֹדֶשׁ _____

1. What does one do if he forgets to say **על הניסים** in his **תפילה**? _____

2. What if he remembers to say it before he reaches **השם**'s name in the following **ברכה**? _____
_____

3. Who is obligated in hearing the **מגילה**, and when? _____
_____

4. When (at what time) can we start reading the **מגילה** at night? _____

5. Old Mr. Kugelmacher is very hungry before **מעריב** and is anxious for the **מגילה** to be read so he can eat something. What does the **רב** tell him he can do in the meantime? _____

6. Where is the best place for the **מגילה** to be read? _____

7. What if there is no **מנין** - how should the people read the **מגילה**? _____
_____

8. When (in which circumstance) does the **בעל קורא** make the **ברכה** before the reading of the **מגילה**? _____

9. When (in which circumstance) doesn't the **בעל קורא** make the **ברכה** before the reading of the **מגילה**, and who else does? _____

10. What is the bare minimum needed so the **ברכה** after **מגילה** can be recited with **השם**'s name? _____

11. What is done if the minimum is not present?
_____

בס"ד

קיצור שוּלְחָן עָרוּךְ

הִלְכוֹת פּוּרִים
סִי' קמא סְעִיפִים י- יד

שמי _____
יום ____ לְחוֹדֶשׁ _____

1. How is the מגילה folded when it is read, and why?
   _____
   _____

2. Which three ברכות are recited before קריאת מגילה? _____
   _____

3. Which ברכה is said after קריאת מגילה? _____

4. What is the הלכה regarding the recital of ברכות for a בעל קורא who is a אבל? _____

5. What should the בעל קורא have in mind when he says the ברכה of שהחיינו? _____
   _____

6. What does the listener have to do to fulfill the מצוה of קריאת מגילה? _____

7. What is the best way to make sure you are being יוצא in the קריאה? _____
   _____

8. What should the בעל קורא be careful of when he reads in a large קהילה (congregation)? _____
   _____

9. Which phrase does the בעל קורא say in one breath? _____

10. When does the בעל קורא raise his voice, and why does he raise it there? _____
    _____

11. When is the מגילה lifted and shaken gently? _____

בס"ד

קִיצוּר שׁוּלְחָן עָרוּךְ

הִלְכוֹת פּוּרִים
סִי' קמא סְעִיפִים טו-יט

שמי _____
יוֹם ____ לְחוֹדֶשׁ _____

1. Moshe has a *printed* copy of the מגילה and is following the reading in it. What should he be careful *not* to do? _____

2. Why should the **בעל קורא** repeat the four verses the **קהילה** says aloud? _____
_____

3. Menachem has heard the מגילה already, but is going to read it to Yonason, who is a patient in the hospital. Who says the **ברכה**? _____

4. Menachem then goes home and reads it for Rochel, his wife. Who says the **ברכה**? _____

5. Moshav-Katan is a small town with only ten Jews. None of them know the **טעמים** (the "tune") of the מגילה. Who should read? _____

6. Is one allowed to write **נקודות** and **טעמים** in the מגילה for the **בעל קורא**? _____

7. Yossi, 13 years old, is reading the מגילה to his friends. Sholom wants to make sure Yossi reads correctly, in the proper tune. What should Sholom *not* do? _____
_____

8. When can a **בעל קורא** say a **ברכה** on a מגילה which is **פסול**? _____

9. When can't he say a **ברכה**? _____

10. What should his listeners do in this case (if he can't make a **ברכה**)? _____
_____

בס"ד | 148 | שמי _____
קִיצוּר שׁוּלְחָן עָרוּךְ | הִלְכוֹת פּוּרִים | יוֹם ____ לְחוֹדֶשׁ ____
סִי' קמא סְעִיפִים טו-יט

1. What can a **אבל** do on **פורים**, different from the rest of the "**שבעה**"? _____
_____

2. Which is the best way a **אבל** should hear the **מגילה**? _____
_____

3. **פורים** falls on a Sunday. Mr. Weiss, a **אבל**, wants to make sure he hears the **מגילה** on **מוצאי שבת**. What should he do? _____
_____

4. What is the proper time of the day a **אונן** should hear **קריאת מגילה**? _____

5. Which portion of the **תורה** is read on **פורים** day? _____
_____

6. Is one supposed to wear **תפילין** during **קריאת מגילה**? _____ Why? _____
_____

7. Rabbi Goldstein has a new baby boy, whose **ברית** is scheduled for **פורים**. When is the best time to have the **ברית**. Why? _____
_____

8. When is the **מגילה** read in the city of **ירושלים**, and what is the reason for this? _____
_____

Siman 140

1/4: How should one who lives in a community without a minyan fulfill his obligation to hear the parshiyos of Zachor and Parah?

- ☺ 1. Read the words on their own
- ☺ 2. Read the words with the proper trop on their own
- ☺ 3. They cannot fulfill their obligation without a minyan

2/4: There are 30 days in Nissan, and 29 days in Adar. If the first day of Adar occurs on Shabbos, on which day of Adar will Parshas Parah be read?

- ☺ 1
- ☺ 8
- ☺ 15
- ☺ 22
- ☺ 29
- ☺ 7 Nissan

3/4: There are 30 days in Nissan, and 29 days in Adar. If the first day of Nissan occurs on Shabbos, on which day of Adar will Parshas Parah be read?

- ☺ 2
- ☺ 9
- ☺ 16
- ☺ 23

4/4: There are 30 days in Nissan, and 29 days in Adar. If the first day of Adar occurs on Friday, on which day of Adar will Parshas Zachor be read?

- ☺ 2
- ☺ 9
- ☺ 16
- ☺ 23

Siman 141

1/15: How many times does one say the bracha of "shehechiyanu" during Purim?

- ☺ 1
- ☺ 2
- ☺ 3
- ☺ 4

2/15: If a bris occurs on Purim, when should it be done?

- ☺ A) Before reading the Megilah
- ☺ B) After reading the Megilah
- ☺ C) After Aleinu
- ☺ D) After davening

3/15: Why should the Ba'al Koreh raise his voice during "balailah hahu nad'dah sh'nas hamelech"?

- ☺ A) Because it reflects the concept of "waking up"
- ☺ B) Because the miracle of Purim begins there
- ☺ C) To ensure that the congregation is awake so far into the reading
- ☺ D) None of the above

4/15: Is a 13 year old boy obligated to give the half-shekel customarily given before Purim?

- ☺ Yes
- ☺ No
- ☺ It depends
- ☺ Machlokes

5/15: Which brachos on the Megilah are recited normally without a minyan?

- ☺ A) The brachos before reading the Megilah
- ☺ B) The brachos after reading the Megilah
- ☺ C) Both
- ☺ D) Neither

6/15: Why do we fast on Ta'anis Esther?

- ☺ A) Because the Jewish People fasted for Esther when she went into Achashverosh's Palace
- ☺ B) Because the Jewish People presumably fasted during the war
- ☺ C) To arouse us to do Teshuva before Purim
- ☺ D) None of the above

7/15: When Purim occurs on Sunday, Ta'anis Esther is pushed to Thursday. If someone accidentally ate on Thursday (forgetting it was a fast day), what should he do?

- ☺ A) Fast on Friday
- ☺ B) Fast after Purim
- ☺ C) He does not have to do anything
- ☺ B) Fast on Shabbos

8/15: Why do we give 3 half-Shekels before Purim?

- ☺ A) Because Klal Yisroel used to give 3 half-Shekels for korbanos
- ☺ B) Because Klal Yisroel used to give 1 half shekel for korbanos
- ☺ C) Because it says the word "T'rumah" 3 times in Ki Sisa
- ☺ D) Because there were 3 donation boxes for the korbanos

9/15: Has a congregation fulfilled their mitzvah of Megilah if the Ba'al Koreh read the word "yoshev" – "he sits", as "yashav" – "he sat"?

- ☺ Yes
- ☺ No
- ☺ It depends
- ☺ Machlokes

10/15: May one eat/drink before reading the Megilah at night?

- ☺ A) Yes
- ☺ B) No
- ☺ C) Yes, but not a Se'udah
- ☺ D) One may only eat what's necessary to stay focused

11/15: May an onain drink wine and eat meat on Purim day?

- ☺ Yes
- ☺ No
- ☺ It depends
- ☺ Machlokes

12/15: How should a congregant without his own kosher Megilah be cautious in regards to hearing every word of the Megilah?

- ☺ A) He should personally read along from his printed Megilah
- ☺ B) He should be extremely vigilant to hear every word from the Ba'al Koreh
- ☺ C) A or B
- ☺ D) None of the above

13/15: What is unusual about the kaddish shalem normally recited during Maariv, on Purim night?

☺ A) We only recite half of it
☺ B) We skip "Oseh Shalom"
☺ C) We skip "Yehai Sh'lamah"
☺ D) We skip "Tiskabel"

14/15: Which of the following is the most ideal to read Megilah from?

☺ A) A Megilah missing a whole concept
☺ B) A Complete Chumash
☺ C) A Megilah missing the first Possuk
☺ D) A Megilah missing 2 pesukim in the middle of the story

15/15: If an onein heard the Megilah before he was able to bury his relative, must he hear the Megilah again after the relative has been buried?

☺ Yes
☺ No
☺ It depends
☺ Machlokes

How are you doing so far?!
They *look* easy huh…?!
Just a few more questions to go!

Siman 142

1/6: Which mitzvah of Purim is the best to spend the most money on?

☺ A) Mishloach Manos
☺ B) The Se'udah
☺ C) Buying wine
☺ D) Matonos la'evyonim

2/6: Which of the following are not an ideal way for a woman to fulfill her obligation of Matonos la'evyonim?

☺ A) Have her husband give for her, to a woman
☺ B) Send money to a poor woman
☺ C) Send money to a poor man
☺ D) Have her husband give for her, to a man

3/6: An Aveil…

☺ A) Should not send mishloach manos
☺ B) Should not be sent mishloach manos
☺ C) Should not send Matonos la'evyonim
☺ D) Should not receive Matonos la'evyonim

4/6: Yosef began his meal a few minutes before Sh'kiah of Purim, and the meal extended hour into Motzei Purim. Has he fulfilled his obligation of eating the Se'udah of Purim?

☺ Yes
☺ No
☺ Machlokes

5/6: May one get married during Purim?

☺ Yes
☺ No
☺ Machlokes

6/6: Yosef has a special robe he wears in honor of Purim, but it's too dirty to wear. May he, ideally, wash the garment during Purim?

☺ Yes
☺ No
☺ Machlokes

מגילת אסתר פרק א א ויהי בימי אחשורוש הוא אחשורוש המלך מהדו ועד כוש שבע ועשרים ומאה מדינה: ב בימים ההם כשבת המלך אחשורוש על כסא מלכותו אשר בשושן הבירה: ג בשנת שלוש למלכו עשה משתה לכל שריו ועבדיו חיל פרס ומדי הפרתמים ושרי המדינות לפניו: ד בהראתו את עשר כבוד מלכותו ואת יקר תפארת גדולתו ימים רבים שמונים ומאת יום: ה ובמלואת הימים האלה עשה המלך לכל העם הנמצאים בשושן הבירה למגדול ועד קטן משתה שבעת ימים בחצר גנת ביתן המלך: ו חור כרפס ותכלת אחוז בחבלי בוץ וארגמן על גלילי כסף ועמודי שש מטות זהב וכסף על רצפת בהט ושש ודר וסחרת: ז והשקות בכלי זהב וכלים מכלים שונים ויין מלכות רב כיד המלך: ח והשתיה כדת אין אנס כי כן יסד המלך על כל רב ביתו לעשות כרצון איש ואיש: ט גם ושתי המלכה עשתה משתה נשים בית המלכות אשר למלך אחשורוש: י ביום השביעי כטוב לב המלך ביין אמר למהומן בזתא חרבונא בגתא ואבגתא זתר וכרכס שבעת הסריסים המשרתים את פני המלך אחשורוש: יא להביא את ושתי המלכה לפני המלך בכתר מלכות להראות העמים והשרים את יפיה כי טובת מראה היא: יב ותמאן המלכה ושתי לבוא בדבר המלך אשר ביד הסריסים ויקצף המלך מאד וחמתו בערה בו: יג ויאמר המלך לחכמים ידעי העתים כי כן דבר המלך לפני כל ידעי דת ודין: יד והקרב אליו כרשנא שתר אדמתא תרשיש מרס מרסנא ממוכן שבעת שרי פרס ומדי ראי פני המלך הישבים ראשנה במלכות: טו כדת מה לעשות במלכה ושתי על אשר לא עשתה את מאמר המלך אחשורוש ביד הסריסים: טז ויאמר מומכן [ממוכן] לפני המלך והשרים לא על המלך לבדו עותה ושתי המלכה כי על כל השרים ועל כל העמים אשר בכל מדינות המלך אחשורוש: יז כי יצא דבר המלכה על כל הנשים להבזות בעליהן בעיניהן באמרם המלך אחשורוש אמר להביא את ושתי המלכה לפניו ולא באה: יח והיום הזה תאמרנה שרות פרס ומדי אשר שמעו את דבר המלכה לכל שרי המלך וכדי בזיון וקצף: יט אם על המלך טוב יצא דבר מלכות מלפניו ויכתב בדתי פרס ומדי ולא יעבור אשר לא תבוא ושתי לפני המלך אחשורוש ומלכותה יתן המלך לרעותה הטובה ממנה: כ ונשמע פתגם המלך אשר יעשה בכל מלכותו כי רבה היא וכל הנשים יתנו יקר לבעליהן למגדול ועד קטן: כא וייטב הדבר בעיני המלך והשרים ויעש המלך כדבר ממוכן: כב וישלח ספרים אל כל מדינות המלך אל מדינה ומדינה ככתבה ואל עם ועם כלשונו להיות כל איש שרר בביתו ומדבר כלשון עמו:

פרק ב א אחר הדברים האלה כשך חמת המלך אחשורוש זכר את ושתי ואת אשר עשתה ואת אשר נגזר עליה: ב ויאמרו נערי המלך משרתיו יבקשו למלך נערות בתולות טובות מראה: ג ויפקד המלך פקידים בכל מדינות מלכותו ויקבצו את כל נערה בתולה טובת מראה אל שושן הבירה אל בית הנשים אל יד הגא סריס המלך שמר הנשים ונתון תמרוקיהן: ד והנערה אשר תיטב בעיני המלך תמלך תחת ושתי וייטב הדבר בעיני המלך ויעש כן: ה איש יהודי היה בשושן הבירה ושמו מרדכי בן יאיר בן שמעי בן קיש איש ימיני: ו אשר הגלה מירושלים עם הגלה אשר הגלתה עם יכניה מלך יהודה אשר הגלה נבוכדנאצר מלך בבל: ז ויהי אמן את הדסה היא אסתר בת דדו כי אין לה אב ואם והנערה יפת תאר וטובת מראה ובמות אביה ואמה לקחה מרדכי לו לבת: ח ויהי בהשמע דבר המלך ודתו ובהקבץ נערות רבות אל שושן הבירה אל יד הגי ותלקח אסתר אל בית המלך אל יד הגי שמר הנשים: ט ותיטב הנערה בעיניו ותשא חסד לפניו ויבהל את תמרוקיה ואת מנותה לתת לה ואת שבע הנערות הראיות לתת לה מבית המלך וישנה ואת נערותיה לטוב בית הנשים: י לא הגידה אסתר את עמה ואת מולדתה כי מרדכי צוה עליה אשר לא תגיד: יא ובכל יום ויום מרדכי מתהלך לפני חצר בית הנשים לדעת את שלום אסתר ומה יעשה בה: יב ובהגיע תר נערה ונערה לבוא אל המלך אחשורוש מקץ היות לה כדת הנשים שנים עשר חדש כי כן ימלאו ימי מרוקיהן ששה חדשים בשמן המר וששה חדשים בבשמים ובתמרוקי הנשים: יג ובזה הנערה באה אל המלך את כל אשר תאמר ינתן לה לבוא עמה מבית הנשים עד בית המלך: יד בערב היא באה ובבקר היא שבה אל בית הנשים שני אל יד שעשגז סריס המלך שמר הפילגשים לא תבוא עוד אל המלך כי אם חפץ בה המלך ונקראה בשם: טו ובהגיע תר אסתר בת אביחיל דד מרדכי אשר לקח לו לבת לבוא אל המלך לא בקשה דבר כי אם את אשר יאמר הגי סריס המלך שמר הנשים ותהי אסתר נשאת חן בעיני כל ראיה: טז ותלקח אסתר אל המלך אחשורוש אל בית מלכותו בחדש העשירי הוא חדש טבת בשנת שבע למלכותו: יז ויאהב המלך את אסתר מכל הנשים ותשא חן וחסד לפניו מכל הבתולת וישם כתר מלכות בראשה וימליכה תחת ושתי: יח ויעש המלך משתה גדול לכל שריו ועבדיו את משתה אסתר והנחה למדינות עשה ויתן משאת כיד המלך: יט ובהקבץ בתולות שנית ומרדכי ישב בשער המלך: כ אין אסתר מגדת מולדתה ואת עמה כאשר צוה עליה מרדכי ואת מאמר מרדכי אסתר עשה כאשר היתה באמנה אתו: כא בימים ההם ומרדכי ישב בשער המלך קצף בגתן ותרש שני סריסי המלך משמרי הסף ויבקשו לשלח יד במלך אחשורש: כב ויודע הדבר למרדכי ויגד לאסתר המלכה ותאמר אסתר למלך בשם מרדכי: כג ויבקש הדבר וימצא ויתלו שניהם על עץ ויכתב בספר דברי הימים לפני המלך:

פרק ג א אחר הדברים האלה גדל המלך אחשורוש את המן בן המדתא האגגי וינשאהו וישם את כסאו מעל כל השרים אשר אתו: ב וכל עבדי המלך אשר בשער המלך כרעים ומשתחוים להמן כי כן צוה לו המלך ומרדכי לא יכרע ולא ישתחוה: ג ויאמרו עבדי המלך אשר בשער המלך למרדכי מדוע אתה עובר את מצות המלך: ד ויהי באמרם [כאמרם] אליו יום ויום ולא שמע אליהם ויגידו להמן לראות היעמדו דברי מרדכי כי הגיד להם אשר הוא יהודי: ה וירא המן כי אין מרדכי כרע ומשתחוה לו וימלא המן חמה: ו ויבז בעיניו לשלח יד במרדכי לבדו כי הגידו לו את עם מרדכי ויבקש המן להשמיד את כל היהודים אשר בכל מלכות אחשורוש עם מרדכי: ז בחדש הראשון הוא חדש ניסן בשנת שתים עשרה למלך אחשורוש הפיל פור הוא הגורל לפני המן מיום ליום ומחדש לחדש שנים עשר הוא חדש אדר: ח ויאמר המן למלך אחשורוש ישנו עם אחד מפזר ומפרד בין העמים בכל מדינות מלכותך ודתיהם שנות מכל עם ואת דתי המלך אינם עשים ולמלך אין שוה להניחם: ט אם על המלך טוב יכתב לאבדם ועשרת אלפים ככר כסף אשקול על ידי עשי המלאכה להביא אל גנזי המלך: י ויסר המלך את טבעתו מעל ידו ויתנה להמן בן המדתא האגגי צרר היהודים: יא ויאמר המלך להמן הכסף נתון לך והעם לעשות בו כטוב בעיניך: יב ויקראו ספרי המלך בחדש הראשון בשלושה עשר יום בו ויכתב ככל אשר צוה המן אל אחשדרפני המלך ואל הפחות אשר על מדינה ומדינה ואל שרי עם ועם מדינה ומדינה ככתבה ועם ועם כלשונו בשם המלך אחשורש נכתב ונחתם בטבעת המלך: יג ונשלוח ספרים ביד הרצים אל כל מדינות המלך להשמיד להרג ולאבד את כל היהודים מנער ועד זקן טף ונשים ביום אחד בשלושה עשר לחדש שנים עשר הוא חדש אדר ושללם לבוז: יד פתשגן הכתב להנתן דת בכל מדינה ומדינה גלוי לכל העמים להיות עתדים ליום הזה: טו הרצים יצאו דחופים בדבר המלך והדת נתנה בשושן הבירה והמלך והמן ישבו לשתות והעיר שושן נבוכה:

פרק ד א ומרדכי ידע את כל אשר נעשה ויקרע מרדכי את בגדיו וילבש שק ואפר ויצא בתוך העיר ויזעק זעקה גדלה ומרה: ב ויבוא עד לפני שער המלך כי אין לבוא אל שער המלך בלבוש שק: ג ובכל מדינה ומדינה מקום אשר דבר המלך ודתו מגיע אבל גדול ליהודים וצום ובכי ומספד שק ואפר יצע לרבים: ד ותבואינה [ותבואנה] נערות אסתר וסריסיה ויגידו לה ותתחלחל המלכה מאד ותשלח בגדים להלביש את מרדכי ולהסיר שקו מעליו ולא קבל: ה ותקרא אסתר להתך מסריסי המלך אשר העמיד לפניה ותצוהו על מרדכי לדעת מה זה ועל מה זה: ו ויצא התך אל מרדכי אל רחוב העיר אשר לפני שער המלך: ז ויגד לו מרדכי את כל אשר קרהו ואת פרשת הכסף אשר אמר המן לשקול על גנזי המלך ביהודיים [ביהודים] לאבדם: ח ואת פתשגן כתב הדת אשר נתן בשושן להשמידם נתן לו להראות את אסתר ולהגיד לה ולצוות עליה לבוא אל המלך להתחנן לו ולבקש מלפניו על עמה: ט ויבוא התך ויגד לאסתר את דברי מרדכי: י ותאמר אסתר להתך ותצוהו אל מרדכי: יא כל עבדי המלך ועם מדינות המלך יודעים אשר כל איש ואשה אשר יבוא אל המלך אל החצר הפנימית אשר לא יקרא אחת דתו להמית לבד מאשר יושיט לו המלך את שרביט הזהב וחיה ואני לא נקראתי לבוא אל המלך זה שלושים יום: יב ויגידו למרדכי את דברי אסתר: יג ויאמר מרדכי להשיב אל אסתר אל תדמי בנפשך להמלט בית המלך מכל היהודים: יד כי אם החרש תחרישי בעת הזאת רוח והצלה יעמוד ליהודים ממקום אחר ואת ובית אביך תאבדו ומי יודע אם לעת כזאת הגעת למלכות: טו ותאמר אסתר להשיב אל מרדכי: טז לך כנוס את כל היהודים הנמצאים בשושן וצומו עלי ואל תאכלו ואל תשתו שלשת ימים לילה ויום גם אני ונערתי אצום כן ובכן אבוא אל המלך אשר לא כדת וכאשר אבדתי אבדתי: יז ויעבר מרדכי ויעש ככל אשר צותה עליו אסתר:

פרק ה א ויהי ביום השלישי ותלבש אסתר מלכות ותעמד בחצר בית המלך הפנימית נכח בית המלך והמלך יושב על כסא מלכותו בבית המלכות נכח פתח הבית: ב ויהי כראות המלך את אסתר המלכה עמדת בחצר נשאה חן בעיניו ויושט המלך לאסתר את שרביט הזהב אשר בידו ותקרב אסתר ותגע בראש השרביט: ג ויאמר לה המלך מה לך אסתר המלכה ומה בקשתך עד חצי המלכות וינתן לך: ד ותאמר אסתר אם על המלך טוב יבוא המלך והמן היום אל המשתה אשר עשיתי לו: ה ויאמר המלך מהרו את המן לעשות את דבר אסתר ויבא המלך והמן אל המשתה אשר עשתה אסתר: ו ויאמר המלך לאסתר במשתה היין מה שאלתך וינתן לך ומה בקשתך עד חצי המלכות ותעש: ז ותען אסתר ותאמר שאלתי ובקשתי: ח אם מצאתי חן בעיני המלך ואם על המלך טוב לתת את שאלתי ולעשות את בקשתי יבוא המלך והמן אל המשתה אשר אעשה להם ומחר אעשה כדבר המלך: ט ויצא המן ביום ההוא שמח וטוב לב וכראות המן את מרדכי בשער המלך ולא קם ולא זע ממנו וימלא המן על מרדכי חמה: י ויתאפק המן ויבוא אל ביתו וישלח ויבא את אהביו ואת זרש אשתו: יא ויספר להם המן את כבוד עשרו ורב בניו ואת כל אשר גדלו המלך ואת אשר נשאו על השרים ועבדי המלך: יב ויאמר המן אף לא הביאה אסתר המלכה עם המלך אל המשתה אשר עשתה כי אם אותי וגם למחר אני קרוא לה עם המלך: יג וכל זה איננו שוה לי בכל עת אשר אני ראה את מרדכי היהודי יושב בשער המלך: יד ותאמר לו זרש אשתו וכל אהביו יעשו עץ גבה חמשים אמה ובבקר אמר למלך ויתלו את מרדכי עליו ובא עם המלך אל המשתה שמח וייטב הדבר לפני המן ויעש העץ:

פרק ו א בלילה ההוא נדדה שנת המלך ויאמר להביא את ספר הזכרנות דברי הימים ויהיו נקראים לפני המלך: ב וימצא כתוב אשר הגיד מרדכי על בגתנא ותרש שני סריסי המלך משמרי הסף אשר בקשו לשלח יד במלך אחשורוש: ג ויאמר המלך מה נעשה יקר וגדולה למרדכי על זה ויאמרו נערי המלך משרתיו לא נעשה עמו דבר: ד ויאמר המלך מי בחצר והמן בא לחצר בית המלך החיצונה לאמר למלך לתלות את מרדכי על העץ אשר הכין לו: ה ויאמרו נערי המלך אליו הנה המן עמד בחצר ויאמר המלך יבוא: ו ויבוא המן ויאמר לו המלך מה לעשות באיש אשר המלך חפץ ביקרו ויאמר המן בלבו למי יחפץ המלך לעשות יקר יותר ממני: ז ויאמר המן אל המלך איש אשר המלך חפץ ביקרו: ח יביאו לבוש מלכות אשר לבש בו המלך וסוס אשר רכב עליו המלך ואשר נתן כתר מלכות בראשו: ט ונתון הלבוש והסוס על יד איש משרי המלך הפרתמים והלבישו את האיש אשר המלך חפץ ביקרו והרכיבהו על הסוס ברחוב העיר וקראו לפניו ככה יעשה לאיש אשר המלך חפץ ביקרו: י ויאמר המלך להמן מהר קח את הלבוש ואת הסוס כאשר דברת ועשה כן למרדכי היהודי היושב בשער המלך אל תפל דבר מכל אשר דברת: יא ויקח המן את הלבוש ואת הסוס וילבש את מרדכי וירכיבהו ברחוב העיר ויקרא לפניו ככה יעשה לאיש אשר המלך חפץ ביקרו: יב וישב מרדכי אל שער המלך והמן נדחף אל ביתו אבל וחפוי ראש: יג ויספר המן לזרש אשתו ולכל אהביו את כל אשר קרהו ויאמרו לו חכמיו וזרש אשתו אם מזרע היהודים מרדכי אשר החלות לנפל לפניו לא תוכל לו כי נפול תפול לפניו: יד עודם מדברים עמו וסריסי המלך הגיעו ויבהלו להביא את המן אל המשתה אשר עשתה אסתר:

פרק ז א ויבא המלך והמן לשתות עם אסתר המלכה: ב ויאמר המלך לאסתר גם ביום השני במשתה היין מה שאלתך אסתר המלכה ותנתן לך ומה בקשתך עד חצי המלכות ותעש: ג ותען אסתר המלכה ותאמר אם מצאתי חן בעיניך המלך ואם על המלך טוב תנתן לי נפשי בשאלתי ועמי בבקשתי: ד כי נמכרנו אני ועמי להשמיד להרוג ולאבד ואלו לעבדים ולשפחות נמכרנו החרשתי כי אין הצר שוה בנזק המלך: ה ויאמר המלך אחשורוש ויאמר לאסתר המלכה מי הוא זה ואי זה הוא אשר מלאו לבו לעשות כן: ו ותאמר אסתר איש צר ואויב המן הרע הזה והמן נבעת מלפני המלך והמלכה: ז והמלך קם בחמתו ממשתה היין אל גנת הביתן והמן עמד לבקש על נפשו מאסתר המלכה כי ראה כי כלתה אליו הרעה מאת המלך: ח והמלך שב מגנת הביתן אל בית משתה היין והמן נפל על המטה אשר אסתר עליה ויאמר המלך הגם לכבוש את המלכה עמי בבית הדבר יצא מפי המלך ופני המן חפו: ט ויאמר חרבונה אחד מן הסריסים לפני המלך גם הנה העץ אשר עשה המן למרדכי אשר דבר טוב על המלך עמד בבית המן גבה חמשים אמה ויאמר המלך תלהו עליו: י ויתלו את המן על העץ אשר הכין למרדכי וחמת המלך שככה:

פרק ח א ביום ההוא נתן המלך אחשורוש לאסתר המלכה את בית המן צרר היהודיים [היהודים] ומרדכי בא לפני המלך כי הגידה אסתר מה הוא לה: ב ויסר המלך את טבעתו אשר העביר מהמן ויתנה למרדכי ותשם אסתר את מרדכי על בית המן: ג ותוסף אסתר ותדבר לפני המלך ותפל לפני רגליו ותבך ותתחנן לו להעביר את רעת המן האגגי ואת מחשבתו אשר חשב על היהודים: ד ויושט המלך לאסתר את שרבט הזהב ותקם אסתר ותעמד לפני המלך: ה ותאמר אם על המלך טוב ואם מצאתי חן לפניו וכשר הדבר לפני המלך וטובה אני בעיניו יכתב להשיב את הספרים מחשבת המן בן המדתא האגגי אשר כתב לאבד את היהודים אשר בכל מדינות המלך: ו כי איככה אוכל וראיתי ברעה אשר ימצא את עמי ואיככה אוכל וראיתי באבדן מולדתי: ז ויאמר המלך אחשורש לאסתר המלכה ולמרדכי היהודי הנה בית המן נתתי לאסתר ואתו תלו על העץ על אשר שלח ידו ביהודיים [ביהודים]: ח ואתם כתבו על היהודים כטוב בעיניכם בשם המלך וחתמו בטבעת המלך כי כתב אשר נכתב בשם המלך ונחתום בטבעת המלך אין להשיב: ט ויקראו ספרי המלך בעת ההיא בחדש השלישי הוא חדש סיון בשלושה ועשרים בו ויכתב ככל אשר צוה מרדכי אל היהודים ואל האחשדרפנים והפחות ושרי המדינות אשר מהדו ועד כוש שבע ועשרים ומאה מדינה מדינה ומדינה ככתבה ועם ועם כלשנו ואל היהודים ככתבם וכלשונם: י ויכתב בשם המלך אחשורש ויחתם בטבעת המלך וישלח ספרים ביד הרצים בסוסים רכבי הרכש האחשתרנים בני הרמכים: יא אשר נתן המלך ליהודים אשר בכל עיר ועיר להקהל ולעמד על נפשם להשמיד ולהרג ולאבד את כל חיל עם ומדינה הצרים אתם טף ונשים ושללם לבוז: יב ביום אחד בכל מדינות המלך אחשורוש בשלושה עשר לחדש שנים עשר הוא חדש אדר: יג פתשגן הכתב להנתן דת בכל מדינה ומדינה גלוי לכל העמים ולהיות היהודיים [היהודים] עתודים [עתידים] ליום הזה להנקם מאיביהם: יד הרצים רכבי הרכש האחשתרנים יצאו מבהלים ודחופים בדבר המלך והדת נתנה בשושן הבירה: טו ומרדכי יצא מלפני המלך בלבוש מלכות תכלת וחור ועטרת זהב גדולה ותכריך בוץ וארגמן והעיר שושן צהלה ושמחה: טז ליהודים היתה אורה ושמחה וששן ויקר: יז ובכל מדינה ומדינה ובכל עיר ועיר מקום אשר דבר המלך ודתו מגיע שמחה וששון ליהודים משתה ויום טוב ורבים מעמי הארץ מתיהדים כי נפל פחד היהודים עליהם:

פרק ט א ובשנים עשר חדש הוא חדש אדר בשלושה עשר יום בו אשר הגיע דבר המלך ודתו להעשות ביום אשר שברו איבי היהודים לשלוט בהם ונהפוך הוא אשר ישלטו היהודים המה בשנאיהם: ב נקהלו היהודים בעריהם בכל מדינות המלך אחשורוש לשלח יד במבקשי רעתם ואיש לא עמד לפניהם כי נפל פחדם על כל העמים: ג וכל שרי המדינות והאחשדרפנים והפחות ועשי המלאכה אשר למלך מנשאים את היהודים כי נפל פחד מרדכי עליהם: ד כי גדול מרדכי בבית המלך ושמעו הולך בכל המדינות כי האיש מרדכי הולך וגדול: ה ויכו היהודים בכל איביהם מכת חרב והרג ואבדן ויעשו בשנאיהם כרצונם: ו ובשושן הבירה הרגו היהודים ואבד חמש מאות איש: ז ואת פרשנדתא ואת דלפון ואת אספתא: ח ואת פורתא ואת אדליא ואת ארידתא: ט ואת פרמשתא ואת אריסי ואת ארידי ואת ויזתא: י עשרת בני המן בן המדתא צרר היהודים הרגו ובבזה לא שלחו את ידם: יא ביום ההוא בא מספר ההרוגים בשושן הבירה לפני המלך: יב ויאמר המלך לאסתר המלכה בשושן הבירה הרגו היהודים ואבד חמש מאות איש ואת עשרת בני המן בשאר מדינות המלך מה עשו ומה שאלתך וינתן לך ומה בקשתך עוד ותעש: יג ותאמר אסתר אם על המלך טוב ינתן גם מחר ליהודים אשר בשושן לעשות כדת היום ואת עשרת בני המן יתלו על העץ: יד ויאמר המלך להעשות כן ותנתן דת בשושן ואת עשרת בני המן תלו: טו ויקהלו היהודיים [היהודים] אשר בשושן גם ביום ארבעה עשר לחדש אדר ויהרגו בשושן שלש מאות איש ובבזה לא שלחו את ידם: טז ושאר היהודים אשר במדינות המלך נקהלו ועמד על נפשם ונוח מאיביהם והרג בשנאיהם חמשה ושבעים אלף ובבזה לא שלחו את ידם: יז ביום שלשה עשר לחדש אדר ונוח בארבעה עשר בו ועשה אתו יום משתה ושמחה: יח והיהודיים [והיהודים] אשר בשושן נקהלו בשלשה עשר בו ובארבעה עשר בו ונוח בחמשה עשר בו ועשה אתו יום משתה ושמחה: יט על כן היהודים הפרוזים [הפרזים] הישבים בערי הפרזות עשים את יום ארבעה עשר לחדש אדר שמחה ומשתה ויום טוב ומשלוח מנות איש לרעהו: כ ויכתב מרדכי את הדברים האלה וישלח ספרים אל כל היהודים אשר בכל מדינות המלך אחשורוש הקרובים והרחוקים: כא לקים עליהם להיות עשים את יום ארבעה עשר לחדש אדר ואת יום חמשה עשר בו בכל שנה ושנה: כב כימים אשר נחו בהם היהודים מאיביהם והחדש אשר נהפך להם מיגון לשמחה ומאבל ליום טוב לעשות אותם ימי משתה ושמחה ומשלח מנות איש לרעהו ומתנות לאביונים: כג וקבל היהודים את אשר החלו לעשות ואת אשר כתב מרדכי אליהם: כד כי המן בן המדתא האגגי צרר כל היהודים חשב על היהודים לאבדם והפיל פור הוא הגורל להמם ולאבדם: כה ובבאה לפני המלך אמר עם הספר ישוב מחשבתו הרעה אשר חשב על היהודים על ראשו ותלו אתו ואת בניו על העץ: כו על כן קראו לימים האלה פורים על שם הפור על כן על כל דברי האגרת הזאת ומה ראו על ככה ומה הגיע אליהם: כז קימו וקבל [וקבלו] היהודים עליהם ועל זרעם ועל כל הנלוים עליהם ולא יעבור להיות עשים את שני הימים האלה ככתבם וכזמנם בכל שנה ושנה: כח והימים האלה נזכרים ונעשים בכל דור ודור משפחה ומשפחה מדינה ומדינה ועיר ועיר וימי הפורים האלה לא יעברו מתוך היהודים וזכרם לא יסוף מזרעם: כט ותכתב אסתר המלכה בת אביחיל ומרדכי היהודי את כל תקף לקים את אגרת הפורים הזאת השנית: ל וישלח ספרים אל כל היהודים אל שבע ועשרים ומאה מדינה מלכות אחשורוש דברי שלום ואמת: לא לקים את ימי הפרים האלה בזמניהם כאשר קים עליהם מרדכי היהודי ואסתר המלכה וכאשר קימו על נפשם ועל זרעם דברי הצמות וזעקתם: לב ומאמר אסתר קים דברי הפרים האלה ונכתב בספר:

פרק י א וישם המלך אחשרש [אחשורוש] מס על הארץ ואיי הים: ב וכל מעשה תקפו וגבורתו ופרשת גדלת מרדכי אשר גדלו המלך הלוא הם כתובים על ספר דברי הימים למלכי מדי ופרס: ג כי מרדכי היהודי משנה למלך אחשורוש וגדול ליהודים ורצוי לרב אחיו דרש טוב לעמו ודבר שלום לכל זרעו: